THE COMPLETE IDIOT'S GUIDE TO

LinkedIn

by Susan Gunelius

ALPHA

A member of Penguin Group (USA) Inc.

To Scott, for continually telling me, "You can do it."

ALPHA BOOKS

Published by the Penguin Group

Penguin Group (USA) Inc., 375 Hudson Street, New York, New York 10014, USA • Penguin Group (Canada), 90 Eglinton Avenue East, Suite 700, Toronto, Ontario M4P 2Y3, Canada (a division of Pearson Penguin Canada Inc.) • Penguin Books Ltd., 80 Strand, London WC2R 0RL, England • Penguin Ireland, 25 St. Stephen's Green, Dublin 2, Ireland (a division of Penguin Books Ltd.) • Penguin Group (Australia), 250 Camberwell Road, Camberwell, Victoria 3124, Australia (a division of Pearson Australia Group Pty. Ltd.) • Penguin Books India Pvt. Ltd., 11 Community Centre, Panchsheel Park, New Delhi—110 017, India • Penguin Group (NZ), 67 Apollo Drive, Rosedale, North Shore, Auckland 1311, New Zealand (a division of Pearson New Zealand Ltd.) • Penguin Books (South Africa) (Pty.) Ltd., 24 Sturdee Avenue, Rosebank, Johannesburg 2196, South Africa • Penguin Books Ltd., Registered Offices: 80 Strand, London WC2R 0RL, England

Copyright © 2012 by Susan M. Gunelius

International Standard Book Number: 978-1-61564-160-4
Library of Congress Catalog Card Number: 2011938630

14   13   12   8   7   6   5   4   3   2   1

Interpretation of the printing code: The rightmost number of the first series of numbers is the year of the book's printing; the rightmost number of the second series of numbers is the number of the book's printing. For example, a printing code of 12-1 shows that the first printing occurred in 2012.

Printed in the United States of America

Note: This publication contains the opinions and ideas of its author. It is intended to provide helpful and informative material on the subject matter covered. It is sold with the understanding that the author and publisher are not engaged in rendering professional services in the book. If the reader requires personal assistance or advice, a competent professional should be consulted.

The author and publisher specifically disclaim any responsibility for any liability, loss, or risk, personal or otherwise, which is incurred as a consequence, directly or indirectly, of the use and application of any of the contents of this book.

Most Alpha books are available at special quantity discounts for bulk purchases for sales promotions, premiums, fund-raising, or educational use. Special books, or book excerpts, can also be created to fit specific needs. For details, write: Special Markets, Alpha Books, 375 Hudson Street, New York, NY 10014.

Publisher: *Marie Butler-Knight*
Associate Publisher: *Mike Sanders*
Executive Managing Editor: *Billy Fields*
Acquisitions Editor: *Tom Stevens*
Development Editor: *Michael Thomas*
Senior Production Editor: *Janette Lynn*
Copy Editor: *Monica Stone*

Cover Designer: *Rebecca Batchelor*
Book Designers: *William Thomas, Rebecca Batchelor*
Indexer: *Angie Bess Martin*
Layout: *Ayanna Lacey*
Senior Proofreader: *Laura Caddell*

Contents

Introduction

Congratulations and welcome to the leading social networking site for business professionals, LinkedIn! Whether your goals for using the site are to build your brand, business, or career, you can do it on LinkedIn. Becoming a LinkedIn member is your first step to broadening your reach to a global audience of people who are interested in sharing, learning, discussing, growing, and helping each other succeed.

You've made another great decision by picking up this book. *The Complete Idiot's Guide to LinkedIn* takes you through the process of setting your LinkedIn goals, creating your strategy, developing a comprehensive profile and company page, and being an active, welcomed member of the LinkedIn community through the various tools, features, apps, and groups available to you. If you read this book cover to cover, you'll learn everything that a beginning LinkedIn user needs to know.

I recommend that you read this book from start to finish to ensure you know everything you need to understand in order to effectively use LinkedIn. However, the book is written in a way that allows you to skip chapters or parts and focus only on the sections you need help with. For example, if you're not interested in creating a LinkedIn Company Page for a business, skip Chapter 4. Similarly, if you have no plans to pay for advertising space on LinkedIn, then you don't have to read Chapter 11.

The Complete Idiot's Guide to LinkedIn is more than just a beginner's guide to creating a LinkedIn account. As a 20-year marketing veteran, I guarantee you'll get access to personal and business marketing tips, strategic planning help, and more. It's this strategic insight that sets this book apart from other beginner's guides to LinkedIn, and you can access it at your fingertips!

How This Book Is Organized

Part 1, Carving Out Your Space on LinkedIn, begins by posing an important question: "Why LinkedIn?" The answer is likely to be slightly different for each person who reads this book because each person has slightly different goals for their LinkedIn efforts. Thus, Part 1 starts by helping you define your LinkedIn goals and put a strategy in place to reach those goals. Next, you learn how to create a powerful profile and Company Page (if you need one for your business) so you can begin to develop your online visibility and build your LinkedIn network of connections. Without an audience, your LinkedIn efforts will go unnoticed. No worries, you'll find your audience if you follow the steps and tips provided in Part 1.

Part 2, Building Your Reputation and Community, is where you learn how to turn your static LinkedIn profile into a powerful communication tool where you can tell your story, develop your reputation, build a network of interested people, and establish your own online influence. Using groups, LinkedIn Answers, apps, recommendations, and more, you can turn your LinkedIn profile into a brand-, business-, and career-building powerhouse.

Part 3, Marketing Yourself Through LinkedIn, teaches you how to promote yourself, your brand, or your business on LinkedIn the right way. Although excessive self-promotion is frowned upon across the LinkedIn member community, there are ways that you can directly and indirectly market your business or yourself through LinkedIn to increase brand awareness, boost sales, or take your career to the next level. You learn all about them in Part 3.

Part 4, Using LinkedIn for Job Searching and Hiring, covers everything you need to know about finding and applying for a job on LinkedIn or posting a job opening on LinkedIn so you can attract applicants, find the right new employee, and expand your talent pool.

Part 5, Analyzing and Retooling Your LinkedIn Strategy, brings your LinkedIn efforts full-circle by teaching you how to analyze those efforts to learn what's helping you reach your goals and what needs to be changed or eliminated. You also learn about the various types of free and paid LinkedIn accounts, so you can feel confident that your account gives you access to the features you need to reach your goals.

The appendixes include an easy-to-understand glossary (Appendix A) where you can get definitions to common LinkedIn terminology, and also links to useful resources where you can find additional help and tools are provided (Appendix B).

Extras

The Complete Idiot's Guide to LinkedIn includes several helpful sidebars to draw your attention to important information. Pay attention to these sidebars when you see them, because they can make your life using LinkedIn easier and enable you to more effectively reach your goals. These sidebars are represented by the following icons:

DEFINITION

As you read this book, you may come across words related to LinkedIn or the internet that you're unfamiliar with. Those words are set off within the text in italics and are defined in these sidebars.

QUICK TIP

Handy information that will help you as you use LinkedIn is called out in "Quick Tip" sidebars. These sidebars often provide helpful ways to save time, work more productively, or just make your LinkedIn experience easier.

WARNING

A "Warning" sidebar cautions you about potentially big problems.

INSIDER SECRET

These sidebars provide hints that advanced LinkedIn users suggest so you can get the maximum benefits from your time and efforts.

Acknowledgments

Thank you to my husband, Scott; to my children, Brynn, Daniel, and Ryan; and to my parents, Bill and Carol Ann Henry. Without each of them I wouldn't be able to do what I do each day and this book certainly wouldn't have been written. They provide me with the daily inspiration, motivation, and sanity checks I need.

A special thank you goes out to my literary agent, Bob Diforio, for bringing this project to me, and to Tom Stevens, Michael Sanders, and everyone at Alpha Books/Penguin Group (USA) who worked on this book and helped bring it to you.

And thank you to all of my LinkedIn connections for making LinkedIn such a useful and meaningful place to spend time. I'll see you online!

Special Thanks to the Technical Reviewer

The Complete Idiot's Guide to LinkedIn was reviewed by an expert who double-checked the accuracy of what you'll learn here, to help us ensure that this book gives you everything you need to know about using LinkedIn to build your business, brand, or career. Special thanks are extended to Viveka von Rosen.

Viveka von Rosen is a nationally renowned LinkedIn speaker, trainer, and consultant, working with business professionals sharing the secrets and strategies of using LinkedIn effectively. She helps clients create a more powerful presence on LinkedIn, grow a truly useful network, and build connection and relationship strategies unique to their company culture.

Trademarks

All terms mentioned in this book that are known to be or are suspected of being trademarks or service marks have been appropriately capitalized. Alpha Books and Penguin Group (USA) Inc. cannot attest to the accuracy of this information. Use of a term in this book should not be regarded as affecting the validity of any trademark or service mark.

Carving Out Your Space on LinkedIn

You've decided to use LinkedIn to build your brand, business, or career, and here you learn about the many parts of LinkedIn and what you should and shouldn't do on LinkedIn before you take another step into the world of professional social networking.

Part 1 of this book teaches you how to define your LinkedIn goals and create your LinkedIn strategy so you're on the path to LinkedIn success from day one. Next, you learn how to create a powerful LinkedIn profile as well as a Company Page, if you need one. Once your home base is set up on LinkedIn, you learn how to find and connect with people.

Why LinkedIn?

In This Chapter

- Learn what's so great about LinkedIn
- Discover how LinkedIn can be used to grow a business, brand, or career
- Get to know the parts of LinkedIn
- Put your LinkedIn goals in writing

Over 120 million people are actively using LinkedIn to network with professionals, build their careers, and grow their businesses and brands. You can do it, too. The sooner you get involved, the better positioned you'll be to leverage the unique features of LinkedIn and open doors to more opportunities than you can imagine.

The challenge is knowing not only how to get started, but also how to strategically use LinkedIn to effect positive change for your business, your brand, and yourself. It starts with defining your goals and understanding the various elements of LinkedIn—and the many ways people and companies are using it. This chapter guides you through the basics, so you're on the track to success from day one of your LinkedIn journey.

What Do You Want from LinkedIn?

Why should a person use LinkedIn? It's a common question. Many people hear about popular websites and tools and think they need to start using them immediately. However, they dive in without understanding the real reasons for leveraging these tools. A social networking site like LinkedIn can open doors, but those doors can vary from one person to another. In short, there are a lot of people using LinkedIn for a lot of different reasons. You can't simply copy what everyone else is doing and expect to be successful. First, you need to understand who is using LinkedIn and the opportunities LinkedIn can create.

LinkedIn is a social networking site targeted to professionals who live and work around the world in diverse industries and in many types of professions. Networking to build your business, brand, and career via LinkedIn works similarly to in-person networking, but you can do it from the comfort of your own home or office at any time of the day or night and for free. You can get started right now. Simply create a free LinkedIn profile that explains who you are and what you do, then reach out and connect with other users, and start join- ing conversations. Naturally, there is more to LinkedIn than a static profile, and that's where the power of LinkedIn, for marketing your business and yourself, is found.

Who Is Using LinkedIn?

Since LinkedIn debuted in 2003, its membership has grown to over 120 million people, and just under half of those users are in the United States. The rest are located in over 200 countries and territories around the world. Just over half of LinkedIn users are male and most users fall into the 25–34 or 35–54 year-old age range. Users work in a wide variety of industries with diverse job functions. Furthermore, it has been reported that every Fortune 500 company has an executive on LinkedIn.

INSIDER SECRET

LinkedIn hiring solutions have been used by nearly 75 percent of Fortune 100 companies as of May 22, 2011. (LinkedIn Statistics Source: press. linkedin.com/about/)

Facebook might be the most popular social networking tool, but in surveys, marketers have repeatedly stated that LinkedIn drives higher marketing return on investment (ROI) results than Facebook. The reason is simple: LinkedIn has far less clutter than Facebook and is far more focused in its member goals. The people who spend time on LinkedIn are there for professional, business purposes. They're not interested in playing games. They have specific goals to learn and grow their businesses or careers. When you connect with people on LinkedIn, you're instantly connecting with an audience that has identified themselves as belonging to a target market of business and career-related professionals. This book teaches you how to use those connections—and your access to that audience—in order to build your own business or personal brand.

LinkedIn Opportunities

LinkedIn enables people to publish content and interact with one another. Your participation can be private or public, and gives you the opportunity to develop your business or personal brand. That means you can use LinkedIn to grow your company or your career. This book will teach you how to use the varied features offered in LinkedIn to jumpstart new opportunities. For example, following are just 20 ways that people use LinkedIn:

- Build relationships with influential people in their industries

- Develop relationships with target customers

- Establish their expertise in a specific subject matter or industry

- Provide valuable and meaningful content and conversations that lead to word-of-mouth marketing

- Acquire new customers

- Gather testimonials and recommendations
- Provide and get answers to questions
- Interact with like-minded people
- Obtain referrals
- Research customers and competitors
- Find vendors and business partners
- Raise funding or donations
- Promote events, new products, and more
- Identify mentors
- Find a new job
- Research a company for potential employment
- Search for new employees
- Acquire incoming links to websites for better search engine rankings
- Offer different ways for people to engage with you and experience your brand in the ways they prefer
- Get on the radar screens of potential clients

The most important thing to understand when it comes to using LinkedIn as a tool to build a business, brand, or career is that LinkedIn is most powerful as an *indirect marketing* tool. That means your LinkedIn activities should not read like an advertisement. LinkedIn should be used as a tool within your overall social media and content-marketing strategy. It is an amazing tool for building long-term, sustainable, and organic business or personal brand growth. However, that growth is dependent on your ability to publish useful content and conversations that help your target audience of existing and prospective customers or employers.

> **DEFINITION**
>
> **Indirect marketing** is any activity that is not intended to result in an immediate action but rather a secondary response. For example, a direct mail campaign is intended to move a consumer to an immediate action such as making a purchase. On the other hand, answering a question on LinkedIn related to your business or area of expertise is meant to directly answer the question, with the opportunity to raise awareness of you, your business, and your brand being the secondary response.

To use LinkedIn effectively, you need to understand what a brand is. In simplest terms, your brand is your promise to your audience and can refer to a business brand or your personal brand. Whether your LinkedIn goal is to boost sales for your company or land your next job, you need to establish your brand promise through your LinkedIn profile, Company Page, content, and activities.

LinkedIn allows you to raise awareness and recognition of your brand (throughout the remainder of this book, *brand* will refer to both business and personal brand). Through your content and conversations on LinkedIn, your connections will develop expectations for you, your brand, and your content. When you continually meet or exceed those expectations again and again through your LinkedIn activities, people will begin to feel secure with your brand. When they feel secure about a brand, they're more likely to try it, talk about it, and become loyal to it.

In other words, your LinkedIn activities can help you build a band of brand advocates who will not only try your products or services but also share your content, talk about your brand to their own audiences, and even protect your brand from naysayers. Brands that consumers become emotionally involved in and loyal to are referred to as relationship brands, and they are the most powerful brands in the world. LinkedIn helps you build those relationships that can transcend micro- and macroenvironmental changes and stand the test of time.

Think of LinkedIn as a long-term strategic tool for building your brand, but you can supplement that long-term strategy with short-term tactics as discussed throughout this book. The worst thing you can do is create an incomplete LinkedIn profile and never return to it again. For LinkedIn to work as a marketing tool to help you build your brand, you need to commit to it for the long haul. Consider the three steps of brand building listed below as you begin your efforts with LinkedIn.

- **Consistency:** All content and communications must consistently represent your brand promise and meet audience expectations for the brand. Otherwise, your audience will become confused and turn away from the brand in search of one that does meet their expectations for it.

- **Persistence:** Brands aren't built overnight. You must be vigilant and continually create content and communications that keep your brand in the audience's mind.

- **Restraint:** Don't be tempted to expand your brand into new ventures that don't consistently match the brand promise and might confuse consumers and do more harm than good.

As you develop your presence on LinkedIn and use the various tools and features available to help you connect with people, keep those three steps of brand building in mind. If an activity doesn't support your brand promise, then it might be better to skip it entirely. Consistency, persistence, and restraint are keys to your long-term business and personal branding success.

The Parts of LinkedIn

Unlike Facebook, which seems to change its features and rules all the time, LinkedIn is a bit more consistent in its offerings. New features are launched, but users typically appreciate changes as delivering added value. LinkedIn features give you the opportunity to create content, join conversations, interact with people, search for jobs, ask questions, recommend other users, and more. The primary parts of LinkedIn are introduced in this chapter and described in more detail throughout this book.

Profile

Your LinkedIn profile is your primary space on LinkedIn. This is where you tell the world who you are, what you've done, and what you can do. It's the face of your online career. Your LinkedIn profile includes your job history, education, awards, website links, recommendations, and your updates feed. You can associate a variety of applications with your LinkedIn profile and modify your profile settings to make all or part of it private or public. A profile is shown in Figure 1.1. Profiles are discussed in detail in Chapter 3.

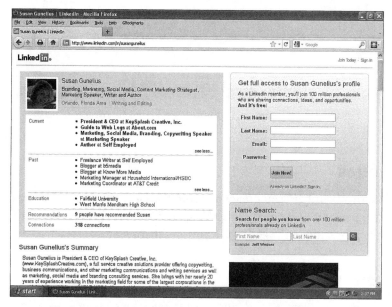

Figure 1.1: *A strong LinkedIn profile tells a complete story.*

Company Page

A Company Page provides a place for a business to have a presence on LinkedIn. It includes information about what the company does and can offer updates, links to employee profiles, career information, product information, and more. A Company Page is shown in Figure 1.2. You can learn more about Company Pages in Chapter 4.

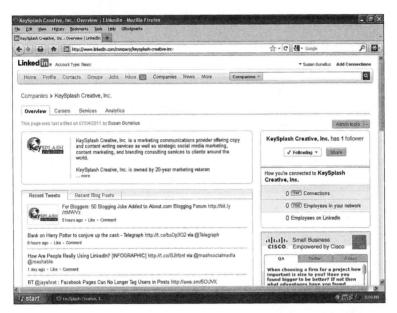

Figure 1.2: *A Company Page offers businesses a space on LinkedIn.*

Groups

LinkedIn members can create and join Groups, where smaller groups of people come together to discuss specific topics through LinkedIn. Learn more about LinkedIn Groups in Chapter 7.

Answers

LinkedIn members can ask and answer questions using LinkedIn Answers. It's a great way for LinkedIn members to gain and share knowledge. LinkedIn Answers is discussed in detail in Chapter 9.

Applications

There are a variety of applications that LinkedIn members can add to their profiles to access features different than those they can get through their standard profiles. For example, members can add events, presentations, portfolios, and more to their profiles using specific applications. In Chapter 6, you can learn more about LinkedIn apps.

Jobs

LinkedIn members can post and apply for jobs using the LinkedIn Jobs feature. Using LinkedIn Jobs to find a job or post a job is discussed in Chapters 14 and 15, respectively.

Ads

LinkedIn members can publish targeted ads through the self-service LinkedIn Ads feature. LinkedIn Ads are discussed in detail in Chapter 11.

Premium Features and Tools

If you upgrade to a paid account on LinkedIn, you get access to a variety of features and tools. For example, with a premium account, you can send LinkedIn *InMails* to any other LinkedIn user rather than just members you're connected to, see more profiles when you conduct a search, save and organize profiles, see additional information about people who have viewed your profile, and more. There are several different kinds of paid accounts, which are discussed in detail in Chapter 16.

DEFINITION

LinkedIn **InMail** is similar to email, but accessible only through LinkedIn members' LinkedIn accounts. A LinkedIn InMail is a private message sent from one LinkedIn member to another.

Defining Your LinkedIn Goals

Now that you know some of the opportunities that LinkedIn offers to you, it's time to define your goals for using it. What do you want to get out of your LinkedIn activities? Do you want to establish your expertise in your industry? Do you want to connect with online influencers to spread the word about your business? Do you want to build relationships with customers? Do you want to find a new job?

If you don't define your reason for using LinkedIn, then your efforts won't drive real results. Don't get overwhelmed or flustered because LinkedIn is an online tool. Just as you have goals when you launch a new marketing campaign or attend conferences, trade shows, or networking and sales events, you should have goals when you use LinkedIn. You can't define your strategy and plan to reach those goals if you don't know what they are, or can't refer back to them to make sure your activities are leading you in the right direction.

Remember, consumers and the online space change quickly, and your goals won't be set in stone. You need to be flexible and modify your goals to adapt to changing consumers, tools, and environments. However, if you don't have goals written down to start with, you'll always feel like you're just treading water rather than moving forward toward the finish line you establish.

Long-Term Goals

Most importantly, you need to identify your long-term goals. After all, the power of LinkedIn comes from its ability to build your business and personal brand for long-term, sustainable, and organic growth. Leverage that power by identifying your long-term stretch goals. For example, if your long-term goal is to boost sales of a specific product, quantify that goal both in terms of time frame and sales volume. On the other hand, if your goal is to raise awareness of a new service, quantify it through incoming links, shared links, and so on.

These are the types of things you'll learn how to do throughout this book. Right now, you need to look to the future and determine what you want to get out of the time and energy you devote to LinkedIn.

Short-Term Goals

Once you know where you want to go as defined by your long-term goals, you need to determine short-term goals to ensure you're on the right path to achieving those long-term goals. There is no point in establishing a three-year goal if you aren't going to support it with short-term goals to ensure you have a chance to meet it.

At the very least, set up quarterly goals that tie into your long-term goals. Your short-term goals depend greatly on your budget and the manpower resources you can devote to LinkedIn. While LinkedIn is easy to use and can be free, it does take time. Don't instantly discourage yourself by setting short-term goals that you can't realistically meet based on the time you can commit to LinkedIn. Don't be discouraged if once you start, you realize LinkedIn takes a bit more time and effort than you originally thought and you have to modify your short-term goals.

Bottom line: Every extra minute you can spend on LinkedIn can only help you reach your business or personal brand goals. However you can effect positive change to your business or personal brand even with just a small amount of time dedicated to LinkedIn each day. Remember, success comes from brand consistency, persistence, and restraint. If you commit to the long haul, you can't fail!

The Least You Need to Know

- People around the world are using LinkedIn for a wide variety of professional and business networking and marketing purposes.
- There are a variety of free LinkedIn features that you can use to develop relationships, establish your expertise, and build your business and personal brands.
- Both individuals and companies can have a presence on LinkedIn.
- LinkedIn should be part of your long-term brand-building strategy.

Build Your LinkedIn Plan

In This Chapter

- Developing your LinkedIn strategy
- Defining your target audience
- Finding the online influencers
- Learning the do's and don'ts of LinkedIn

Once you make the decision to use LinkedIn as a tool to build your business, brand, and career, you need to put together a plan of action, so you can meet your goals. Remember, LinkedIn is a powerful tool in your marketing and branding toolbox that can help you establish your personal and business authority across a global audience, but you can't do it without a solid strategy. This chapter teaches you how to develop your own LinkedIn strategy and a plan to implement that strategy.

As with most online tools that enable you to publish your own content and conversations, there are some unwritten do's and don'ts of acceptable LinkedIn behavior that you need to understand and adhere to if you want to be a welcome member of the social networking community. In this chapter, you learn those unwritten rules, as well as the written rules and terms of service that all LinkedIn users must comply with at all times. Review those rules and make sure you follow them, or your account could be disabled.

Develop Your Strategy

Before you can develop your LinkedIn strategy, you need to understand the difference between three key terms that are used throughout this book:

- **Strategy**   Your LinkedIn strategy is an implied or implicit statement of how you will achieve your objectives. Your strategy provides the direction *and* the decisions, related to your personal or business brand, that your LinkedIn presence and activities will communicate. This includes your brand promise, brand positioning, target audience, and the LinkedIn features available to you as well as your time, resource, and monetary investments. In other words, your LinkedIn strategy provides broad direction to all other functions related to your business, brand, or career development.

- **Tactics**   The short-term actions you perform in an effort to execute your LinkedIn strategy.

- **Plan**   Your LinkedIn plan is a written document that analyzes where you are currently in terms of meeting your LinkedIn goals, what your competitors are doing, where your target audience is, and what are your resources and budget. Based on your LinkedIn strategy, your LinkedIn plan outlines a long-term roadmap filled with short-term tactics and strategic steps to achieve your goals.

INSIDER SECRET

Your LinkedIn strategy defines where you want to go, and your LinkedIn plan defines how you're going to get there.

In order to develop a comprehensive LinkedIn strategy, you need to first define your goals as discussed in Chapter 1. Next, take the time to fully evaluate where you are today (personally or in terms of your business), what your competitors are doing on LinkedIn, and what your audience is doing on LinkedIn. You need to look for potential opportunities and threats, and you need to determine what are your strengths and weaknesses.

In marketing practice, this process is referred to as creating a SWOT Analysis. SWOT stands for strengths, weaknesses, opportunities, threats. The key is to look for gaps and fill them. Those gaps could be new opportunities that you can fill or gaps that you must fill to defend yourself against competitive threats. You cannot create an effective LinkedIn strategy for the future if you don't take time to understand the environment where you'll be spending time (i.e., LinkedIn) and where you can fit into that environment.

B2B or B2C

What type of audience do you want to connect with? Are you trying to build a business that offers services to another business or government agencies? Do you want to build a consumer product brand to sell more products to people? These are some of the first questions to ask yourself as you develop your LinkedIn strategy.

LinkedIn is often referred to as the social site for *business-to-business (B2B)* sales, marketing, networking, and career development because the majority of members are professionals working either directly or indirectly in the world of business. However, the LinkedIn user base offers a lot more than B2B conversations, wants, and needs. *Business-to-consumer (B2C)* initiatives have a place on LinkedIn, too.

 DEFINITION

Business-to-business (B2B) refers to a business, company, individual, or organization that markets its products and services to other businesses. For example, an advertising agency is a B2B company.

Business-to-consumer (B2C) refers to a business, company, individual, or organization that markets its products and services to consumers. For example, your local drugstore is a B2C company.

The LinkedIn audience comes from the worlds of finance, marketing, self-employment, government, nonprofit, legal, and more. They're executives, professors, middle management, students, entrepreneurs, and so on. In other words, they're a diverse group of people, but they typically share a common focus on personal or business professional growth. That is why LinkedIn has gained a reputation as a B2B social media and content marketing tool, while

Facebook—which has a much broader audience of users—has gained a reputation as a place for B2C marketing. However, every LinkedIn user is a consumer. They purchase products to live their lives each day, so excluding B2C marketing and brand-building activities from your LinkedIn strategy would mean missed opportunities. Bottom line: Even B2C has a place on LinkedIn.

Your LinkedIn strategy should appropriately reflect your efforts B2B or B2C. Even if you're solely using LinkedIn as a tool to find your next job, your LinkedIn strategy should reflect your efforts B2B. While your efforts will focus on connecting with other people within your industry for career networking, your goal is to market yourself and your services as an employee to those businesses.

Networking Strategy

The concept of networking to build a career, business, or brand isn't a new one. For as long as one can remember, people have been informally and formally networking to gather business and career leads, get on important people's radar screens, and open doors to new opportunities. Whether it's an informal cocktail hour after work with colleagues or a planned conference or event that brings larger numbers of people together for a common purpose, socializing with people at in-person networking events is common around the world.

With the debut of social networking sites in the late 1990s and early 2000s, the concept of networking for business, brand, and career growth evolved. No longer was it necessary to meet in-person to network with other people. By the mid-2000s, social networking moved from being an ancillary tactic for career and business development into an essential strategic priority. Today, if you're not participating in social networking through a site like LinkedIn, you're limiting your chances for success in whatever field or endeavor you choose.

Therefore to reach your goals on LinkedIn, you must define your networking strategy. LinkedIn should not replace your in-person networking efforts, but it should enhance those efforts. It's simply not feasible to travel around the world and attend every conference, seminar, and trade show related to your career or business. Fortunately, LinkedIn offers tools such as groups, questions and answers, and messaging that enable you to converse with other people, schedule and promote online and offline events, and share and learn.

Determine the type of networking you want to do on LinkedIn to enhance your offline efforts and your other online efforts, then integrate those networking needs into your LinkedIn strategy. For example, if you want to connect with experts in a specific field to learn and to open doors for future business partnerships or sales, search for a LinkedIn group that is targeted to that audience and join it. (You can learn more about LinkedIn Groups in Chapter 7.) Alternatively, if you want to build relationships with people who work at a specific company to open doors to work with that company in the future, search for employee profiles (discussed in Chapter 5) or visit that company's LinkedIn page and browse through employee profiles directly from that page (discussed in Chapter 14).

Again, you need to know why you want to network with people on LinkedIn before you can develop a strategy and plan to network effectively with them.

Content Strategy

Every word, image, video, presentation, and so on, that you publish on LinkedIn is a form of content, and all of that content can be considered part of your overall LinkedIn content marketing strategy. In simplest terms, content marketing is a method of indirectly promoting a company using words, images, and video that are published online or offline. There are three primary forms of content to consider when you're talking about content marketing strategy:

- **Long-form content**   Content that takes more than a couple of minutes to create and consume is considered long-form content. For example, most blog posts, articles, videos, white papers, e-books, and presentations would be considered long-form content. When you share a link to one of your sales presentations through your LinkedIn profile, you're promoting your useful long-form content and indirectly marketing yourself, your business, and your brand.

- **Short-form content**   Content that takes fewer than a couple of minutes to create and consume is considered short-form content. For example, Twitter posts, shared links on social bookmarking sites like Digg.com or StumbleUpon. com, and pictures or animated GIFs would be considered short-form content. When you share your Twitter posts feed via your LinkedIn profile updates, you're promoting your short-form content and indirectly marketing yourself, your business, and your brand.

- **Conversational content**   Content that is published to start or be part of an online conversation or two-way dialogue is considered conversational content. For example, a blog post comment, a forum post, a LinkedIn or Facebook update to another user or in a group, a comment on a video or image, or a Twitter update in reply to another user are all types of conversational content. When you publish a comment in response to another comment in a LinkedIn group that you belong to, you're indirectly promoting yourself, your business, and your brand through useful conversational content.

As a member of LinkedIn, you can publish short-form and conversational content on the site, and you can also share and promote short-form, conversational, and long-form content that is published off of LinkedIn. For example, you can (and should) publish a link to your most recent blog post related to your business, brand, or career in your LinkedIn profile feed (discussed in Chapter 5). As you create (and inevitably modify) your LinkedIn strategy and plan, you must determine the type of content you are comfortable creating and understand where and how to create and publish that content both on LinkedIn and off of LinkedIn. Tips and suggestions for content creation are included throughout this book, so help is always at your fingertips.

Keep in mind, for content marketing to work your content should be useful and meaningful to your target audience, not self-promotional. While it's perfectly acceptable to share links to your useful content on your blog or other site, and it's also acceptable to publish an occasional promotional piece of content (for example, if you're holding a special sale), it's not acceptable to use LinkedIn as a place to continually promote yourself. LinkedIn is not your marketing brochure.

Marketing Strategy

Review your ultimate goals that made you consider using LinkedIn in the first place. What do you want to get out of your time on LinkedIn? Your marketing strategy depends on those goals. As mentioned in the preceding section, LinkedIn is not your marketing brochure, but it is a powerful social media and content-marketing tool. Through your social interactions and the content you publish on LinkedIn, you can effectively market yourself, your brand, and your business to large targeted audiences. It's time to put your strategy for marketing yourself or your business on LinkedIn into writing.

As discussed in the definition of strategy (provided earlier in this chapter), your marketing strategy for LinkedIn must include both information and direction related to your macro- and microenvironments wherever you do business or represent yourself for career purposes. It needs to include directions related to your brand promise and position, as well as directions related to your competitor and customer analyses. Finally, it must include information about your budget and resources, and all of these parts must tie into your goals.

Put together a 12-month marketing strategy for how you plan to use LinkedIn to build your business, brand, or career; then turn that strategy into an actionable LinkedIn marketing plan that addresses the following strategy definitions and tactics to reach your strategic goals.

- **Objectives:** What do you want to do in the next 12 months?

- **Target audience:** Who do you want to talk to in the next 12 months and where can you find them? (Demographic and behavioral segmentation are discussed in the next section.)

- **Influencers:** Who can help you spread your messages and where can you find them (i.e., who they are, where they are, how they can help you, how you can build relationships with them)?

- **Content:** What kind of content do you and your competitors publish? What content does your target audience want? What content do influencers share with their own audiences?

- **Content forms:** What types of long-form, short-form, and conversational content will you publish?

- **Marketing integration:** How will your LinkedIn efforts tie in with your overall marketing strategy and build your business, brand, and career? How will you cross-promote to boost your results?

- **Results tracking:** How will you gather metrics to track your performance?

Don't let the process of defining your LinkedIn strategy and plan become overwhelming. Remember, the social web is a constantly evolving environment with new tools and features debuting every day. Your LinkedIn strategy and plan should not be etched in stone. Instead, both should be working documents that change as you learn—and grow along with—your target audience, competitors, and the tools available to you. What works today might not work tomorrow in the fast-moving world of social media. You need to be prepared to adapt your efforts if you want to attain the best results.

Define Your Target Audience

As you learned in the previous section of this chapter, developing your LinkedIn strategy requires that you define your target audience. In marketing terminology, your target audience is the segment of the larger population that you focus your efforts on in order to best meet your overall business and brand objectives. You have to analyze and define several specific demographic and behavioral attributes to define your target audience.

For example, you can segment a broader audience using demographic characteristics such as these:

- Age
- Gender

- Income

- Education

- Location (where they live and work)

- Work (employer, industry, profession, and so on)

You can also segment a broader audience using behavioral characteristics. Social networking and online behaviors are particularly helpful in segmenting your target audience for your LinkedIn initiatives. Examples of behavioral attributes can include ...

- Social sites where they have active profiles.

- Groups, blogs, and forums where they actively publish content and conversations.

- The type of content they like based on social sharing tools such as Facebook's Like button, Google+'s +1 button, Digg. com, StumbleUpon.com, Twitter's Retweet button, and so on.

- The people they follow and interact with on social sites.

- The types of products, businesses, and brands they publish reviews about online.

Use these traits to develop a profile of your best customer or the ideal person you want to connect with on LinkedIn to reach your goals. As you spend more time analyzing the broader audience and determining what type of people you want to connect with based on demographic and behavioral characteristics, you'll begin to learn where similar people spend time online, what they talk about, what's important to them, and how they like to be contacted on and off LinkedIn. Use these findings to develop your LinkedIn strategy, so your efforts are spent interacting and building relationships with the right people.

QUICK TIP

It's true that all conversations can be helpful to you, but there are only so many hours in the day. Focus your efforts on your target audience in order to achieve the highest return on your time investment.

Simply connecting with people on LinkedIn, as you'll learn to do in Chapter 5, isn't enough. If you want to reach your goals, you need to know who to connect with and what to say to them in order to get them emotionally involved with you, your business, and your brand. That's the critical step to building relationships with people, and that's where LinkedIn can help you meet your goals.

Emotional involvement with you, your business, and your brand leads directly to loyalty and brand advocacy (people talking about you, sharing your content, and joining your conversations). This is a concept that I like to explain as the 3 Ss of customer loyalty.

- **Stability**   People feel emotionally involved with you, your business, and your brand when you send them a consistent message in every interaction.

- **Sustainability**   People feel emotionally involved with you, your business, and your brand when they believe that you'll be with them for a long period of time.

- **Security**   People feel emotionally involved with you, your business, and your brand when you give them a feeling of peace of mind.

In other words, people will feel loyal to you and your relationships will be stronger when they understand what to expect from you, and can trust you to deliver on those expectations every time they interact with you. This is a fundamental principle of brand building that applies to your efforts to build your business or personal brand through LinkedIn, too. Bottom line: Your LinkedIn activities and persona have to be reliable and trustworthy. If they are not, it will be nearly impossible to gain the emotional involvement you need to build relationships that lead to brand advocacy and word-of-mouth marketing.

If no one talks to you, with you, or about you on LinkedIn, then you're just talking to yourself and you'll never reach your goals. Define your target audience and deliver the content, conversations, and experiences that they want and need from someone like you. Carve out your niche and your position on LinkedIn as the go-to person for your area of expertise, and then live that brand promise in all of your LinkedIn activities. Not only will the LinkedIn audience take notice, but online influencers will, too, as you'll learn in the next section.

Find the Influencers

Who are the people who have influence over large groups of your target audience? When you network offline to build your business, brand, or career, there are always certain people you want to connect with who can introduce you to key individuals who can truly help you reach your goals. If you're using LinkedIn to build your business, then you need to look for people on and off LinkedIn who have the eyes and ears of your target consumers. If you're trying to build your career, then you need to look for people on and off LinkedIn who have the eyes and ears of employers and recruiters who work with and hire people in your line of work.

Not everyone on LinkedIn is an influencer, and influence isn't solely about the number of connections a person has on LinkedIn. Influence is primarily about quality connections, not quantity. In other words, it's better to have 100 connections on LinkedIn with people who value what you say, share your content, converse with you, and talk about your content with their own audiences than it is to have 500 LinkedIn connections who click the **Connect** button and then are never heard from again. The same theory holds true for online influencers. An online influencer who has 100 quality connections can do far more for you in terms of word-of-mouth marketing than an online influencer with 500 connections who hasn't logged in to LinkedIn for a year.

INSIDER SECRET

There are times when the theory of quality over quantity might not hold true on LinkedIn. For example, some people might actively work to build their LinkedIn profiles, but they do have influence over large audiences outside of LinkedIn. You must evaluate each person individually to determine their true influence.

By definition, influencers can affect the way their loyal audiences think and act. Influencers have earned trust among their audiences, so if you can get influencers to talk about you, share your content, and join your conversations, their audiences will see those interactions and get to know you. In time, the goal is to build strong enough relationships with online influencers that they understand the value and usefulness you add to the online conversation and they *want* to share your content with their own audiences. In other words, they trust that what you have to say is reliable and meets the expectations of their own audiences.

Online influencers are powerful, and you need to tap into their reach by developing real relationships with them. The first step is identifying who has the eyes and ears of your target audience. In Chapter 5, you learn specific steps to find and connect with people on LinkedIn, but before you can actively search for people on LinkedIn, you need to know what you're looking for. Therefore, you have to spend time poking around LinkedIn to determine the keywords online influencers use in their LinkedIn profiles to identify themselves, the types of groups they belong to on LinkedIn, their titles, specific companies that influencers might work for, specific education or schools they list in their LinkedIn profiles, and so on.

Using various directory and search tools available to you in LinkedIn, you can find people who are similar to each other based on the information in their profiles and their LinkedIn activities. Just as you created a profile of your best customers to define your target audience, you can create profiles of online influencers, so you can find more of them on LinkedIn. It just takes some research and time, but those influencers are on LinkedIn waiting to connect with people like you who can offer meaningful content and conversations that they want to discuss and share with their own audiences. This is the type of word-of-mouth marketing that money can't buy, and it's at your fingertips through LinkedIn!

The Do's and Don'ts of LinkedIn

There are a variety of unwritten do's and don'ts that define LinkedIn rules of etiquette and are tips for success. Think of it this way: you wouldn't stand in front of a crowd at an in-person networking event and state that you despise your boss. You shouldn't do it in your LinkedIn updates or conversations either.

Your words can live online for a very long time and you never know where they might show up in the future thanks to links and copied content. Even after you delete an inappropriate picture or comment from your LinkedIn account, it might be too late. That picture or comment may have already been indexed by Google and other search engines, it may have been copied by another person and republished on their blog, or it could have been tweeted by more than one person to huge audiences. Did you know that the Library of Congress archives all public Twitter updates? The rules of behavior that you live by in offline professional networking apply online, too, and LinkedIn is not an exception to that rule.

WARNING

If you wouldn't do it in front of your boss, don't do it on LinkedIn.

Following are a number of LinkedIn do's and don'ts that can keep you out of trouble and position you for success rather than failure:

- Do include a professional picture with your profile.
- Do write an honest and complete profile.
- Do customize links in your profile to state where those links lead and what they contain.
- Do write a LinkedIn profile headline that explains what you do rather than providing generic information.
- Do include a personal message with your LinkedIn connection requests.
- Do personalize your LinkedIn profile URL.
- Do think like the boss (or customer) you want to connect with, and create a profile that speaks to that person.
- Do update your LinkedIn profile often.
- Do add value to every conversation you join on LinkedIn.

- Do acknowledge others, join their conversations, and share their content.

- Do work to create a profile that is 100 percent complete.

- Do customize your profile header and summary to let people know who you are and what you do, which will entice people to click on and read your entire profile.

- Do include keywords in your profile titles and specialties to help people find you in LinkedIn searches.

- Do make your profile public to boost your exposure.

- Do use LinkedIn apps and tools to add useful information to your profile and audience.

- Do disconnect from members who participate in activities that could be considered spam, illegal, inappropriate, or in violation of LinkedIn policies.

- Don't spam other LinkedIn members with self-promotional messages and updates.

- Don't spam the system and try to get around the rules in order to send connection requests to people you don't know.

- Don't publish anything you don't want the world to see.

- Don't replace personal updates entirely with updates from automated tools.

- Don't feel obligated to accept every connection request you get. Accept connection requests based on your LinkedIn goals.

- Don't think of your LinkedIn profile as a résumé. How boring would it be if someone handed you their résumé at an in-person networking event?

- Don't violate any laws or LinkedIn policies.

Even if your LinkedIn goals are limited in scope and your profile is private, the do's and don'ts still apply to you. LinkedIn is considered to be the social networking site for professionals, and as such, professional behavior is expected at all times.

Understand LinkedIn Rules and Terms of Service

LinkedIn has a clearly written list of rules for users, which are provided in the site's terms of service user agreement (accessible through the **User Agreement** link in the site's footer as shown in Figure 2.1). The document covers rules that every member must comply with or risk account deactivation. There are 5 do's and 28 don'ts included in the LinkedIn user agreement, so make sure you read them and abide by them in all of your LinkedIn activities.

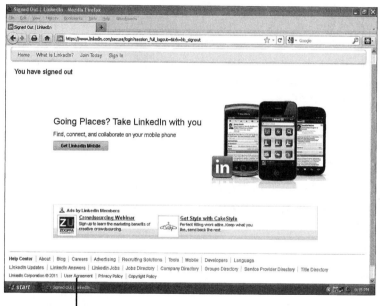

User Agreement link

Figure 2.1: *Click the* **User Agreement** *link in the LinkedIn.com footer to review the site's terms of service.*

QUICK TIP

To read the complete LinkedIn rules and policies before you start your profile, follow these links:

- User Agreement—linkedin.com/static?key=user_ agreement&trk=hb_ft_userag
- Copyright Policy—linkedin.com/static?key=copyright_ policy&trk=hb_ft_copy
- Privacy Policy—linkedin.com/static?key=privacy_policy&trk=hb_ ft_priv

The best rule to follow is this: If you're unsure whether a LinkedIn activity is acceptable, don't do it. It's better to be safe than sorry, so erring on the side of caution ensures that your hard work in building up your LinkedIn profile and audience isn't wasted over a single action. If you act professionally, ethically, honestly, and legally on LinkedIn, you should be safe and a welcome member of the LinkedIn community.

The Least You Need to Know

- To develop your LinkedIn plan, you must define your networking, content, and marketing strategies.
- Determine who you want to connect with (your target audience) to reach your LinkedIn goals.
- Online influencers can help spread your words and your authority wider and farther than you can alone.
- There are both written and unwritten rules of LinkedIn that you must follow at all times.

Creating Your Profile

In This Chapter

- Starting strong
- Going public
- Reaching 100 percent complete
- Developing a powerful profile
- Configuring settings, a URL, and more

Your LinkedIn profile is your space on the most popular professional social networking site in the world. With that in mind, you need to create a powerful profile that clearly explains who you are, what you can do, and where you want to go in your business or career. As you spend more time on LinkedIn, you'll be able to separate the powerful profiles from the weaker ones. Make sure your LinkedIn profile is one you want people to see and tells the story you want to share, in order to reach your goals.

From content to settings, there is more to your LinkedIn profile than your name and job title. This chapter teaches how to make your profile as strong as it can be from your first day on LinkedIn.

Focus and Lead with Your Strengths

A fundamental rule of branding says that a focused brand is a strong brand, and that rule applies to your online brand, too. Whether you're using LinkedIn to grow your business or career, your LinkedIn profile communicates your personal online brand, which reflects on all other aspects of your life and work. Therefore it needs to be focused to reach its full potential.

When people find your LinkedIn profile, they're unlikely to scroll through your entire profile and read every part and piece of information. Instead, they'll read through the information that appears *above the fold* and judgments will be formed as to whether or not they'll continue reading or connect with you on that information alone.

DEFINITION

Content that appears in a person's web browser window without having to scroll is considered to be **above the fold.** The term originally referred to content that can be seen in the top half of a newspaper page without turning the paper over.

If the content at the beginning of your LinkedIn profile doesn't tell the story it needs to in order to attract the target audience that you want to connect with, you'll lose connection opportunities; your exposure and success will be limited. That's why it's absolutely critical to lead with your strengths as they apply to your LinkedIn goals. Use the suggestions provided throughout this chapter as you create your LinkedIn profile to ensure it hypes your strengths and stays focused.

Make It Public

LinkedIn is an important part of your overall social media and content marketing plans. Everything you say and do on LinkedIn can boost your online exposure and open new doors for you. A private

LinkedIn profile only puts you in front of people you are connected to on LinkedIn. However, a public LinkedIn profile puts you in front of the world and allows anyone searching for people using keywords contained in your profile to find you.

WARNING

If there are things in your LinkedIn profile you don't want the world to see, then you should consider deleting them. Remember, LinkedIn is a professional networking site, so keep it clean.

If your profile touts your strengths, you're on your way to getting in front of the audience you need in order to reach your goals. Don't hide behind a private LinkedIn profile. Instead, make it public by signing in to your LinkedIn account and clicking on your name in the upper-right corner of the page that opens. Next, click on the **Settings** link from the drop-down menu, then click on the **Edit Your Public Profile** link under the Helpful Links heading, as shown in the lower portion of Figure 3.1.

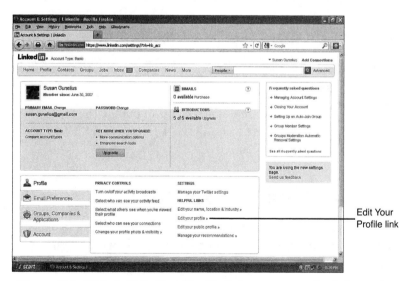

Figure 3.1: *Click the Edit Your Profile link to access your LinkedIn profile.*

As shown in Figure 3.2, you can click check boxes to select each part of your profile that you want to make publicly visible. Keep in mind, this is the profile that even people who are not logged in to LinkedIn can see.

Figure 3.2: *Select the check boxes next to information you want the world to see in your LinkedIn profile.*

The more parts of your profile that you make public, the more chances there are for people to find it via keyword searches on Google, Yahoo!, Bing, and so on.

The Completeness Bar

As you create your LinkedIn profile, you'll notice a Completeness Bar located on the right side of your screen, as shown in Figure 3.3. Your goal should be to reach 100 percent profile completeness.

Figure 3.3: *Try to reach 100 percent profile completeness.*

A 100 percent complete LinkedIn profile includes the following:

- Photo
- Executive summary
- Specialties skill set
- Education
- Three recent positions
- Three recommendations from your connections

You can provide all of the information to create a 100 percent complete LinkedIn profile except for three recommendations. However, you can send recommendation requests to your connections to reach 100 percent completeness. Recommendations are discussed in full detail in Chapter 8.

Developing a Powerful Profile, Section by Section

It's time to learn how to create your own LinkedIn profile one piece at a time. First, take some time to review your goals as discussed in Chapter 2. Next, determine your profile focus and the strengths you want to lead with. Finally, visit LinkedIn.com (see Figure 3.4), enter the requested information into the Join LinkedIn Today box, and click the **Join Now** button to create your own LinkedIn account.

Figure 3.4: *Enter the requested information to create your LinkedIn account.*

After you click the **Join Now** button, you'll be taken through a series of screens with questions that might vary depending on the information you input. These questions enable you to create a skeleton profile.

Depending on the type of email account you have, you might have to complete an extra step to verify your email account before your LinkedIn account will be fully functional. This step simply involves clicking on a link that is sent to the email address you provide during the LinkedIn registration process to verify and register that address with your LinkedIn account.

Once your account is created, you can start working on developing a comprehensive LinkedIn profile section by section.

Write a Captivating, Keyword-Rich Headline

Which sounds better as a profile headline?

- Owner, ABC Mobile
- Mobile app developer, mobile marketing consultant

The first headline is very literal. It tells people exactly what the LinkedIn member's title is and what company he works for. On the other hand, the second headline tells more of the LinkedIn member's story. It communicates his strengths in just six words and includes more than one keyword phrase that people might use to find industry experts via LinkedIn searches or search engines.

Your LinkedIn profile heading should accomplish two things: tell your story and strengths, and make your profile search-friendly. What are the most important things that you want to be known for? What do you want people to know about you before they even view your complete LinkedIn profile? What keywords are people using to find others with skills and goals similar to yours? These are the questions you need to answer in order to create a truly useful LinkedIn profile heading.

QUICK TIP

Use free tools like the Google Keyword Estimator Tool (adwords.google.com/select/KeywordToolExternal) and the Google Traffic Estimator (adwords.google.com/select/TrafficEstimatorSandbox) to research keywords.

To edit your LinkedIn profile heading, log in to your LinkedIn account and click on the **Profile** link in the top navigation bar. The Edit Profile page opens. Click on the **Edit** link next to your name to open the Basic Information editing page shown in Figure 3.5. Just type a new headline into the Headline text box, and click the **Save Changes** button to make your changes go live immediately.

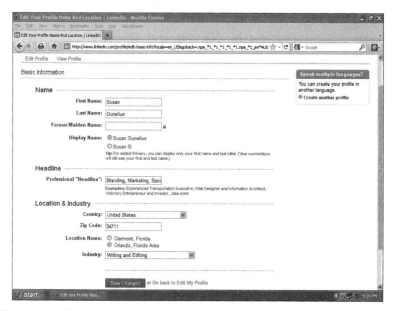

Figure 3.5: *Enter your headline into the Basic Information section of your profile.*

Basic Information

In addition to editing your headline in the Basic Information section of your LinkedIn profile, you can also edit your name, location, and industry information, as shown in Figure 3.5. This is the information that appears in your LinkedIn profile snapshot along with your photo.

Keep in mind, people might search LinkedIn members by industry, location, name, or keywords. Be sure to complete all fields in the Basic Information section of your LinkedIn profile, so as many people as possible can find you.

Photo

In the Edit Profile view of your LinkedIn account, you can click on the **Edit** link in the top-left corner of your profile to edit the photo that is displayed with your live LinkedIn profile. Just click the **Browse** button to locate the photo from your computer's hard drive that you want to upload to your account. Make sure the file is under 4 MB and is in JPG, GIF, or PNG format.

Once you upload your photo, you can choose to make it visible to your connections only, your entire network only, or to everyone. It is recommended that you make your photo visible to everyone in order to give you the most exposure, but if your LinkedIn goals are more limited in scope, you can choose a more private setting.

Summary

The summary section of your LinkedIn profile is where you can really tell your story. From the Edit Profile page of your LinkedIn account, you can click the **Add Summary** link to add a summary to your LinkedIn profile or click the **Edit** button next to the Summary heading if you've already created your summary and need to revise it.

The Summary page opens as shown in Figure 3.6. Here you can enter a written description of your professional experience and goals, as well as enter a list of your specialties. Be sure to use keywords in this section to increase the chances for people to find your profile via searches.

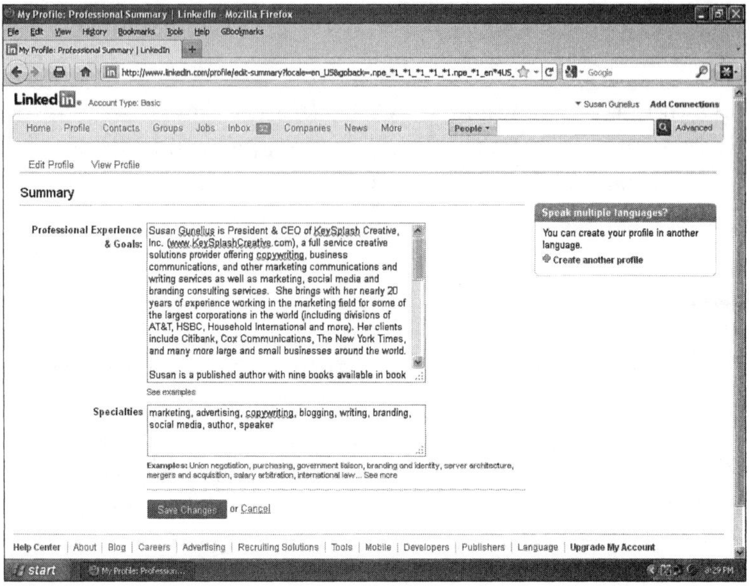

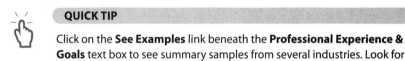

Figure 3.6: *Enter your story in the Summary section of your profile.*

Click on the **See Examples** link beneath the **Professional Experience & Goals** text box to see summary samples from several industries. Look for this link as you edit other profile sections, too.

Your summary is your opportunity to really sell yourself. Don't be modest. However, your summary is limited to 2,000 characters. You also shouldn't try to include everything about you in the summary. Instead, focus on your strengths and the most important things you want your target audience to know about you in order to meet your goals. Your summary should encourage the right people to want to learn more about you and connect with you.

When you're satisfied with your summary, click the **Save Changes** button and see how it looks on your live profile. Be sure to proof-read it!

Experience

The Experience section of your LinkedIn profile is where you can provide information about all of the jobs you've held and work you've done. Many companies are already included in the LinkedIn directory, so as you enter your positions, you should be sure to provide the company name, your job title, the start and end dates of your employment, and a description of your job. If the company you worked for is not already in the LinkedIn directory, you'll need to enter the company's industry and website address as well.

To enter your experience, simply go to the Edit Profile page of your LinkedIn account and click the **Add a Position** link to the right of the Experience heading. The Add Position window opens as shown in Figure 3.7.

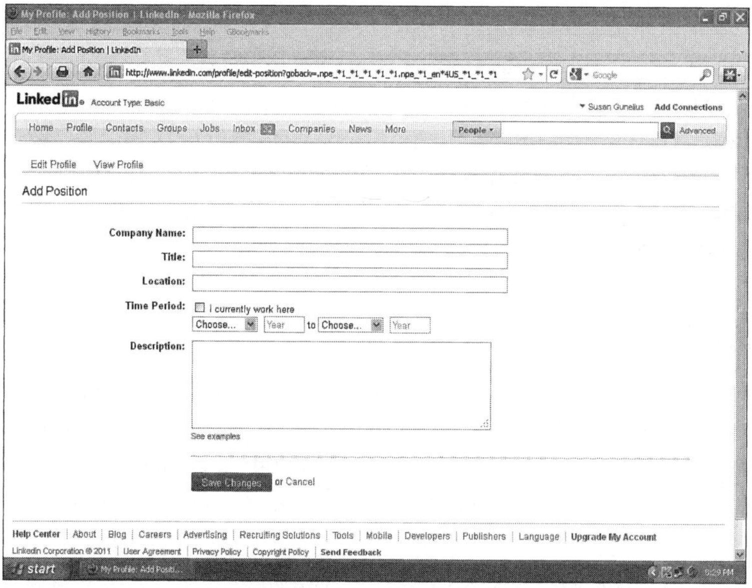

Figure 3.7: *Enter details about your jobs using the Add Position form.*

In order to add a position to your LinkedIn profile, you must provide a job title, company name, and dates of employment. The other fields in the Add Position form are optional. You can add as many positions as you want, including freelance work, consulting work, and so on.

The goal is to show everything you've done and can do, particularly as it relates to your LinkedIn profile focus and goals. People search for other people on LinkedIn by company, job title, and experience keywords. You don't want to miss a chance to be found by leaving jobs out of your profile.

For example, if you're looking for a job in graphic design but your only experience in the field has been designing websites for friends, you can enter that work as a position and refer to it as "Freelance Graphic Designer." While you don't want to be deceptive in your profile, you do want to make sure all relevant experience is included.

> **QUICK TIP**
>
> Jobs are listed in your LinkedIn profile chronologically based on start dates. The position with the most recent start date is listed first. There is no way to reorder jobs unless you change start dates.

If you're currently employed in a specific job, be sure to check the **I Currently Work Here** box in the Add Position form. This removes the end date from the position. Also, uncheck the **Update My Headline** button unless you want LinkedIn to automatically overwrite your existing profile headline with information from the new position.

Education

Completing the education section of your LinkedIn profile makes it easy to reconnect with old classmates and tells people who find your profile more about you. You can add your high school, college, graduate school, law school, medical school, vocational school, and so on, to your LinkedIn profile.

Just click on the **Add a School** link to the right of the Education heading in the Edit Profile section of your LinkedIn account to open the Add Education form shown in Figure 3.8.

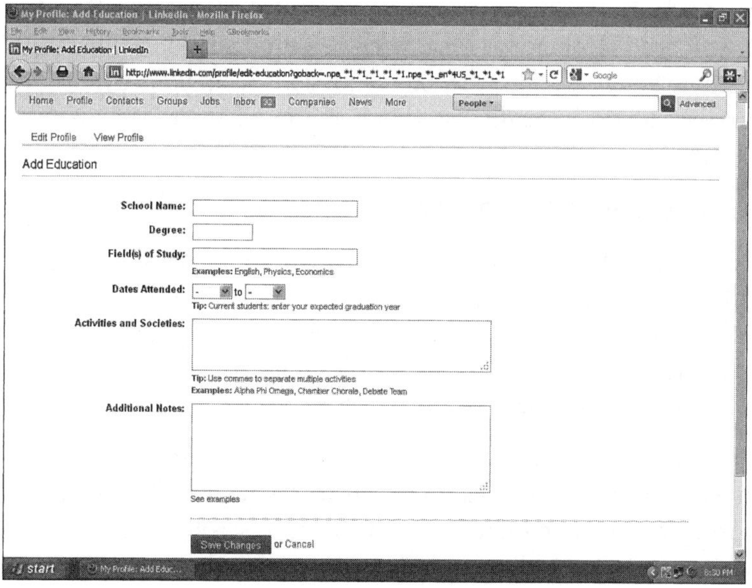

Figure 3.8: *Enter information about each school that you attended.*

Enter your school name, the degree you earned, fields of study, dates attended, activities and societies, and any other relevant information into the form, and then click the **Save Changes** button. Make sure the information looks good on your live profile, and then add any additional schools you want to include in your profile.

> **QUICK TIP**
>
> You can view your profile as others will see it at any time by selecting the **Profile** link in the top navigation bar when you're logged in to your LinkedIn account. A drop-down menu appears where you can click the **View Profile** link to view your live LinkedIn profile.

Recommendations

As you complete your profile, you'll notice in the Edit Profile view, that beneath each job and school listing is a link that says, Ask for recommendations. Recommendations are a powerful feature of LinkedIn that allows members to provide testimonials about other members they have worked with or attended school with.

In order to reach 100 percent completeness of your LinkedIn profile, you need to obtain at least three recommendations. These links are where you can request recommendations from your connections. Recommendations are discussed in detail in Chapter 8.

Additional Information

The Additional Information section includes four sections that can help you make your profile more comprehensive. Remember, the more information you can give to tell your story, the better. Therefore, if you can enter information into the Additional Information section of your LinkedIn profile, do it.

To complete this section, go to the Edit Profile page in your LinkedIn account and click on the **Edit** link next to the Additional Information heading (you'll probably have to scroll down to see this section). The Additional Information form shown in Figure 3.9 opens.

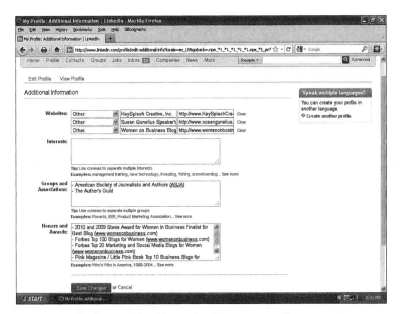

Figure 3.9: *Enter as much additional information to tell your story as you can.*

The Additional Information section of your LinkedIn profile provides space for you to enter the following details:

Websites: Enter the URL for any websites, blogs, forums, or other online destinations that you own. Be sure to personalize the URLs so they're not given generic labels such as "Personal Website." To do this, click on the **Choose** drop-down menu to the left of the URL text box, and select **Other** from the list. A new text box appears where you can enter a custom name for your link. This is a very important step that can boost traffic to your content and conversations that happen off of LinkedIn.

Interests: You can enter professional and personal interests into this text box. What do you want people to know about you that might not already be reflected in your LinkedIn profile? Enter it here in 750 characters or fewer.

Groups and Associations: If you belong to any groups or associations that can help tell your story or get your LinkedIn profile in front of your target audience, be sure to include them in this section, which is limited to a maximum of 750 characters.

Honors and Awards: Show off the honors and awards you've received in this section of your LinkedIn profile. Again, you can use up to 750 characters.

Once you've entered all of your information into the Additional Information form, click the **Save Changes** button and review it on your live LinkedIn profile. Make sure there aren't any spelling errors!

Other LinkedIn Profile Sections

LinkedIn has launched several new sections that you can add to your LinkedIn profile to tell more of your story. These sections don't apply to everyone, so you need to click the **Add Sections** link beneath your LinkedIn profile summary (while in the Edit Profile page of your account) to find them. However, depending on your skills and experience, one or more of these sections could be very important to you.

QUICK TIP

You can change the order of the sections in your LinkedIn profile from the Edit Profile page of your account. Just hover over the section you want to move and click on the crosshair/four-way arrow handle located to the left of a section heading in your profile. Drag it to the location where you want it to appear. A gray box will appear, indicating positions where you're able to relocate sections within your profile. When you're satisfied with the location, release the mouse and the section is instantly repositioned to that spot.

Publications: If you have authored any published books or articles that you want to feature as part of your LinkedIn profile, simply click on the **Add Sections** link to open the Add Sections pop-up window, and select the **Publications** link from the list of sections provided. You'll be asked to provide the publication name, publisher, date of publication, link to the publication, and a description. You can also add other authors if you co-wrote the publication.

Certifications: You can highlight any special certifications you've received by adding the Certifications section to your LinkedIn profile. Just click on the **Certifications** link in the Add Sections pop-up window and complete the form provided.

Languages: For many people, highlighting the various languages they speak is a critical part of their LinkedIn profile. You can add a languages section to your profile by clicking on the **Languages** link in the Add Sections pop-up window and entering the information requested.

WARNING

Don't confuse the Languages section of your LinkedIn profile with a complete profile created in another language. To create your profile in a different language, click on the **Create Your Profile in Another Language** link near the top of the right column in the Edit Profile page of your account.

Patents: If you own any patents, then you should add the Patents section to your LinkedIn profile. Click on the **Patents** link in the Add Sections pop-up window to do it.

Skills: Not only is it useful to add the Skills section to your LinkedIn profile so you can provide a quick list of your most important and marketable skills, but it's also a great way to add keywords to your profile! Click on the **Skills** link in the Add Sections pop-up window to create your skills list.

LinkedIn frequently launches new tools and features, so keep an eye out for announcements on the LinkedIn blog: blog.linkedin.com/.

Configuring Profile and Account Settings

You're in complete control of your LinkedIn profile. You can edit your profile at any time. Remember it's your story, so set up your profile and account in the ways that best communicate that story to your audience.

To modify your settings, log in to your LinkedIn account and click on your name in the top-right corner of your window; a drop-down menu appears. Click on the **Settings** link from that menu to open the main settings page. As shown in Figure 3.10, on the left side of this page is a box with quick links to complete common tasks such as changing your password or email address.

In the lower-left corner of Figure 3.10 is a box with four tabs: Profile; Email Preferences; Groups, Companies & Applications; and Account. This is where all of your various settings can be found. By default, the Profile tab is selected and visible.

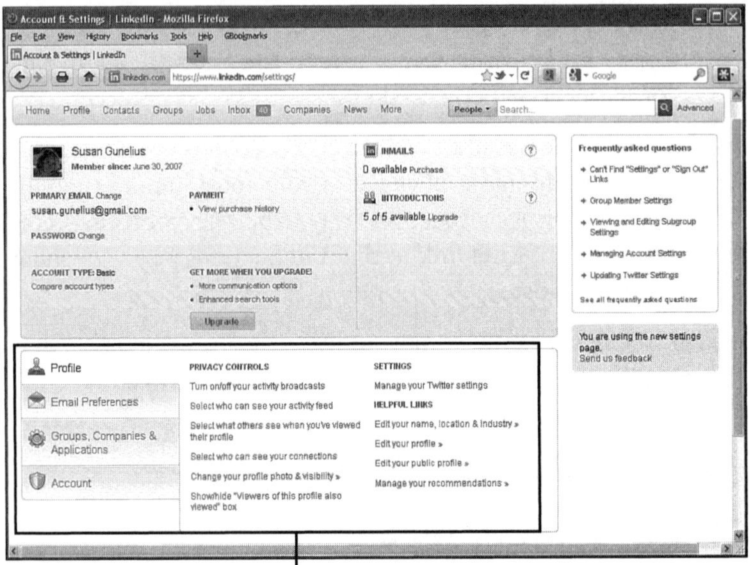

Manage all of your account settings here

Figure 3.10: *The Settings page is where you can customize all configurations for your profile and account.*

Profile

There are a wide variety of settings you can configure to make your LinkedIn profile look the way you want it to. Don't be afraid to experiment with the different settings. You can't break anything, and reverting to previous settings is as easy as a click of the mouse.

As shown in Figure 3.10, the Profile tab offers a list of links. When you click on those links, you can modify the following:

Turn on/off your activity broadcasts: Just click the check box to let people know when you edit your profile, make recommendations, or follow companies on LinkedIn. When this setting is checked and turned on, all of your activity updates will appear in your LinkedIn activity feed. This is a great way to stay on your connections' radar screens.

WARNING

If you're looking for a new job and don't want your current employer to see your LinkedIn activities, you might consider turning the activity broadcast feature off.

Select who can see your activity feed: If you don't want anyone to see your LinkedIn activities at all, you can modify this setting by selecting **Only You** from the provided drop-down menu. For greater levels of exposure, however, you can select to make your activity feed visible to only your connections, your entire network, or everyone. For maximum exposure, choose the **Everyone** setting.

Select what others see when you've viewed their profile: Depending on your LinkedIn goals, you might want to change this setting in your profile. You can select to make your name and headline visible to members whose profiles you view, or you can choose to show an industry-specific anonymous profile where only your industry and title will be visible. You can also choose to be totally anonymous, so other members won't see any information about you when you view their profiles. Again, for the most growth and opportunities, display your name and headline.

QUICK TIP

If you choose either of the available anonymous settings for others to see when you view their profiles, you won't be able to view your Profile Stats, which tell you who has viewed your own profile.

Select who can see your connections: You can allow all of your connections to view your entire list of connections or you can keep your list of connections private by choosing the **Only You** option when configuring this profile setting. Keep in mind, mutual connections will always be visible to members in your network. Furthermore, one of the primary purposes of social networking is *networking*, so making connections visible to others is an important part of meeting new people and building new relationships based on mutual goals and interests. With that in mind, it is recommended that you make your connections visible.

Change your profile photo & visibility: This link provides another way for you to edit your profile photo as discussed earlier in the Photo section of this chapter.

Show/Hide "Viewers of this profile also viewed" box: If you want your profile visitors to see links to other profiles that previous visitors have looked at in addition to your profile, click this link and select the check box to display the "Viewers of this profile also viewed" box on your profile.

Manage your Twitter settings: If you use Twitter, it's extremely easy to update your LinkedIn profile with your tweets automatically. Just click the **Manage your Twitter settings** link followed by the **Add Twitter Account** link in the settings page that opens to link your Twitter account with LinkedIn. That's all there is to it. Be sure to select the check box next to **Display your Twitter account on your LinkedIn profile** once you've successfully added your Twitter account.

You can also limit the tweets you share from your Twitter account. For example, if you don't want all of your tweets to appear in your LinkedIn profile, you can select the check box next to the **Share only tweets that include #in**, within this settings page. Anytime you write a tweet that you want to be published in your LinkedIn profile, make sure you include the **#in** *hashtag*. Only those tweets with that hashtag will publish to your LinkedIn profile when this setting is selected.

> **DEFINITION**
>
> A **hashtag** is a keyword preceded by the # symbol used in a tweet. Hashtags help Twitter users quickly find content related to a specific subject.

You can also choose to show rich link display where possible, including a picture, page title, and short description. Just select the check box under the Tweet Display heading.

Edit your name, location & industry: This is a quick link to edit the basic information in your profile as discussed earlier in the Basic Information section of this chapter.

Edit your profile: This is a quick link to take you to the Edit Profile page as discussed in the Profile section earlier in this chapter.

Edit your public profile: As mentioned earlier in this chapter, you can make your LinkedIn profile public by selecting this link in the Profile settings section of your LinkedIn account. Pick and choose the sections of your profile (in the Customize Your Public Profile box on the right side of the page) that you want to make visible to everyone who sees it (whether or not they're logged in to LinkedIn).

Scroll down to the Your Public Profile *URL* box and click on the **Customize Your Public Profile URL** link. This is a very important setting to configure because it allows you to personalize your LinkedIn profile URL, making it easier for you to share your profile link and for people to find your profile on LinkedIn.

> **DEFINITION**
>
> **URL** stands for Uniform Resource Locator. It represents the unique address of a web page.

For example, instead of having a generic numeric LinkedIn profile URL, you can choose your own 5–30 letter personalized URL extension. All LinkedIn Profile URLs include the same parts except for the final extension that signifies the specific profile, as follows linkedin.com/in/YourPersonalizedInfo. My LinkedIn profile URL is linkedin.com/in/SusanGunelius. That's so much better than a generic URL. You can make your personalized URL anything you want, as long as it hasn't already been taken by someone else. Personalizing your URL also helps boost your Google search rankings when people enter your name into the Google search box.

Manage your recommendations: This is where you can request, send, and administer recommendations on LinkedIn. Recommendations are discussed in detail in Chapter 8.

Email Preferences

To avoid being inundated with email related to your LinkedIn activities and connections, you can modify your email preferences by selecting the Email Preferences tab on the Settings page in your LinkedIn profile as shown in Figure 3.11.

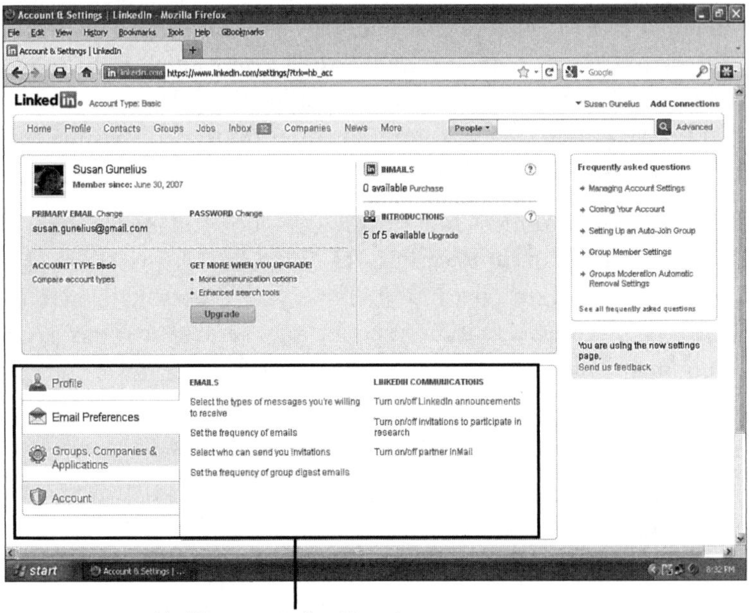

Modify your email settings here

Figure 3.11: *Configure your email and LinkedIn communications preferences.*

Select the types of messages you're willing to receive: You can configure your LinkedIn account so you receive messages notifying you of new introductions from other members and private email messages via the LinkedIn messaging tool, InMail. Alternatively, you can receive only introduction messages. I highly recommend that you choose the former setting, so other members can easily contact you. Why are you on LinkedIn if you don't want to communicate with other members?

You can also select the check boxes next to each item listed under the Opportunities heading: career opportunities, expertise requests, consulting offers, business deals, new ventures, personal reference requests, job inquiries, and requests to reconnect. These preferences appear in the Contact section of your LinkedIn profile and give other members a better idea of the types of communications you're interested in. Finally, you can enter any advice to people who contact you in the text box provided.

Set the frequency of emails: This is where you can modify how frequently you receive notification emails from LinkedIn related to your connections, groups, invitations, and so on. You can set each of the following emails to be sent to you individually (as they happen), weekly (in a digest format), or not at all:

- **InMails, Introductions, and OpenLink** messages come from outside your network, and you can choose to accept or decline them at any time.

- **Invitations** to join other members' networks.

- **Profile forwards** sent from other members who think you might be interested in the profile owners.

- **Job notifications** sent from other members who think you might be interested in job openings.

- **Questions from your connections.**

- **Replies/messages from connections** in response to messages you sent.

- **Invitations to join groups.**

- **Network activity** updates on your connections' major activities.

- **Network activity discussion** updates. These are updates to discussions you've participated in.

- **Referral Center.** Sent from LinkedIn when Referral Center has identified connections that could be a good fit for open jobs at your company.

- **Receive Actionable Emails** from other members.

- **Connection Suggestions** sent from other members.

- **Top articles news digest.** An aggregated list of top headlines being discussed by people in your industry.

Select who can send you invitations: The best choice is to allow anyone on LinkedIn to send you invitations to connect. You can always accept or decline individual invitations; so to grow your network, allow anyone to send you an invitation. If you'd prefer, you can choose to receive invitations only from people who know your email address or appear in your Imported Contacts list (if you imported a contacts list as discussed in Chapter 5). For the least growth potential, you can allow invitations only from people on your Imported Contacts list.

Set the frequency of group digest emails: If you belong to any LinkedIn groups (discussed in Chapter 7), you can configure how frequently you receive emails about group activity updates to daily, weekly, or not at all.

Turn on/off LinkedIn announcements: If you select the check box in this setting, you'll receive messages from LinkedIn with announcements, tips, and information about new products and services. These messages are useful, so I recommend that you activate this setting and give it a try. You can always turn it off later if you don't like the messages.

Turn on/off invitations to participate in research: LinkedIn invites users to participate in market research studies based on non-personal information contained in their LinkedIn profiles. If you'd like to participate in online research studies, select the check box in this setting.

Turn on/off partner InMail: LinkedIn Partner InMails are sent by third parties for marketing purposes. You can opt out of all or some third party InMail messages by deselecting the check boxes in this settings page.

Groups, Companies & Applications

Select the **Groups, Companies & Applications** link on the main Settings page in your LinkedIn account to reveal links to modify settings related to groups, companies, applications, and privacy controls as shown in Figure 3.12.

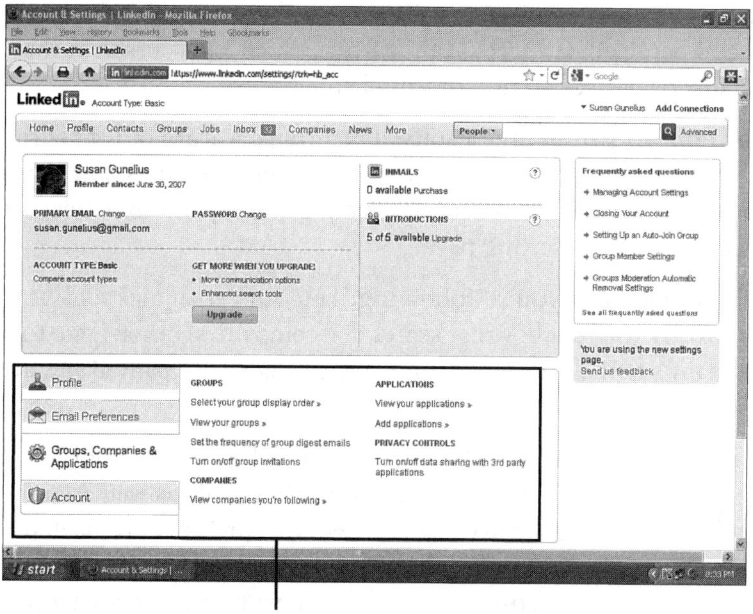

Manage your groups, companies, and applications settings here

Figure 3.12: *Configure your preferences related to groups, companies, and applications.*

Select your group display order: Click on this link to change the order of the groups you belong to in your LinkedIn profile. Most people belong to multiple groups, and some groups are more useful in telling your story than others. Put those more useful groups at the top of your groups list by entering numbers into the boxes under the Order heading on this settings page.

QUICK TIP

You can also click the **Member Settings** link to the right of any group name on this settings page to modify individual group settings. Groups are discussed in detail in Chapter 7.

View your groups: Get a quick look at the groups you belong to, groups you might like, groups you're following, and the groups directory from this settings page. You can also create a group here. Again, groups are discussed in Chapter 7.

Set the frequency of group digest emails: This is simply another place where you can access this setting, which is discussed in the Email Preferences section of this chapter.

Turn on/off group invitations: The groups feature of LinkedIn is an important part of networking with other members, but if you don't want to receive invitations to join groups, you can deselect the check box on this setting page.

View companies you're following: You can get a quick look at the companies you're following, search for companies, or navigate to a company's home page from this settings page. Company Pages are discussed in detail in Chapter 4.

View your applications: You can get a quick view of all of the applications you've added to your LinkedIn profile as well as any external websites you have given access to your LinkedIn profile. You can remove any application or external website from your profile permanently by selecting the check box next to it and clicking the **Remove** button. Applications are discussed in detail in Chapter 6.

Add applications: This settings page lists available applications that you can add to your LinkedIn profile. Again, applications are discussed in Chapter 6.

Turn on/off data sharing with third party applications: There are many applications that are not owned by LinkedIn but can add features to your LinkedIn user experience and profile. Make sure the check box in this setting is selected so your data can be shared with third party applications. You will always be prompted to allow individual applications to access your data when you add them to your profile, so I recommend that you turn this setting on and allow or disallow apps to access your data on a case-by-case basis in the future.

Account

You can configure your main LinkedIn account settings by clicking on the **Account** tab on the main settings page and revealing links to privacy controls, settings, email and password, and helpful links as shown in Figure 3.13.

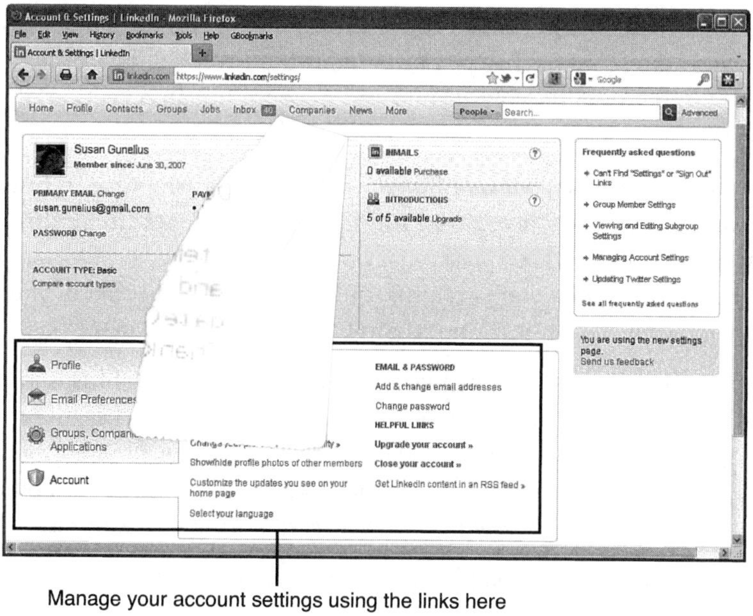

Manage your account settings using the links here

Figure 3.13: *Modify your account settings from the Account tab.*

Manage Social Advertising: It's highly likely that you'll want to turn this setting off by deselecting the check box in the settings window. If this setting is selected, then your name and photo could show up in related ads shown to LinkedIn members when you recommend people and services, follow companies, or take other actions.

> **QUICK TIP**
>
> The Manage Social Advertising setting defaults to *on*, so you need to go in and manually deselect that check box to turn it off.

Turn on/off enhanced advertising: LinkedIn partners with third party companies to show ads to members based on nonpersonally identifiable information in their profiles. If you don't want to see these ads, you should deselect the check box in this setting.

Change your profile photo & visibility: This is just another way to access the same setting you find under the Profile tab described earlier in the Configuring Profile and Account Settings section of this chapter.

Show/hide profile photos of other members: If you want to limit the member profile photos that you see as you navigate LinkedIn, you can configure those preferences on this settings page. Options include viewing everyone's photos, only photos from people in your network, only your connections' photos, or no one's photos.

Customize the updates you see on your home page: This is a particularly useful setting to modify to meet your needs because it lets you reduce the clutter of updates displayed on your home page. You can choose to view or hide the following updates on your home page by selecting or deselecting the corresponding check boxes:

- New connections in your network
- Updates from your extended network
- Status updates from your connections
- Posts from your connections
- When connections change profile information
- When connections change profile photos
- When connections receive recommendations
- When connections upgrade to a premium account
- Questions from your connections
- Answers from your connections
- Jobs you may be interested in
- Events your connections are interested in or attending
- Polls from your connections
- Groups your connections have joined or created
- Discussions from your groups
- Application updates from your connections

- When connections modify or add a Company Page
- When connections follow news

Select your language: You can change the primary language of your profile to any of those offered through this settings page.

Add & change email addresses: You can add, delete, or edit the email addresses you want associated with your LinkedIn account from this settings page. Select your preferred email address as the primary email address for your account. This is where all notifications and email messages related to your account will be sent. You should also enter all other email addresses that you use to provide more ways for people to find you. Taking this additional step also eliminates messages to your alternate email addresses inviting you to join LinkedIn when other members invite you using those addresses.

Change password: Choose a password that is at least 6 characters and enter it into the password form.

Upgrade your account: You can upgrade to a paid account by clicking this link. Upgraded accounts are discussed in detail in Chapter 16.

Close your account: If you want to delete your account entirely, this is where you do it.

Get LinkedIn content in an RSS feed: If you want to be able to view LinkedIn content via your preferred *feed reader* you can enable an *RSS* feed for your network updates or access the RSS link for any category in LinkedIn Answers (LinkedIn Answers are discussed in detail in Chapter 9) through this settings link.

DEFINITION

An acronym for Really Simple Syndication, **RSS** is a technology that creates web content syndication and allows web users to subscribe to websites and blogs. RSS subscribers receive the content for their various website and blog subscriptions in an aggregated form. That content is read in a single location through a **feed reader.** Popular online feed readers include Google Reader and NewsGator.

As you spend more time on LinkedIn, you might find that you want to change some of your LinkedIn settings. That's absolutely fine. You should be flexible in using LinkedIn to meet your goals. Don't be afraid to experiment and learn in order to build the most effective and powerful LinkedIn profile.

The Least You Need to Know

- A public LinkedIn profile offers the most exposure and opportunity for growth.
- A powerful profile is focused, highlights your strengths, tells your story, and is 100 percent complete.
- You should take advantage of all sections and personalization options available to you to make your LinkedIn profile stronger.
- Configure your profile, email, and account settings to ensure that your LinkedIn profile and account work the best way to meet your goals.

Developing a Company Page

In This Chapter

- Why you need a Company Page
- Creating your Company Page
- Raising awareness of your Company Page
- Developing a powerful profile
- Configuring settings, a URL, and more

LinkedIn offers a place for businesses, too. Any business can create a Company Page on LinkedIn that can be used to tell the company's story, recruit new employees, share product and service information, gather testimonials, and more. Whether your company has 10,000 employees or one, you can create a Company Page for free.

There are approximately 2 million Company Pages on LinkedIn. With tens of millions of LinkedIn members viewing those pages, it can be assumed that potential customers, employees, business partners, investors, and more want to learn more about these companies and connect with them. Your company should be represented, and this chapter teaches you how to get started.

Features and Uses for Company Pages

Your LinkedIn Company Page is your business's space on the most popular professional social networking website. When I teach people about social media marketing, one of the first things I explain is how important it is to have a core-branded location online that all of your online activities lead back to. This is the central hub of your online presence, where you have control, and can tell your company's complete story.

A LinkedIn Company Page is a great choice for a business's core-branded online destination because it's interactive and easily connected to all of your online activities. Your free Company Page can help you ...

- Make your company more human through engaging content and conversations.
- Put faces to your brand by highlighting employees.
- Describe your company culture and work environment.
- Feature your products and services.
- Receive and display recommendations and testimonials.
- Announce job openings.
- Describe employee benefits.
- Publish news, product updates, and useful information.
- Share your blog posts, Twitter updates, YouTube videos, and more.
- Hype special discounts and offers.
- Promote events, conferences, and so on.
- Offer links to your company's other websites.
- Gather analytics about people who visit your Company Page.
- Compare your Company Page to similar pages.

Your LinkedIn Company Page is primarily an indirect marketing tool, but by using specific features, you can also use it for direct marketing such as promoting events, announcing sales, and so on. However, as with your personal LinkedIn profile and efforts, the vast majority of the activities on your Company Page should offer useful, meaningful information rather than sales pitches.

> **QUICK TIP**
>
> There are more people looking at your Company Page than potential customers and employees. Investors, purchasing managers, recruiters, journalists, and more might look, too. Make sure your content matches that diverse audience and leverages the opportunities those people present.

Your LinkedIn Company Page is divided into four specific parts identified by tabs: Overview, Careers, Products & Services, and Analytics. Each part offers different ways for you to publish content, engage with visitors, and share useful information.

Overview: The Overview section of your LinkedIn Company Page is your welcome page. Here you can:

- Describe your company.
- Identify your company's industry, location, revenue, size, website, and date founded.
- Display your blog and Twitter feeds.
- Share news about your company.
- Highlight your company's LinkedIn activity feed.
- Display your employees and new hires.

Careers: The Careers section enables visitors to research your company for potential employment. With a free Company Page, you can display open job opportunities.

Products & Services: The Products & Services section allows you to tell more of your company story. You can …

- List and describe your products and services.

- Publish videos and images.

- Request and display recommendations.

- Promote special offers.

Analytics: The Analytics section is only visible to your page's administrator(s) and allows you to gather metrics related to your free Company Page's performance. You can …

- Track the number of followers your Company Page has.

- Identify what your visitors click on your page.

- Track page views and visitors.

- Compare your page's performance to similar companies' page performance.

You can set up a skeleton LinkedIn Company Page in just a few minutes and add to it at any time. A Company Page can only benefit your company in terms of spreading awareness and boosting word-of-mouth marketing, so if you don't have a Company Page already, you should create one as soon as possible.

How to Create a Company Page

Anyone who has a company email address, and who is a current employee of that company, is authorized to create a Company Page for that company if they have a LinkedIn account. Just sign in to your LinkedIn account, click the **Companies** link in the top navigation bar, and then click the **Add Company Page** link near the top right of the Companies page. This opens the Create a Company Page shown in Figure 4.1.

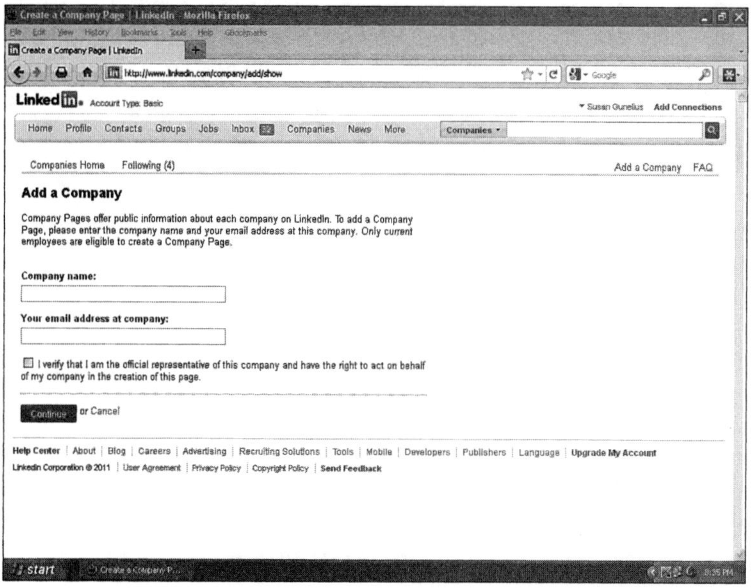

Figure 4.1: *Enter the requested information into the form to create a Company Page.*

> **QUICK TIP**
>
> You can visit linkedin.com/company/add/show to go directly to the Create a Company Page form.

Simply enter your company email address and your name, click the **Verification** check box, and click the **Continue** button. Your Company Page opens in edit mode with the Overview tab ready for you to develop as shown in Figure 4.2.

Overview

There are several sections of the Overview tab that you can develop. Try to provide as much information as you can to tell the best story for the LinkedIn audience.

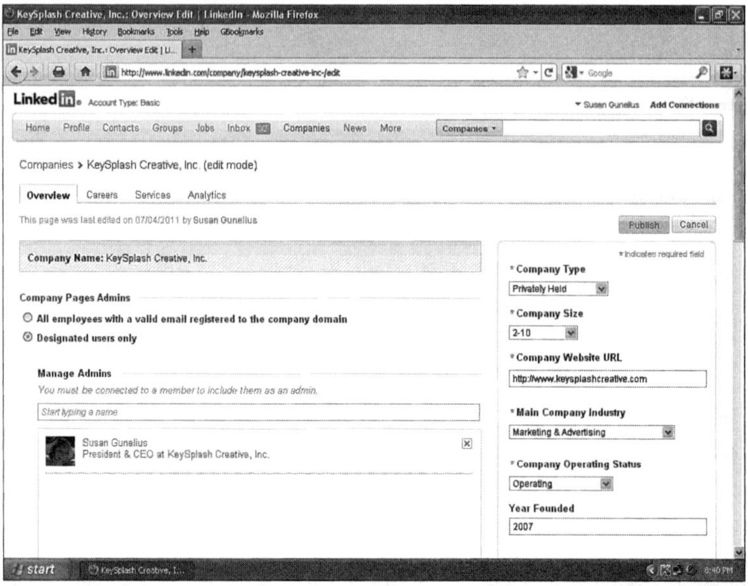

Figure 4.2: *Enter your company's Overview information in the **Overview** tab.*

Company Pages Admins: This section is shown in Figure 4.2, and it's where you identify who can edit your Company Page. You can opt to allow everyone with a valid company email address to edit your Company Page, or you can identify designated users by email address. Just click the corresponding radio button to make your selection.

> **QUICK TIP**
>
> If you choose the Designated Users Only option, the screen expands to reveal a text box where you can enter approved admin email addresses.

On the right side at the top of the Overview tab edit screen is a section where you can enter your company information as follows:

1. Click the drop-down menu under the **Company Type** heading and select the correct option for your company.

2. From the **Company Size** drop-down menu, identify how many employees work for your business.

3. Enter your Company Website URL.

4. Select your **Main Company Industry** from the provided drop-down menu.

5. Identify your **Company Operating Status** by selecting the appropriate option from the drop-down menu.

6. Enter the **Year Founded**.

7. Provide up to five **Company Locations** (shown in Figure 4.3).

Logos: As shown in Figure 4.3, you can upload a standard logo of 100×60 pixels to appear with your profile and a 50×50 pixel logo to appear in network updates related to your Company Page.

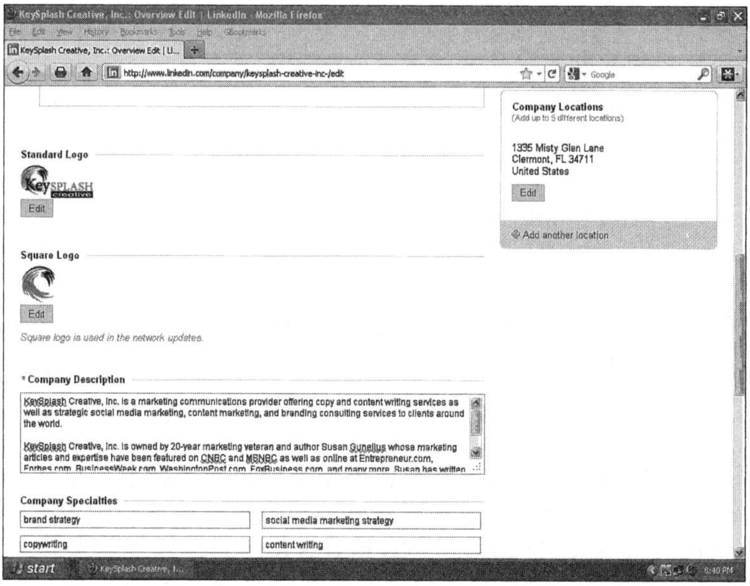

Figure 4.3: *Upload your logo and describe your company and specialties.*

Company Description: Enter a compelling description of your company that describes what you do, the benefits you bring to customers and employees, and what you can offer.

Company Specialties: Enter keywords related to your company's specialties in the text boxes provided. You can add more specialties by clicking the **Add More Specialties** link.

Twitter ID: If you have a Twitter profile where you tweet content for your company (at least part of the time), then you should enter your Twitter handle into the **Twitter ID** text box provided (as shown in Figure 4.4) to display your Twitter stream on the Overview tab of your LinkedIn Company Page.

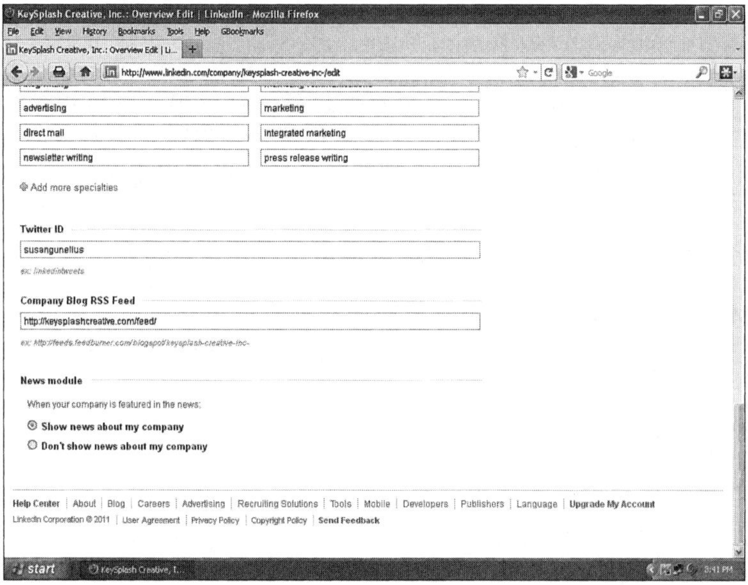

Figure 4.4: *Enter your Twitter username in the **Twitter ID** text box to show your Twitter feed on your Company Page Overview tab.*

Company Blog RSS Feed: If you publish a company blog, then you should display a feed of your recent posts on your Company Page by entering your blog RSS feed URL in this text box.

INSIDER SECRET

If you haven't set up your company blog's RSS feed, you can find an easy guide at: google.com/support/feedburner/bin/topic.py?topic=13055.

News module: You can display links to news about your blog that appears across the web by selecting the **Show News About My Company** radio button in this section. News comes from a variety of sources and is identified contextually, so you cannot control what appears in this module. If you'd prefer not to show news from other sources in your Company Page, select the **Don't Show News About My Company** radio button.

When you've completed all sections of the Overview tab, click the **Careers** tab to customize that section of your Company Page.

Careers

The Careers tab is only personalized on your Company Page when you post a job through LinkedIn. Free Company Pages offer the basic Careers tab, which displays a list of the active job postings you've published on LinkedIn. Simply click the yellow **Post a Job** button shown in Figure 4.5 to get started.

> **WARNING**
>
> There is a fee to post a job on LinkedIn for 30 days. The cost varies based on the location of the job (e.g., $195 in Orlando vs. $295 in New York City). Discounts are offered when multiple jobs are posted at the same time.

Figure 4.5: *Click the **Post a Job** button to publish a job opening.*

The Post a Job page opens: here you can enter all relevant information and publish your job opening. Once the job opportunity is
published, it automatically appears on your LinkedIn Careers tab as
shown in Figure 4.6. Posting jobs is covered in detail in Chapter 15.

Figure 4.6: *Your posted jobs appear on your Company Page Careers tab.*

If your company is extremely serious about using LinkedIn for
recruiting and hiring, then you should contact LinkedIn Corporate
Recruiting Solutions through the **Contact Us** button at talent.
linkedin.com to discuss premium career pages. LinkedIn offers
Gold and Silver career page packages that can turn your company's
career page into a complete information center.

QUICK TIP

The LinkedIn Company Page has a premium careers page that you can
view at: linkedin.com/company/linkedin/careers. It offers a special display
banner, jobs, employee recommendations, video, benefits, culture, and
more.

Keep in mind, the Gold and Silver career page packages are not cheap. LinkedIn doesn't advertise the prices for these packages, but as part of its Corporate Recruiting Solutions offerings—discussed in detail in Chapter 15—they are offered through one-year contracts and can cost tens of thousands of dollars per year.

Products and Services

The Products tab is where you can showcase your products and services, complete with descriptions and recommendations. Note that the heading of this tab will reflect the types of products and services you add to your page. For example, if you only add products, the tab will simply say "Products," but if you add products and services, it will say "Products and Services," or simply "Services" if you only add services.

Just click the arrow on the **Admin Tools** button to reveal your editing options and select **Add a Product or Service** to add a new product or service to your Products & Services tab. The edit Product & Services page opens as shown in Figures 4.7 and 4.8. Here you can enter all of the requested information about your product or service.

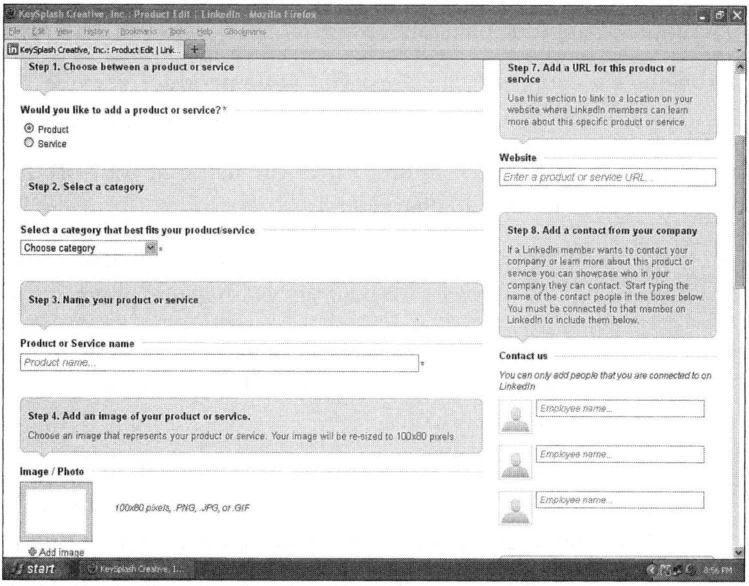

Figure 4.7: *Complete the form to add a product or service to your Company Page.*

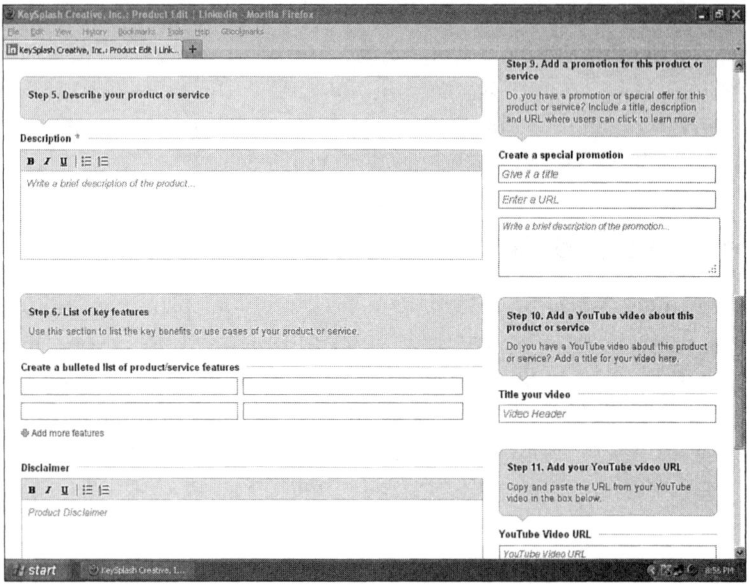

Figure 4.8: *Scroll down to complete all fields in the form.*

Provide the requested information to add your product or service as follows:

1. **Would you like to add a product or service?** Select the appropriate radio button.

2. **Select a category that best fits your product/service.** Choose the best category from the drop-down menu.

3. **Product or Service name.** Enter the name of your product or service (up to 100 characters).

4. **Add an image of your product or service.** Click the **Add Image** link to upload a 100×80 pixels image or photo in .png, .gif, or .jpg format.

5. **Description.** Enter a description (up to 2,000 characters) of your product or service.

6. **Create a bulleted list of product/service features.** Enter up to eight key benefits in the text boxes provided (up to 100 characters each). Click the **Add More Features** link to display additional text boxes. Note that this step includes a

Disclaimer box, where you can enter any necessary legal notices related to your product or service.

7. **Website.** Enter a URL in the text box in the upper-right column. The URL should direct visitors to your website or a particular page on your website, where they can learn about your product or service in more detail.

8. **Contact us.** In the text boxes provided, enter the names of employees you are connected to on LinkedIn who can respond to inquiries on behalf of your company.

9. **Create a special promotion.** This is where you can offer discounts and other promotions. Just enter a title, URL, and description of your special promotion.

10. **Title your video.** You can add a YouTube video about your product or service. Enter a title for the video in this text box.

11. **YouTube video URL.** Enter the URL of the YouTube video about your product or service into the text box. The video will be embedded into your product/service page.

WARNING

You can only add 25 products or services to your Company Page, so choose your best products for the LinkedIn audience if you have a large product line.

Once you add a product to your Company Page, you can edit it, delete it, or add more by clicking the **Admin Tools** button on the right side of your Company Page (above your page follower count) to reveal the admin drop-down menu. You can see a published product from the Dell Company Page on LinkedIn in Figure 4.9. Note that individual recommendations are published beneath the product description box. Visitors to your page can recommend individual products and services by clicking the Recommend button beneath the product name as shown in Figure 4.9.

Figure 4.9: *Dell has received 62 recommendations on this product.*

You can also view your main products and services page, where all of the products you added to your Company Page are listed with the images and descriptions you provided. You can see part of Dell's product list in Figure 4.10.

Analytics

The final tab of your LinkedIn Company Page is the Analytics tab. This is where you can track the performance of your Company Page. Here you'll find charts telling you how many page views and visitors each tab in your Company Page receives. You can also learn what people click on in your Company Page and how many LinkedIn members are following your page. For deeper analysis, you can compare your statistics with similar companies' statistics.

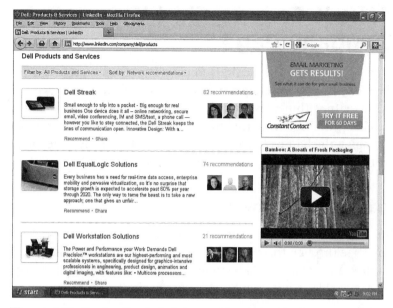

Figure 4.10: *Product lists include images, descriptions, and recommendation information.*

Use the metrics provided in these charts to identify trends, learn what is and isn't working, and modify your efforts for the future. For example, if you launch a special campaign to increase followers, you can analyze how visits and page views were affected during the campaign, as well as how many new followers your page received during that time.

The statistics offered in the Analytics tab should be used in conjunction with your own analysis of recommendations, brand sentiment in terms of conversations and sharing related to your Company Page and the content published there, and so on. Of course, you should also consider any other metrics and analytics tools that you use to track your online activities and performance to develop a complete picture of how your LinkedIn efforts and Company Pages are doing in terms of helping you meet your goals.

Make It Easy to Find Your Company Page

As you develop your LinkedIn Company Page, don't feel over-whelmed. It's easy to set up a simple page and claim your space on LinkedIn within a few minutes, but to create a comprehensive Company Page, you need to invest some time and thought into developing the best page possible. Once your Company Page looks just the way you want it to, it's time to spread the word about it!

Search and Discovery

There are many ways that LinkedIn members can find your Company Page through their daily LinkedIn activities or through specific searches. Your goal should be to make your Company Page as easy to find as possible so it is seen by as many people as possible.

As you create your Company Page, be sure to include as much information related to your industry and specialties as you can. Write with keywords in mind, so people have a greater chance of finding your Company Page when they conduct searches for companies with your products and services using the LinkedIn company search feature.

At the same time, you need to stay active on LinkedIn to ensure your Company Page pops up in as many places as possible. For example, people can stumble on your Company Page when:

- They hover the mouse over your company name in one of your employee's personal LinkedIn profiles, and a pop-up preview of your Company Page appears onscreen.

- They receive a notification that one of their LinkedIn connections recommended one of your products or services.

- They see your company in the list of Companies You May Be Interested in Following provided automatically by LinkedIn.

- They see your company in the list of Jobs You May Be Interested In when they're searching the jobs section of LinkedIn.

- One of their connections shares a link to your content.

- Your company is mentioned or you participate in a group that a member belongs to and that interaction appears in their news feed.

> **INSIDER SECRET**
>
> Make sure your employees are accurately identified in their LinkedIn profiles as working for your company. Also, monitor employee listings on your Company Page. If you find people listing themselves as your employees who have never worked for your company, email customer_service@linkedin.com to have them removed.

All of your activities on LinkedIn provide potential ways for people to hear about your company. This indirect way of raising awareness of your LinkedIn Company Page is an essential component of social media marketing that can be a powerful form of word-of-mouth marketing and brand building. Don't underestimate its reach.

You can also promote your Company Page off of LinkedIn. For example, include a Follow Us on LinkedIn button on your website, blog, email signature, business card, and so on. You can even create your own Company Profile plugin using the LinkedIn developer network plugins at: developer.linkedin.com/community/plugins.

Figure 4.11 shows what a Company Profile widget with a follow button can look like. It's perfect for a sidebar or footer—particularly on your company blog.

Just choose the button layout that you like and click on the **Get It** button to open the Build a Company Profile plugin page shown in Figure 4.12.

Figure 4.11: *Show your company profile with a follow button on your website or blog.*

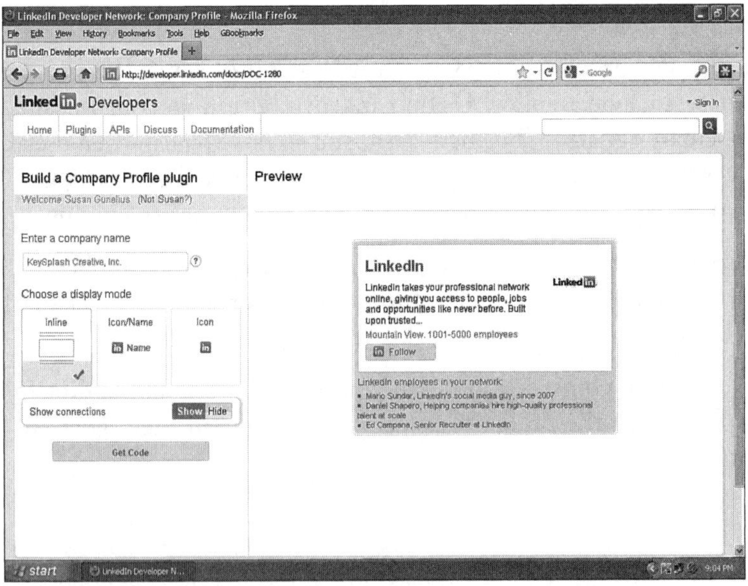

Figure 4.12: *Enter the requested information to create your Company Profile plugin.*

QUICK TIP

You need to sign in with a LinkedIn developer account to complete the plugin form. Just click the **Sign In** link at the top of the form to link your LinkedIn account to the developer network.

Complete the form by providing your company name, selecting the layout you prefer for the button, and whether or not you want people's LinkedIn connections to be shown. Then click the **Get Code** button to get your personalized embed code, which you can copy and paste into your web page. That's all there is to it!

Recommendations

Product and service recommendations do more than provide testimonials to boost your company credibility and sales. They also help people find your Company Page on LinkedIn. You can click the **Request Recommendation** link on any product or service listing on your Company Page to send recommendation requests to people in your LinkedIn network.

Any time a customer buys from you, why not send a recommendation request? Even if you're not connected to that customer on LinkedIn, you can send an email inviting them to follow your Company Page on LinkedIn and write a recommendation. To boost response rates, you can offer a discount on a future purchase. Don't be afraid to get creative in encouraging people to follow you and recommend your products and services. Those testimonials are meaningful, and research shows that consumers trust recommendations over any form of advertising or marketing. Make it a priority to get them.

You can also solicit recommendations from your own website using the product or service recommendation button that LinkedIn offers to web developers. You can create a recommendation button for each product or service listed on your LinkedIn Company Page and add each unique button to the corresponding product page on your website. With a single click of the button, visitors to your website can recommend a product or service on your LinkedIn Company Page (of course, they have to sign in to LinkedIn to write their recommendation).

Through the LinkedIn developer network, you can easily create your own product and service recommendation buttons. Just visit developer.linkedin.com/community/plugins, scroll down to the Recommend with LinkedIn section, and click the **Get It** button beneath the button you want to use on your website.

The Build a Recommend Button page opens; here you enter your company name and product ID (which is the numeric part of each specific product's page URL), and choose the orientation for your button. Click the **Get Code** button, and copy and paste the provided code into your web page where you want the button to appear. Now people can recommend your product or service on LinkedIn with a click of the button!

Ads

If you have money in your budget to advertise your Company Page, you can do so with LinkedIn Ads. There are four primary types of ads to choose from: text, display, recommendation, and recruitment ads.

LinkedIn Ads vary in price depending on the type of ad you run and your targeting criteria. You can learn all about LinkedIn Ads in Chapter 11.

The Least You Need to Know

- If you have a company email and a LinkedIn account, you can create a Company Page for your business.
- Basic Company Pages offer space for you to publish company, product, and service information. More features are available with sizeable price tags.
- LinkedIn members can publish recommendations on your Company Page for each product or service you list.
- You can promote your Company Page to increase awareness.

Making Connections and Increasing Your Visibility

In This Chapter

- Bringing your own connections to LinkedIn
- Finding people to connect with
- Letting LinkedIn find connections for you
- How to send invitations
- Being visible with updates and messages

LinkedIn is a social networking site. Notice the two keywords used in the previous sentence: *social* and *networking*. LinkedIn is nothing without people who interact with one another. If you simply create your LinkedIn profile and walk away, you've missed the point of being on LinkedIn.

This chapter teaches you how to find people (both people you already know and new people) and add them to your LinkedIn connections while expanding your overall LinkedIn network of contacts. What good are your LinkedIn efforts if no one knows about them? Making connections is essential to your LinkedIn efforts or you won't be able to reach the goals you learned to set in Chapter 1.

Degrees of Separation

To understand the importance of building your LinkedIn network, you must understand how LinkedIn connections are classified. As a LinkedIn member you can connect with other people, which allows you to view their complete profiles, their activity feeds, and send them private messages (depending on their account privacy settings). These people are called your *first-degree connections.*

Your LinkedIn network is made up of your first-degree connections as well as second- and third-degree connections. These are the people you're connected with *through* your first-degree connections. People who belong to the same LinkedIn groups that you belong to are also considered part of your LinkedIn network.

To better understand the concept of LinkedIn degrees of separation, think of the pop-culture game "Six Degrees of Kevin Bacon." According to this game, every famous person can be connected to Kevin Bacon in six degrees or less. Here's an example to connect Kevin Bacon to Mick Jagger:

1. Mick Jagger was in *Freejack* with Emilio Estevez.

2. Emilio Estevez was in *The Outsiders* with Tom Cruise.

3. Tom Cruise was in *A Few Good Men* with Kevin Bacon.

It's that simple. If Kevin Bacon and Mick Jagger were on LinkedIn and both were connected to Emilio Estevez but not personally connected as a first-degree connection with each other, they would be second-degree connections through their mutual connection with Emilio Estevez. There are many ways that Kevin Bacon can be connected to Mick Jagger, and each second- or third-degree connection offers opportunities for them to get on each other's radar screens, learn about each other, and ultimately connect with each other.

As you actively participate on LinkedIn, watch for recommendations about people you might know—or want to connect with—from your extended network. LinkedIn automatically offers these types of links and suggestions, and you'll see them as you use LinkedIn. They might appear as a sidebar box, in public profiles, and so on. Figure 5.1 shows a list of connection recommendations on the LinkedIn home page when you're logged in to your account.

People You May Know recommendations

Figure 5.1: *LinkedIn suggests people for you to connect with based on your LinkedIn profile and activities. Watch for People You May Know and similar connection recommendations.*

Send connection requests and introduction requests whenever you find someone who can add value to your LinkedIn experience and help you meet your goal—just as you would do at in-person networking events. You can do this with your first-, second-, and third-degree connections on LinkedIn. Leveraging the ability to see who is in your extended network on LinkedIn allows you to connect with not just your first-degree connections but potentially thousands (or millions) of second- and third-degree connections, too!

Import Contacts

Once your LinkedIn profile is created and effectively tells your story, it's time to start connecting with other LinkedIn users. Before you

start making connections on LinkedIn, understand the three ways
that connections can happen:

- **Invitations**   You can send an invitation to another LinkedIn
  member asking them to connect with you directly. You can
  also send invitations to people who aren't using LinkedIn yet
  and invite them to join and connect with you.

- **Introductions**   If you want to connect with someone you
  don't know, you can look for a mutual connection via your
  second- and third-degree network, and request that person to
  make an introduction for you. If you have a Basic LinkedIn
  account, you can have five outstanding introductions open at
  one time. You can pay for a premium account to get more.

- **InMail**   InMails are used to communicate directly with
  anyone on LinkedIn who you are not connected to in any
  way. When you send an InMail, the recipient's private information is not revealed to you unless they respond to your
  InMail and provide it. Basic LinkedIn profile users can
  receive InMail messages, but to send InMail messages, you
  have to upgrade to a premium account.

> **QUICK TIP**
>
> InMail is different from the free private messaging system that LinkedIn
> connections can use to communicate with one another. The free system
> is accessible through the Inbox link in the top navigation bar when you're
> logged in to your LinkedIn account.

If you already have a long list of contacts in a spreadsheet or in your
email account, you can import those contacts directly into LinkedIn.
It's a great way to start building your connections with people you
already know. You can send invitations to connect to your contact
lists individually or in bulk (meaning you send a single connection
request to a list of people).

The first step to importing your contacts is to log in to your
LinkedIn account and click the **Add Connections** link under the

Contacts heading in the top navigation bar. This opens the Add Connections page shown in Figure 5.2 with the Add Connections tab already selected.

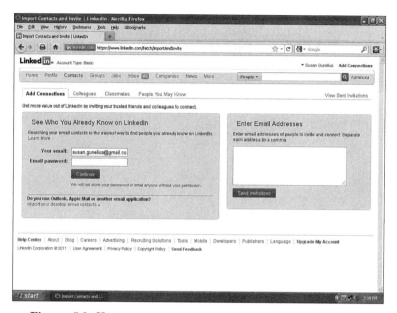

Figure 5.2: *You can import contacts from the Add Connections page.*

There are three options available to you on this page. You can:

Import webmail contacts. Find people who already have LinkedIn accounts whose email addresses are in your web-based email contact list (such as Gmail, Yahoo! Mail, Hotmail, etc.). Just enter your email address and email password into the form and click the **Continue** button.

Import desktop email contacts or contacts from other lists. Import contacts from your desktop email account (such as Microsoft Outlook, Apple Mail, etc.) or from a file of contacts that you upload to your LinkedIn account. Just click the **Import Your Desktop Email Contacts** link and the import entry form changes to the file import form as shown in Figure 5.3. Here you can upload a .csv, .txt, or .vcf file of contacts.

INSIDER SECRET

Click the **Learn More** link above the Contacts File text box to access directions for downloading a .csv file from popular webmail providers. You can also get this information directly from your webmail provider.

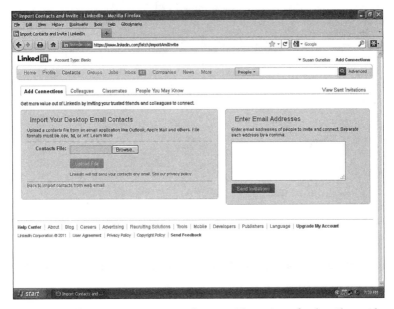

Figure 5.3: *You can import contacts from a wide variety of webmail providers.*

Enter individual contact email addresses. If you only want to import a small number of people, then you can simply enter their email addresses into the Enter Email Addresses form on the right side of the Add Connections page.

Once you import your contact lists, you can pick and choose who you want to connect with on LinkedIn. Now you can send connection requests to people with existing LinkedIn accounts, and invitations to join LinkedIn to nonmembers. It's a good idea to include a personalized message with invitations you send to LinkedIn members and follow up on invitations sent to nonmembers with a personal email message to explain the invitation to them.

WARNING

You can't personalize your invitation message when you send connection requests in bulk.

Searching for People

As you're building a network, it's always best to start connecting with people you know first. Importing your existing contacts is just the first step of finding people to connect with through LinkedIn. There are certainly more people that you know on LinkedIn than people you have in your contact list.

Furthermore, LinkedIn can only find your contacts if the email addresses you have for them match the email addresses in their LinkedIn profiles. People change their email addresses all the time and most people have more than one email account. If all of those email addresses aren't listed in their account profiles, you might not find them when you import your contact list. That's where your search for people on LinkedIn begins!

QUICK TIP

Make sure your LinkedIn profile account settings include all of your email addresses so people have the best chances of finding you, too!

One of the simplest ways to search for a person on LinkedIn is to enter their name into the search box in the top-right corner of your screen when you're signed in to your LinkedIn account. (Make sure the People option to the left of the search box is selected.) However this isn't always effective, particularly if you're searching for someone with a common name. Don't worry! Your search has just begun.

Finding Colleagues, Classmates, and People You May Know

Fortunately, LinkedIn offers a variety of other ways to find people. When you visit the Add Connections page in your LinkedIn account as shown in Figure 5.2, you can click on any of the tabs at the top of the page to search for people.

Just click the **Colleagues** tab to search for people on LinkedIn who have worked at the same companies that appear in your LinkedIn profile. You can also click the **Classmates** tab to find people who have attended the same schools that appear in your LinkedIn profile. You can click the **People You May Know** tab to access a list of people that LinkedIn thinks you might know based on the information included in your LinkedIn profile (such as industry, company, school, and so on). You can find a lot of people quickly using these search features.

> **QUICK TIP**
>
> In order to appear in the Colleagues and Classmates lists on LinkedIn, that person needs to have the exact same company or school name identified in his profile.

Don't hesitate to follow trails on LinkedIn to find people. For example, look at who your own connections are linked to and follow links to second- and third-degree connections when you see them. There is a huge audience of people on LinkedIn who could be very interested in networking with you!

Advanced People Search

The Advanced Search tools on LinkedIn are where you can really get into detailed searches for people. Click the **Advanced** link to the right of the search box in the top-right corner of your screen when you're logged in to your LinkedIn account. The Advanced Search screen opens with the Advanced People Search tab already selected from the tabs at the top of the screen as shown in Figure 5.4.

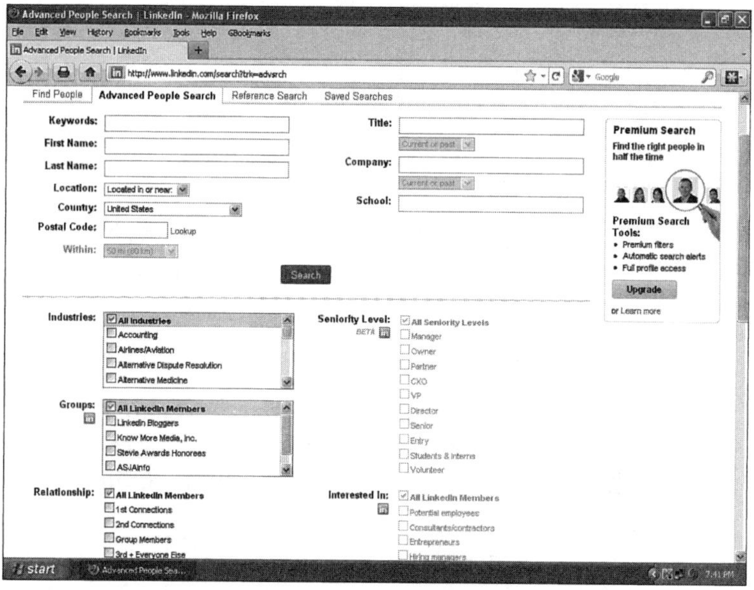

Figure 5.4: *You can find people using a wide variety of variables through the Advanced People Search tool.*

Now it's time to get serious about finding people on LinkedIn! Scroll through the Advanced People Search form and notice the many ways you can narrow your people searches to find specific people. Basic account holders can select from the following search options:

- Keywords

- First Name

- Last Name

- Location

- Country

- Postal Code (use the **Within** drop-down menu to narrow your results to a specific geographic radius)

- Title (use the **Current or past** drop-down menu to narrow your results)

- Company (use the **Current or past** drop-down menu to narrow your results)

- School

- Industries

- Groups

- Relationship

- Language

- Sort By (use the drop-down menu to sort results by Relevance, Relationship, Relationship + Recommendations, Connections, or Keywords)

- Views (you can see results in basic or expanded view)

- Premium account holders can also search using Function, Company Size, Seniority Level, Interested In, Years of Experience, Recently Joined, and Fortune 1000 filters

To the right of the varied Advanced People Search form options are additional criteria that are in beta as of this writing. Look for these additional options to be available when you conduct your own searches, as they'll help narrow your results even more.

INSIDER SECRET

The Advanced Search tool is only as useful as the information LinkedIn members input into their profiles.

The LinkedIn Advanced Search tool does not allow wildcard searches, but it does support some common search techniques. For example, you can:

- Surround keywords with quotes to search for a complete phrase.

- Exclude results with specific keywords by entering NOT before the keyword.

- Narrow results to those that include one or two keywords by entering OR between the two keywords.

- Find results that include two different keywords (not necessarily together as a single phrase) by entering AND between the words.

• Find results that combine several terms by using parentheses with the preceding options. For example, you can search on *CEO OR (president AND corporation)*.

Find People

Another way to search for people on LinkedIn is to click the **Find People** tab in the Advanced Search section of LinkedIn. When you click on the tab (shown in Figure 5.4), the Find People page opens, which you can see in Figure 5.5.

Figure 5.5: *Use the Find People tools to find people within your extended LinkedIn network.*

The Find People tool makes it easy for you to find your first-, second-, and third-degree connections as well as people you're connected to through groups that you belong to. This is a powerful tool to locate people in your existing extended network so you can send invitations to connect with them. Once you're connected, you can jump-start or deepen your relationships with them.

The Find People tool offers a variety of useful filters to help you narrow the list of people provided:

- Search (click the **More** link to reveal the search fields available in the Advanced People Search section discussed in the "Advanced People Search" section of this chapter)

- Current Company

- Relationship

- Location

- Industry

- Past Company

- School

- Profile Language

- Premium account filters and beta filters include Groups, Years of Experience, Function, Seniority Level, Interested In, Company Size, Fortune 1000, and Recently Joined (upgrading your account is discussed in Chapter 16)

For each of the search options listed above, click the **Show More** link to select from a list of choices or enter custom criteria.

You can search through your hundreds or thousands of extended network connections using these search options. For example, following are five strategic searches you could conduct to find people who can help you build your LinkedIn network for indirect business-to-business marketing purposes:

- **Search by Industry and Location** to find people in a specific geographic area who work in industries that your business targets.

- **Search by Industry and Title** (click the **More** link under the search text box in the upper-left corner of the Find People page as shown in Figure 5.5 to reveal the Title search feature) to connect with purchasing managers, executives, or other individuals and decision-makers who might be interested in the type of work you do.

- **Search by Company name** to find everyone who currently works for a specific company that you want to connect with. Next, find the most appropriate people on that list to help you meet your goals and send invitation requests to them.

- **Search by Current Company and Past Company** to find people who work for or worked for your competitors. Next, browse through their public profiles to see whom they're connected with (there are likely to be some people you should also connect with in those lists).

- **Search by Industry, Postal Code, Distance Within, and Keywords** to find people who are highly focused on your area of business and live or work in a specific area.

The search options offered by LinkedIn are extremely useful. They can help you find business partners, vendors, investors, employees, a job, customers, publicity opportunities, and more. Don't underestimate the power of finding and connecting to people in your extended LinkedIn network and beyond.

Reference Search and Saved Searches

In the Advanced Search section of your LinkedIn account (shown in Figure 5.4), you can find people by clicking on the **Reference Search** tab to open the page shown in Figure 5.6. Keep in mind, the Reference Search tool is only available to people with paid accounts.

If you have the frequent need to confirm work history for people or find references for people who worked at the same company during the same period, then the Reference Search tool might be useful to you. Just enter the company name, candidate name, and dates of employment into the Reference Search form, and a list of references is delivered to you.

Figure 5.6: *Search for job applicant or business prospect references through LinkedIn Reference Search (paid accounts only).*

Basic LinkedIn account holders can also save up to three searches. Just search on a name or keyword using the Advanced People Search form discussed earlier in this chapter and click the **Save** button at the top of the results page. Your saved searches appear on the Saved Searches page shown in Figure 5.7.

Figure 5.7: *Basic LinkedIn account users can save up to three searches.*

Once you save a search, you can also set up an email alert so you're notified each time a new LinkedIn member adds or changes a profile to match your search. If you need to save more searches and alerts, you can upgrade to a paid account as discussed in Chapter 16.

Title Directory

If you want to find people who hold specific types of jobs, you can use the Advanced Search tools discussed earlier in this chapter, or you can browse through the Title Directory at: linkedin.com/directory/title/.

INSIDER SECRET

You can only access the Title Directory when you're not logged in to LinkedIn. Click the **Title Directory** link in the footer of the LinkedIn home page to open it. However, you can't view profile results until you log in to your LinkedIn account.

This directory is challenging to navigate, but it could lead you to profiles that you might not stumble upon otherwise. You can browse the directory by title, or you can browse titles included in the directory by region or company. With each click of the mouse on a link in the directory, your results get more and more targeted until a list of matching profiles is delivered.

Group Members

If you belong to groups on LinkedIn, which are discussed in detail in Chapter 7, then you have additional ways to find more people on LinkedIn. Not only do group members appear in your extended network in the Find People tab of the Advanced Search tool discussed earlier in this chapter, but you can also search through group members as you interact within the group.

You don't have to have a first-degree connection with another group member in order to send them a connection request or private message. Don't just think of joining groups as a way to interact within the group setting, it's also a great way to find new people to connect with directly and deepen relationships outside the group discussions.

Connecting with Other LinkedIn Members

Now that you know the primary ways to find people on LinkedIn, it's time to learn how to actually connect with them. As you learned earlier in this chapter, you can send connection invitations to LinkedIn members whom you know, and you can invite people to join LinkedIn who are not already members.

To prevent someone from spamming large numbers of people with LinkedIn invitations, LinkedIn limits the number of people you can invite to join and connect with. This helps to ensure users only try to connect with people they know and for legitimate networking purposes.

If you run out of invitations, visit: help.linkedin.com/app/ask/ subject/Invitation%20Increase%20Request to request an invitation increase. Your ratio of sent invitations to accepted invitations is a primary factor in LinkedIn approving this request.

Send and Receive Invitations

When you find an existing LinkedIn member whom you want to add to your connections, you can visit his or her profile and click the **Add to Your Network** button as shown in Figure 5.8.

> **QUICK TIP**
>
> You can also find an **Add to Your Network** link with Member Profile listings in search results and with LinkedIn Recommended Connections for people who are in your existing extended LinkedIn network.

When you want to add another LinkedIn member within your extended LinkedIn network of second- and third-degree connections and mutual group members, you are prompted to complete the Invite to Connect on LinkedIn form shown in Figure 5.9.

Click this button to add a person to your LinkedIn connections

Figure 5.8: *Click the **Add [person's name] to Your Network** button to invite LinkedIn members to connect with you.*

Figure 5.9: *Identify how you know the LinkedIn member and include a personalized message to invite them to connect.*

To complete the form, you must identify how you know the person you're trying to connect with. LinkedIn expects users to only try to connect with people they legitimately know to retain its usefulness as a professional networking site, so be honest when you make your selection.

If you select the **Colleague, Classmate,** or **We've Done Business Together** radio button to identify your relationship with the other person, you'll be prompted to select the appropriate company or school from those listed in your LinkedIn profile.

If you're friends or acquaintances with another person but have not actually worked with them or attended school with them, you can either select the **Friend** radio button or the **Other** radio button. If you select the **Other** option, you'll be prompted to enter the other person's email address to verify that you know them. Keep in mind, if the person does not have the email address you enter into the form saved in her LinkedIn account settings, the invitation won't be delivered.

WARNING

If you select the **I Don't Know [person's name]** radio button, you'll be prompted to seek an introduction from another LinkedIn member or send an InMail.

Finally, enter a personal message into the message text box to explain who you are and why you want to connect on LinkedIn. Select the **Send Invitation** button to send your invitation to the other LinkedIn member.

When you (or another LinkedIn member) receive invitations to connect with another member, those invitations appear within your LinkedIn Inbox, which is accessible through the **Inbox** link in the top navigation bar. Simply click the **Inbox** link, and then click the **Invitations** tab that appears at the top of the page to view your invitations (as shown in Figure 5.10).

Figure 5.10: *View your invitations through your LinkedIn Inbox.*

When you receive an invitation, you have an opportunity to review the sender's LinkedIn profile and accept or decline the invitation.

QUICK TIP

You can configure your email settings within the Settings of your LinkedIn account to identify who can send you invitations and to receive notification via email when someone sends you an invitation.

You can also invite people who are not already LinkedIn users to join LinkedIn and connect with you by clicking the **Add Connections** link in the top-right corner of the screen when you're logged in to your LinkedIn account. Then enter individual email addresses into the **Enter Email Addresses** text box on the right side of the screen and click the **Send Invitations** button as described in the "Import Contacts" section earlier in this chapter.

Request an Introduction

When you want to connect with someone you don't know personally (but who is a second- or third-degree connection to you through your extended LinkedIn network), you can send a request for an introduction to a member that you and that person are both connected to.

For example, in the example used earlier in this chapter, Mick Jagger could send an introduction request to Emilio Estevez asking Emilio to introduce Mick to Kevin Bacon. When Emilio receives the introduction request from Mick, he can decide whether or not he wants to forward the request to Kevin so he and Mick can connect.

You can do the same thing to connect with people at key companies or who have skills and interests that are of interest to you and can help you meet your LinkedIn goals. Simply select the **Get Introduced** link on a second- or third-degree connection's profile as shown in Figure 5.11 to get started.

Figure 5.11: *Click the **Get Introduced** link to open the introduction form and connect with people you don't know.*

Next, you are asked to identify which mutual connection you'd like to send your introduction request to (if there is more than one to choose from), and complete the Request an Introduction form shown in Figure 5.12.

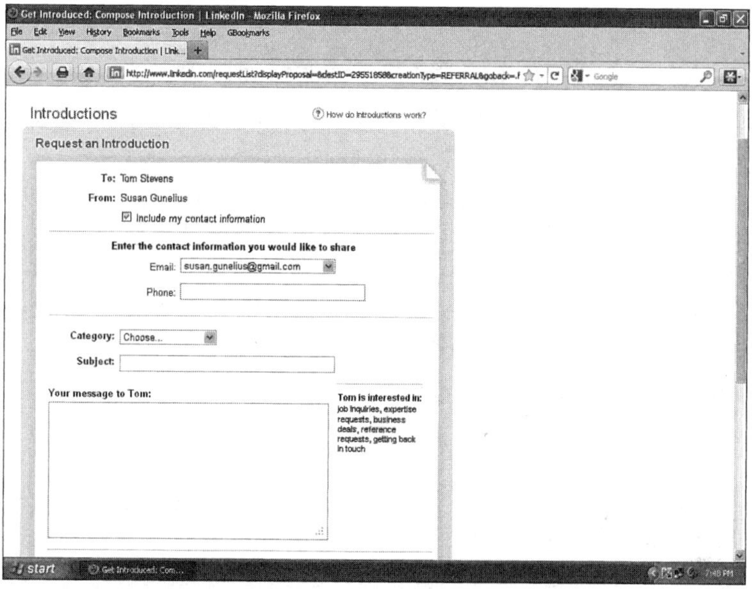

Figure 5.12: *Complete the Request an Introduction form to have a first-degree connection introduce you to a second- or third-degree connection.*

When requesting an introduction, make sure you ask only those who know both you and the person with whom you're trying to connect. You don't want to make someone feel obligated to make an introduction they're not comfortable with. In other words, don't jeopardize your existing relationships to make new connections on LinkedIn.

Send an InMail

If you want to connect with someone you don't know, who is not in your extended network, or whom you're not comfortable asking anyone in your network to introduce you to, you can send him an InMail. As mentioned earlier in this chapter, basic LinkedIn account holders can receive unlimited InMail messages; but if you want to send InMail messages, you will have to upgrade to a premium LinkedIn account.

If you find a person on LinkedIn whom you want to send an InMail message to, just click the **Send InMail** link on their profile. You'll be prompted to click an **Upgrade** button to choose the type of premium account you want. Premium accounts are discussed in detail in Chapter 16.

Staying on Users' Radar Screens

The easiest way to stay on your LinkedIn connections' radar screens is to be active on LinkedIn. Participate in conversations, share other users' content, comment on their updates, join groups and participate, feed your blog and Twitter content into your LinkedIn update stream, and be visible. You can learn more about all of these activities and opportunities in Parts 2 and 3 of this book, but first, you must understand what LinkedIn updates and activity feeds are.

In simplest terms, everything that you do on LinkedIn is considered an update, which can appear in your activity feed. Depending on how you configured your account privacy settings (discussed in Chapter 3), some or all of your updates could be visible to your LinkedIn connections and network.

Let's assume you've configured your LinkedIn profile for maximum growth and made all of your updates public within your activity feed. You can view your activity feed or your connections' activity feeds by visiting a profile and clicking the **See More Activity** link in that person's activity box, as shown in the lower right-hand corner of Figure 5.13.

You can also click the **Home** button in the top navigation bar (when you're logged in) and scroll down to the activity updates section on the left side of the page to view your connections' activities in a variety of useful ways. For example, as shown in the center of Figure 5.14, you can view All Updates, Shares, or Groups, or you can click the **More** link to select **Profiles, Recommendations, Companies, Answers, Connections, Photos,** or **News**. Click on any of these links to view only specific types of activities such as when a person edits his profile, receives a profile recommendation, adds new connections, or uploads a photo. You can even click the **Search Updates** link to search for updates using specific keywords.

The See More Activity link

Figure 5.13: *Click the **See More Activity** link in a person's profile to view more of their LinkedIn updates.*

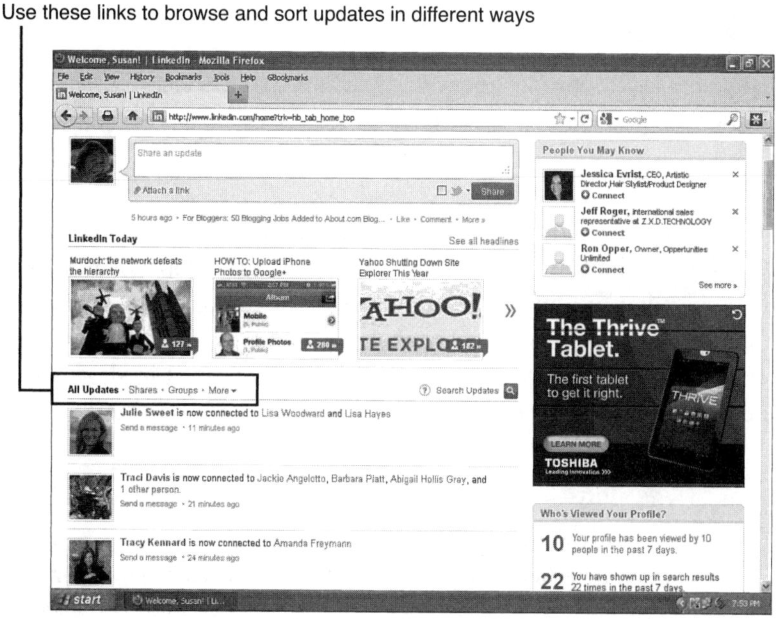

Use these links to browse and sort updates in different ways

Figure 5.14: *You can view activity feeds in a variety of ways to reduce update clutter and focus on updates that matter most to you.*

Select the **More** link and choose **See Additional Views** from the drop-down menu to open the Category View page shown in Figure 5.15. Here you can view the most recent connection activities by category (such as Updates, Recently Connected, Group Activity, and more), by individual connection, all of your connections' updates, or just your own updates.

Figure 5.15: *From the Category View page, you can select tabs to view updates by connections, notifications, and more.*

If you want to pare down the updates that appear on your home page, you can click the **Customize** link from the **More** drop-down menu on your LinkedIn home page. This opens the Account settings window discussed in Chapter 3. The Account settings window is where you can pick and choose the types of updates you want to show and hide as well as how many updates to show on your home page.

> **WARNING**
>
> If you haven't configured your profile, updates, and activities to be visible to your connections and network, then they won't see them in their network activity feeds. Be sure to follow the instructions provided in Chapter 3 to configure your profile so your activities get the type of exposure you want them to.

There are many ways that your name, knowledge, expertise, and personality can be seen on LinkedIn through your activities and updates. Don't be shy if you want your efforts to deliver the results you need to be successful.

Publishing Content and Participating in Conversations

You can tell your LinkedIn connections what you're doing, publish your thoughts, offer tips and education, share content you like, and more through your LinkedIn status updates. Just log in to your LinkedIn profile and you'll see a text box at the top of your LinkedIn home page inviting you to Share an Update as shown in Figure 5.16.

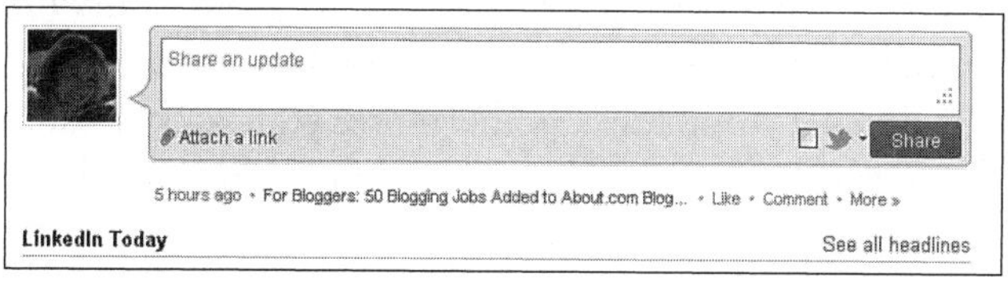

Figure 5.16: *Type your update into the text box and click the* **Share** *button.*

Type the message you want to publish in your activity feed into the text box. You can click the link labeled **Attach a Link** to include a link to content on another web page in your update. You can also simultaneously publish your update on your Twitter account by selecting the check box next to the Twitter bird icon (if you've linked a Twitter account to your LinkedIn profile as discussed in Chapter 6).

When your update is published, it is visible to everyone you've allowed it to be visible to through your account configuration settings. When people see your updates in their network activity feeds, they can comment on your update, like it, or share it with their own audiences. When they do those things, it puts your updates in front of their LinkedIn connections via their network activity feeds. That's more exposure for you!

You can also comment, like, or share updates published by your connections that you find in your network activity feeds. Simply click the **Comment** link beneath an update that you want to discuss. The original publisher sees your comment, as does anyone who received the original update in their network updates (regardless of whether or not they're connected to you). Your comment can jump-start a conversation and help you build your relationship with that person and their audience. At the same time, your comment appears in both your update feed and the original publisher's network activity feed.

When you click the **Share** link on one of your connection's updates, you share just the link, not the original commentary or comments other people have posted to the original update. You can add your own message with the shared link. While this option isn't conversational like the commenting feature, it does show that you are spreading another LinkedIn member's content and gives that member additional exposure. You can opt to share content by posting it to your own updates (to notify your network), to groups only (to notify group members), or to individuals only (to send a direct message to individual LinkedIn Inboxes). Furthermore, your activity shows up in your own activity feed and the original publisher's feed.

Finally, you can click the **Like** link to show that you like a connection's update. You can also add a comment when you like an update. When you like an update, the activity appears in your own network activity feed and a network update is sent to all of your connections. Of course, the original poster also sees that you liked their update in their activity feed.

QUICK TIP

You can click the **Unlike** link on any update you've liked to remove your endorsement of it.

To help you get started on the right foot with useful LinkedIn activities and network updates that position you for success, following are 10 tips you can use immediately:

- **Publish useful and meaningful updates** that your connections would find valuable. Don't clutter their activity updates with irrelevant information.

- **Use the Category view of network updates** to quickly find recent updates that you can comment on, share, or like. Real-time conversation is a powerful thing.

- **Be sure to include a comment** when you share or like another user's update. Never miss an opportunity to strike up a conversation.

- **Post a return comment** if someone comments on your update. Would you ignore someone who tried to talk to you in person? Don't ignore them on LinkedIn.

- **Conduct network activity keyword searches** to monitor updates that matter most to you and jump into relevant conversations. Set up and save a keyword search with an email notification to follow specific activities.

- **Check out the Profiles network activity view and comment on recent promotions, awards, job changes, and so on.** A simple congratulations can mean a lot.

- **Ask a question in your status updates.** You'd be surprised how many people will answer as your network grows.

- **Click the *Like* button** and help your connections get more exposure for their great content. What goes around comes around.

- **Monitor Company network activity** to see which of your connections are following new companies and which companies you're following are looking for new employees. Share job opportunities related to your industry with your connections. You never know who you might be helping find their next career.

- **Click the *Send a Message* link under an update** to send a private message to a connection and discuss that update with them in greater detail. It's a great way to reach out to someone personally and get to know them better.

Using Private Messages to Deepen Relationships

Public conversations via network updates is a great way to stay visible on LinkedIn and make sure people recognize you and get to know what you're about, but don't forget the private messaging tool available to you. Click the **Inbox** link in the top navigation bar when you're signed in to your LinkedIn account to open your private LinkedIn messaging tool. You can send private messages to any of your first-degree connections, receive private messages, manage invitations, and search for messages from your LinkedIn Inbox page.

The private messaging system in LinkedIn is a way to leverage one-to-one marketing by getting to know people better on a personal level.

However, don't inundate people with unsolicited marketing messages. First and foremost, your LinkedIn efforts should always be about building meaningful relationships which lead to organic indirect marketing of yourself, your business, and your brand. The LinkedIn community is adamant in its intolerance for overt marketing and sales.

The Least You Need to Know

- Your LinkedIn network extends to three degrees of separation, putting you in front of more people than you probably know.
- You can communicate with your LinkedIn connections via public updates and private messages.
- Even if you don't know someone on LinkedIn, you can connect with him or her through an introduction or InMail.
- Your LinkedIn updates appear in your connections' network activity feeds, so be active to stay visible.

Building Your Reputation and Community

You've set up your LinkedIn profile and Company Page. You've connected with people and built your network. Now, it's time to start using that profile and Company Page to build your reputation, influence, and community.

Part 2 teaches you how to use the various tools and applications available to you to enhance your profile, demonstrate your expertise, show off your work and accomplishments, and more. You also learn how to use groups, recommendations, and LinkedIn Answers to reach your LinkedIn goals.

Useful Tools and Apps

6

In This Chapter

- Using LinkedIn with Twitter
- Connecting your Twitter updates to your LinkedIn profile
- Feeding your blog updates to LinkedIn
- Using apps to tell more of your story

LinkedIn offers a variety of tools and applications that you can add to your profile to tell more of your story. For example, you can show off samples from your portfolio, share your Twitter and blog updates via LinkedIn, announce events, and more. It's unlikely that you'll use every tool and application available to you. However this chapter introduces those that enhance your profile, so you can pick the ones that will help you meet your goals.

You can always remove a tool or app from your LinkedIn profile, and most are free—or at least offer free trials—so you can test them out. Always keep your LinkedIn goals in mind and leverage applications and tools that can help you achieve the success you want and need.

Twitter Tool

LinkedIn works seamlessly with Twitter. You can tweet your LinkedIn status updates without leaving LinkedIn, and you can automatically publish your tweets to your LinkedIn activity feed (if your Twitter profile is configured as public).

In Chapter 3, you learned how to associate your Twitter account with your LinkedIn account through the Edit My Profile process. Just click the **Add Twitter Account** link next to the Twitter feed in your Edit Profile screen, enter your **Twitter ID**, and follow the instructions to verify your Twitter account name and password. As long as you enter the correct Twitter account name and password, verification happens immediately and your Twitter account will be linked to your LinkedIn account.

Next, you are asked to choose how you want to share your tweets on LinkedIn. You have two choices: share all tweets (all of your Tweets are published to your LinkedIn activity feed) or share only tweets that contain #in (only Tweets that include *#in* will be published to your LinkedIn activity feed).

You can also share your LinkedIn status updates through your Twitter profile by selecting the check box next to the Twitter icon and **Share** button beneath the LinkedIn Share an Update text box as shown in Figure 6.1.

The Twitter icon

Figure 6.1: *Select the Twitter check box next to the Twitter icon to share your LinkedIn update on your Twitter profile and your Twitter timeline, too.*

The first time you select this check box to post a LinkedIn update to your Twitter profile, you'll be asked to verify your account name and password one more time. Once you do this step, you won't be asked to verify your account again.

Social networking happens on a variety of websites. The simple truth is that some people prefer to use LinkedIn while others might only use Twitter. Your strategic goal should be to surround your target audience with branded online experiences, so they can self-select how they want to interact with you and your brand. That means you should have a presence on LinkedIn, Twitter, Facebook, and other social media sites for maximum growth. However, managing all of those accounts is time consuming! That's where automation tools like the Twitter tool on LinkedIn can help you *save* time and spread your content to wider audiences at the *same* time.

Enable more people to find and consume your updates and content by publishing them in multiple places, but don't fall into the trap of relying on automation. Your personal participation, conversations, and activities are the most important part of building your online brand. No one wants to connect with an automated LinkedIn or Twitter profile.

Enhance Your Profile with Apps

Third party apps bring some amazing enhancements to LinkedIn profiles. A list of current LinkedIn apps is always available at linkedin.com/static?key=application_directory.

> **QUICK TIP**
>
> You can access all LinkedIn apps by clicking the **More** link in the top navigation bar when you're logged in to your account, and choose **Get More Applications** from the drop-down menu.

Keep in mind, LinkedIn can introduce or remove an app at any time. The apps discussed in this chapter, as well as those introduced in Chapters 10 and 13, could change at any time. Always check for updates to the app list to see if new apps are available to make your LinkedIn profile even more powerful.

Blog Link

The Blog Link application makes it extremely easy to connect your blog to your LinkedIn profile, so updates are automatically published to your LinkedIn activity feed whenever you publish a new blog post. The update will include your blog post title and a link for people to visit your blog to read the complete post.

You can also choose to show the Blog Link box on your LinkedIn home page (when you're logged in to your account) as shown in Figure 6.2.

The Blog Link app box on a LinkedIn profile

Figure 6.2: *Promote your blog posts with the Blog Link app (located on the right-hand side of this figure).*

If you want to see recent blog posts from your connections who use Blog Link, click the **From My Contacts** tab at the top of the Blog Link box.

Again, this app helps you put your content in front of a wider audience by showcasing your blog posts through your LinkedIn profile. And remember, your posts also appear in the From My Contacts tab on other users' Blog Link boxes. It's a simple and effective way to indirectly promote your expertise and your brand.

Box.net Files

Box.net Files is a popular online and mobile document storage and collaboration tool. You can share and add files to your LinkedIn profile in a snap with the Box.net Files app. This is a great feature if you're looking for a job or new clients. You can upload your résumé, portfolio samples, presentations, white papers, a rate sheet, audio files, or just about any other kind of document that helps to tell more of your story.

This is the space in your LinkedIn profile where you can display marketing materials to tell more of your story, as well as useful documents your connections would find valuable.

E-Bookshelf

Through the E-Bookshelf app, FT Press (a division of *Financial Times*) provides access to finance, investing, business, marketing, sales, management, and scientific content and articles written by its team of expert authors. You can add this app to your LinkedIn profile and access content with the three free credits that come with the app. After you use those credits, you have to purchase more to access additional content.

If you're in the business field, this content could be useful to help you learn, stay on top of news and expert opinion, and even find content to write and talk about on LinkedIn, your blog, and so on.

GitHub

GitHub is a popular website for open-source web-development collaborative projects. If you're a web developer, or you already use GitHub, then the GitHub app might be a useful addition to your LinkedIn profile. Once you add the GitHub app, you can show off your GitHub projects on your LinkedIn profile, and you can share your GitHub activities with your LinkedIn audience through network updates.

You can also manage some GitHub activities without leaving LinkedIn. For example, you can find out which of your existing LinkedIn connections are active on GitHub and take a look at the projects they're working on. If you find a LinkedIn connection who uses GitHub, you can follow them and watch their projects on GitHub without leaving your LinkedIn account. It's an easy way to increase your network of developers!

Google Presentation

Do you create presentations through the Google Docs presentation tool? Do you create PowerPoint presentations for sales and marketing? You can upload those presentations to your LinkedIn account with the Google Presentation app. There are many types of presentations that you could add to your LinkedIn profile to indirectly market yourself, your business, and your brand. You could upload ...

- A recent sales presentation.

- A presentation that accompanied a lecture.

- A presentation from a web-based seminar or course.

- A presentation that displays samples from your portfolio.

- A presentation that delivers results from research or other analytics reports.

- A presentation that showcases your résumé and accomplishments in a visual way.

Just add this application to your LinkedIn profile, upload your presentations, and pick the ones you want to show on your profile. It really is that simple!

Huddle Workspaces

Huddle is a popular collaboration and content-management tool that offers a LinkedIn app you can use to collaborate and develop content with others through LinkedIn. You can add the Huddle app to your LinkedIn profile, create private workspaces, and invite LinkedIn connections to a workspace to collaborate on documents and projects.

The Huddle app allows you to ...

- Work with unlimited connections in varied private workspaces.

- Converse with other workspace members through a forum.

- Access 1 GB of secure storage space for document creation and collaboration.

- Create and edit documents online without any additional software.

- Publish comments on documents and content.

- Request and receive approvals.

INSIDER SECRET

If you already use Huddle, you can synchronize your LinkedIn activities through the Huddle app with your other Huddle activities—and even access all of your activities (even those you didn't start through the LinkedIn app) through LinkedIn.

The possibilities for using a tool like Huddle to streamline existing work activities and create new opportunities to collaborate privately with people around the world are limitless.

Lawyer Ratings

If you're an attorney, then you should consider using the Lawyer Ratings app. This app is provided by Martindale-Hubbell, which is an organization that gathers and reports information about lawyers in a database that connects people with attorneys.

When you add the Lawyer Ratings app to your LinkedIn profile, your Martindale-Hubbell Client Review and Martindale-Hubbell Peer Review ratings are highlighted on your profile. Visitors to your profile can also click the **Review Now** button to submit their own review of your services to the Martindale-Hubbell Lawyer Ratings application and database.

Consumers trust testimonials more than any type of advertising or marketing. Including reviews and making it easy for people to submit reviews about you on your LinkedIn profile is just one more way to demonstrate your abilities and the positive results you deliver.

Projects and Teamspaces

The Projects and Teamspaces app is offered by Manymoon and makes the company's popular online project management and productivity platform available through your LinkedIn profile. You can add this app and get free access to unlimited workspaces, tasks, documents, and connections.

The Projects and Teamspaces app allows you to track feeds related to projects, tasks, and teams. You can also share tasks, files, and conversations with your LinkedIn connections who are also using the app and assigned to the same workspaces. If you're looking for an app that can help you and your team boost productivity and more efficiently manage projects and tasks, then the Projects and Teamspaces app could be a good tool for you to try.

Reading List by Amazon

If you're a book reader (or author), then the Reading List by Amazon app can help you share the books you love and find more books to read based on your connections' lists and recommendations. Simply add the Reading List by Amazon app to your LinkedIn profile and follow the simple instructions to create a list of books you're reading now or want to read, you have already read, or want to recommend (such as books you or friends have written). The list is displayed as part of your LinkedIn profile.

You can also learn what your connections are reading if they use the Reading List by Amazon app, too. You can even follow updates to lists created by your connections, other people in your industry, or other LinkedIn members whom you want to network with and get to know better. At the same time, other users can also see the updates you make to your own list.

SlideShare Presentations

SlideShare is one of the most popular social websites for uploading and sharing presentations. As shown in Figure 6.3, when you add the SlideShare app to your LinkedIn profile, your recently uploaded SlideShare presentations can appear in your LinkedIn profile.

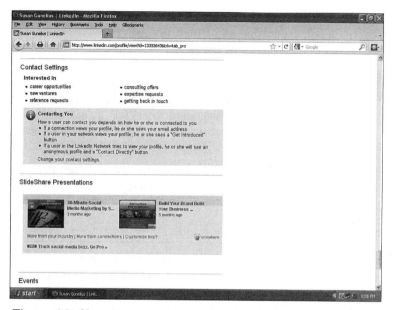

Figure 6.3: *Showcase your presentations on your LinkedIn profile with the SlideShare app.*

You can use SlideShare to upload a variety of file types in addition to traditional PowerPoint and Mac Keynote presentation files. You can even add video and audio to create web-based seminars. It's a great way to market yourself, your brand, or your business!

Tweets

The Tweets app offers a different way to publish and access Twitter content without leaving your LinkedIn profile. When you add Tweets to your LinkedIn account, you link a Twitter account with your LinkedIn account, and your recent tweets are displayed on your LinkedIn profile. You can also see tweets from people you follow on Twitter on your LinkedIn home page, and publish tweets and LinkedIn updates simultaneously.

Tweets provides more functionality than the Twitter tool that you can edit as part of your LinkedIn profile. Tweets works more similarly to a Twitter client, because you can publish tweets, retweet other people's posts, and reply to other people's tweets on your

Twitter profile. However, you can do all of those things through LinkedIn, which saves time and makes life easier.

INSIDER SECRET

There are many Twitter clients and tools that enable you to manage a wide variety of social accounts and activities from a single place. HootSuite.com and TweetDeck.com are two of the most popular options.

If you like the idea of managing Twitter activities through your LinkedIn profile, then give the Tweets app a try.

WordPress

If you use WordPress as your blogging application, then the WordPress app for LinkedIn takes the work out of synchronizing your blog post updates to your LinkedIn updates. Just install this app, and follow the steps to configure your WordPress blog settings. You can even filter posts with a special LinkedIn tag to control your LinkedIn updates. Once you've configured the app, your blog post updates will automatically publish as LinkedIn updates and will be sent as network activity updates to everyone in your LinkedIn network.

Both the WordPress app and the Blog Link app are popular. If you use WordPress, then you can give both a try and see which app you prefer. As with most LinkedIn apps, they're free!

The Least You Need to Know

- You can automatically publish your Twitter updates to your LinkedIn activity stream.
- Use the tools and apps available to you through LinkedIn to automate processes, save time, and boost your productivity.
- LinkedIn apps can give you a way to show off your work and promote yourself, your brand, and your business.
- Most LinkedIn apps are free to use and can be added or removed at any time without negatively affecting your LinkedIn profile or account.

Working with Leverage Groups

In This Chapter

- Finding groups that matter to you
- Taking the plunge and joining groups
- Creating your own group
- Getting involved and automating processes

Groups offer many opportunities to grow your business, brand, and career. Of course groups let you start and join discussions with people who are interested in the same topics, but they also let you get in front of members that you might not meet otherwise.

When you join a group, every other member of that group becomes part of your LinkedIn extended network, which expands your reach significantly. Remember, the power of LinkedIn comes from your network, which enables you to connect with large targeted audiences very quickly. This chapter teaches you how to find, join, create, and participate in groups, so you can get involved immediately.

Searching for Groups

There are just over one million groups on LinkedIn, and the vast majority of the approximately 100 million LinkedIn members belong to at least one group. Think of all the networking opportunities at your fingertips through the LinkedIn Groups feature! The challenge is finding the right groups to join, so you can meet your goals for LinkedIn.

You can join up to 50 groups on LinkedIn and another 50 subgroups, which are smaller *niche* groups for targeted conversations and engagement within a larger group. Each group can have up to 20 subgroups. That gives you a lot of room to work with in terms of joining groups, evaluating their potential for helping you meet your goals, and deciding whether you want to stay in the group or leave it, ultimately.

When you search for groups on LinkedIn, you're likely to find multiple groups focused on the same topics and targeted to the same types of people. Look for active groups that stay on topic and have a membership that adds value to conversations with their knowledge and experience. Even if a group is recommended to you by another LinkedIn member, you'll have to join the group and get involved to determine whether or not it's the right group for you.

Group Search Feature

You can search for a group using keywords at any time by clicking the drop-down arrow next to the search text box in the top-right corner of your screen when you're logged in to your LinkedIn account. Just choose **Groups** from the drop-down menu that appears, and then type your keywords into the search box as shown in Figure 7.1.

Figure 7.1: *Enter your group keyword(s) into the Groups search text box in the upper-right corner—in this case, "content marketing."*

Click the magnifying glass to get a full list of results in the Groups Directory as shown in Figure 7.2.

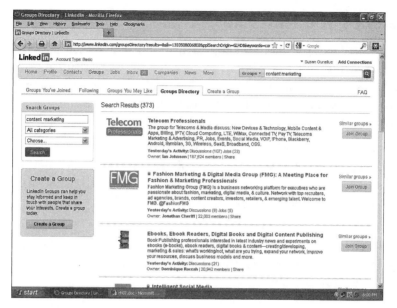

Figure 7.2: *You can search for groups using the Groups Directory.*

Groups Directory

You can also access the Groups Directory at any time by clicking the **Groups** link in the top navigation bar when you're signed in to your LinkedIn account. Next, click the **Groups Directory** link in the drop-down menu to visit the Groups Directory shown in Figure 7.2.

It's easy to narrow your search results using the Search Groups form on the left side of the screen in the Groups Directory. You can enter keywords, choose a group category, and select a group language using the search text box and drop-down menus in the form. Click the **Search** button, and matching groups are returned to you, which you can scroll through and evaluate. Just click the **group name** link in each entry to visit the group page and poke around.

QUICK TIP

Click the **Similar Groups** link above the **Join Group** button in each Groups Directory–search result listing to find groups that are deemed to be similar by LinkedIn.

Groups You May Like

Click the **Groups** link in the top navigation bar, and then select the **Groups You May Like** link to access a list of groups that LinkedIn believes matches your interests. LinkedIn identifies groups you may like based on the information in your LinkedIn profile and the information in existing group members' profiles.

It is possible that you could visit this page in your account and find no groups listed. There are a couple of reasons that might happen. First, you may have already joined all of the groups that LinkedIn has identified as good matches for you. Second, there might not be any group matches at a given time.

Don't check the Groups You May Like list once and never view it again. New groups open all the time, so you never know what you might find on this list!

Other Profiles

One of the best ways to find groups that can help expand your reach and achieve your LinkedIn goals is to check out the groups that your LinkedIn connections belong to. Visit the profiles of your connections who are in your target audience, and scroll down to see the groups they belong to. When you find an interesting group on a connection's profile, send that person a message and ask them what they think of the group. It's a great way to evaluate the group and strike up a conversation to deepen your relationship with that person.

> **QUICK TIP**
>
> You can view the group memberships of any LinkedIn user with a public profile.

Remember, the power of LinkedIn comes not just from your first-degree connections, but from your entire expanded network. Trolling their profiles for interesting and useful groups is a perfect example of how you can make your expanded network work for you.

Join Groups and Subgroups

The first step to getting involved with a group that interests you on LinkedIn is to join that group. There are three types of LinkedIn groups:

- **Open groups**   Any LinkedIn member can join an open group. All discussions are visible to LinkedIn and non-LinkedIn members, can be shared on Twitter, and are indexed by search engines.

- **Public (members-only) groups**   Any LinkedIn member can join a public group, but discussions are only visible to LinkedIn members (regardless of whether or not they are a member of that group). These groups are designated with a padlock icon next to the group name.

- **Private groups**   Private groups do not appear in the LinkedIn Groups Directory, which limits the number of people who are likely to find them. Membership is by invitation only or by sending a request to join. Discussions are only visible to group members.

QUICK TIP

It's up to each individual group manager to decide whether requests to join are automatically approved or require moderator approval.

There are two ways to join a group: you can respond to an invitation that you receive in your LinkedIn Inbox asking you to join (like the one shown in Figure 7.3), or you can click the **Join Group** button visible on any group page to join. Depending on how the group manager set up the group, you might be able to join the group instantly, or your request to join might be sent to a group moderator who will determine whether your request is approved.

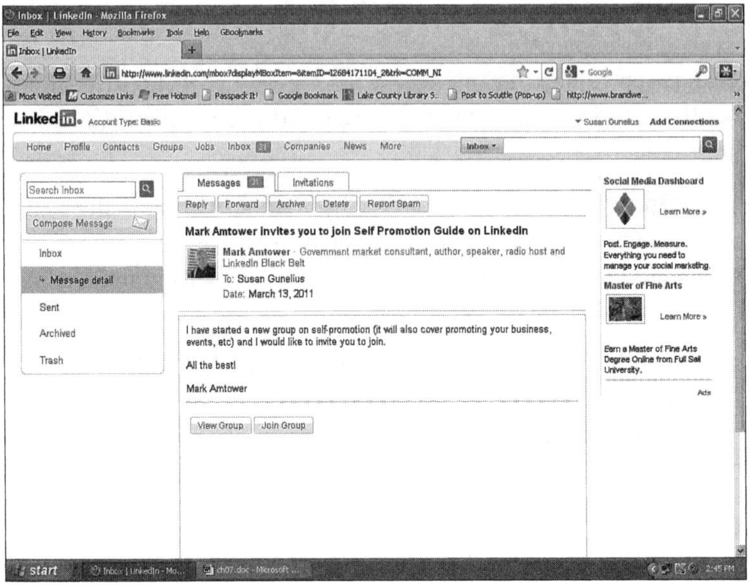

Figure 7.3: *Group invitations arrive to your LinkedIn Inbox.*

As shown in Figure 7.4, just click the **Join Group** button on any group page to join it.

Figure 7.4: *Click the Join Group button to join a group.*

If the group is configured to auto-approve requests to join, then you'll immediately be taken to the group page as a member after you click the **Join Group** button as shown in Figure 7.5. If the group requires that your request to join be approved, you'll have to wait until you receive acknowledgement that a group moderator has approved your membership before you can participate in the group.

Keep in mind, group owners determine how each group is set up. Depending on the group settings, you might be able to join discussions without being a member of the group.

Figure 7.5: *When you join a group, you might be able to immediately participate in conversations, depending on the group's settings.*

After you join a group, take a minute to configure your group settings by clicking the **Here** link at the top of the page as shown in Figure 7.5 ("You can adjust your settings **here**"). This opens your Settings page shown in Figure 7.6. You can access the Settings page anytime in the future under the **More...** tab on a group page.

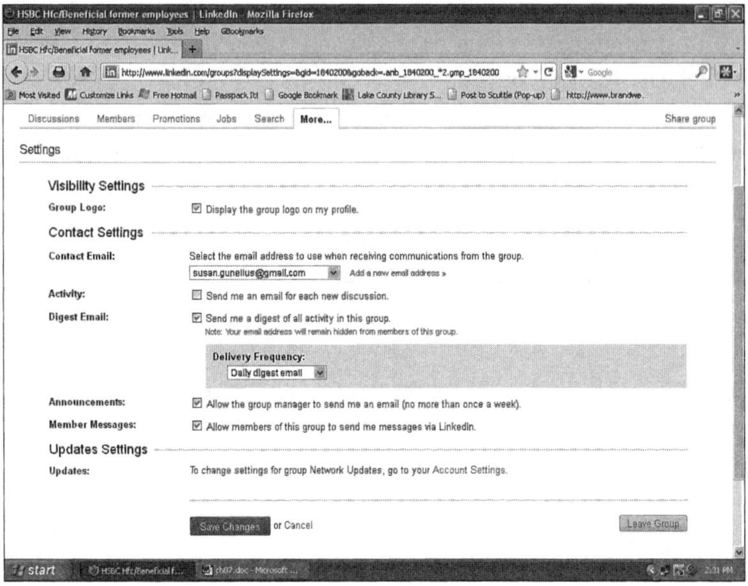

Figure 7.6: *Configure your contact and notification settings for your group membership.*

Here you can determine whether or not you want to display the group logo on your LinkedIn profile, how you want to be contacted by group members, and how frequently you want to receive notification emails related to group updates. Once you configure your group member settings, be sure to click the **Save Changes** button or your settings won't be updated.

INSIDER SECRET

You can leave a group at any time by clicking the **Leave Group** button on your group member Settings page.

Some group managers preapprove potential group members. If you request to join a group that you've been preapproved to be a part of, your request will be automatically approved, giving you instant access to the group discussions, activities, and so on. This is a particularly useful feature for group managers who want to make it easy for people with specific email addresses to join, such as everyone with an email address from their company.

The process for joining subgroups within a LinkedIn group works similarly. You can find subgroups in the LinkedIn directory and click the **Join Subgroup** link, or you can respond to an invitation to join a subgroup.

> **WARNING**
>
> You must be a member of the parent group in order to join a subgroup.

You can find subgroups for groups that you already belong to by clicking the **More...** tab at the top of the group page and selecting the **Subgroups** link from the drop-down list. All subgroups that have not been set to Private will be listed, and you can join those that interest you.

Keep in mind, the same auto-approve and manual approval processes apply in subgroups that were described earlier in this section for joining groups. That means you might be able to join a subgroup and instantly participate, or you might have to wait to receive approval before you can actively engage in the subgroup discussions.

If you have an idea for a new subgroup, you can always suggest one to the group managers by starting a new discussion about it within the parent group.

Start a Group

If you can't find an existing LinkedIn group that meets your needs, all hope is not lost. You can start your own! Any LinkedIn member can start a group and create a focused place for people with like interests to converse. Believe it or not, you can create a group in just a few minutes.

Before you create your own group, it's important to understand that there are limits that apply to LinkedIn members' group activities. Following are some of those limitations:

- You can own or manage up to 10 parent groups and 20 subgroups at one time.

- Each parent group and subgroup can have only one owner.

- Each parent group and subgroup can have up to 10 managers.

- You can be a member of up to 50 parent groups and 50 sub-groups at the same time.

- You can be a moderator of up to 50 groups at one time.

- Each parent group and subgroup can have up to 50 moderators.

- You can follow up to 20,000 group members at one time.

- Each group can have up to 20,000 members before the owner has to request a limit increase from LinkedIn.

- You can create up to 20 subgroups for each parent group.

Click the **Groups** link in the top navigation bar when you're logged in to your LinkedIn account and click the **Create a Group** link from the drop-down list. This opens the Create a Group page shown in Figures 7.7 and 7.8.

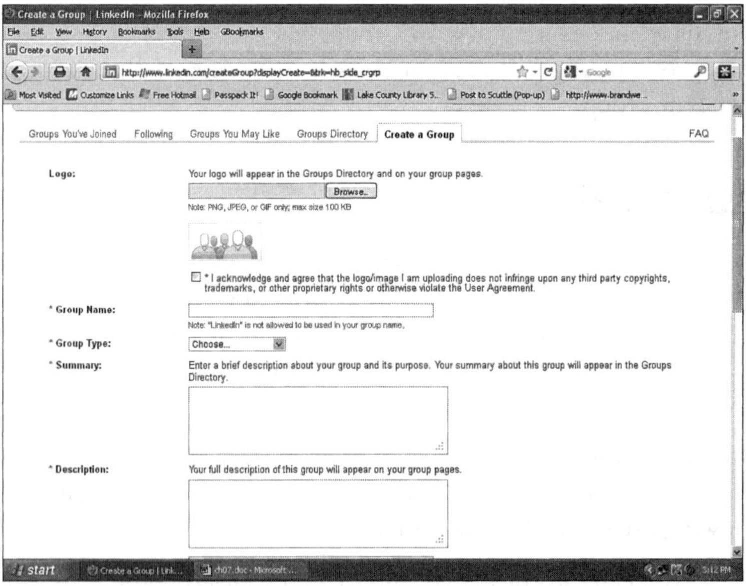

Figure 7.7: *Give your group a name and description that will make it easy for people to find it.*

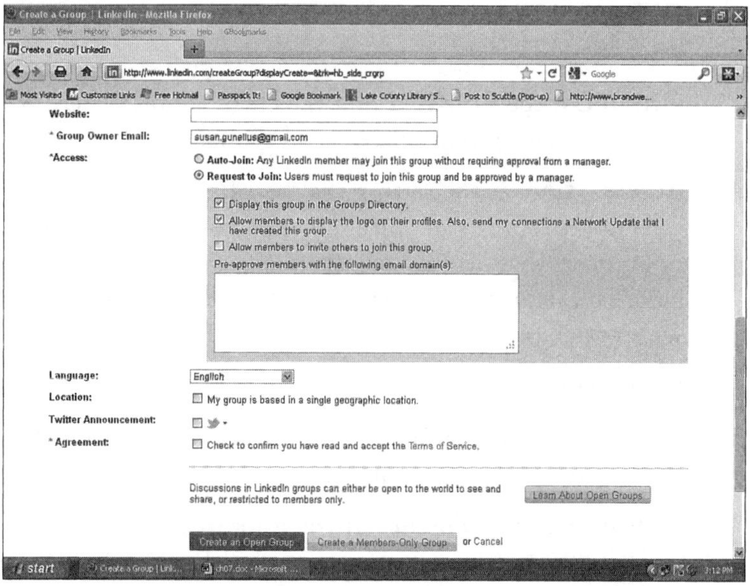

Figure 7.8: *Configure access settings for your new group.*

You can create your group by filling out the Create a Group form as follows:

1. **Logo**   Upload a logo to represent your group. This appears on the group page and in members' profiles (unless you make the logo private). Note that you must have permission to use your group logo or own the copyright to it. If you do, check the box beneath the **Groups** icon.

2. **Group Name**   Choose a name that describes your group and includes keywords so it's easy to find in searches.

3. **Group Type**   Choose the appropriate category from the list to define your group.

4. **Summary**   Enter a descriptive summary of your group that includes keywords. This will appear in group search results and the Groups Directory, so tell your story well.

5. **Description**   Enter a complete description of your group, it will appear on all group pages.

6. **Website**   If there is a website associated with your group, enter the URL here.

7. **Group Owner Email**   Enter the email address where you want to receive group-related correspondence.

8. **Access**   Choose the setting that best fits your needs. You can allow people to automatically join your group, or you can require that people request to join and must be approved before they can actually be part of the group. You can also set up some preapproval and privacy settings here.

9. **Language**   Choose your primary group language.

10. **Location**   If your group is based on a specific geographic area (such as a local group), enter it here.

11. **Twitter Announcement**   If you want to announce your group on Twitter, check this box and make sure the correct Twitter ID is shown.

12. **Agreement**   Read the terms of service and check this box.

13. **Create Group**   Click the **Create an Open Group** button to make your group open to all LinkedIn members and visible to everyone on the internet, or click **Create a Members-Only Group** to make your group open and visible only to LinkedIn members.

Your group is instantly created. Take some time to create a list of preapproved members, send invitations, add group managers, create subgroups, define group rules, and more. All of these settings are available from the Manage tab that will be visible to you at the top of your group pages. You can also set member permissions through the Manage tab in order to reduce spam and irrelevant discussions that can damage the user experience.

QUICK TIP

You can set any member of your group to a manager role by visiting your group's Manage tab, clicking the **Participants** link, and then clicking the **Members** tab. Find the member, and click **Change Role** to make that person a group manager.

Remember it's your group, so you configure it to work the way you want it to. The goal is to create a group experience that people want to be a part of, and that comes by first being a group member yourself and learning how to effectively participate in a LinkedIn group setting.

Participate

The real power of LinkedIn groups comes from your participation in groups that put you in contact with—and in front of—people who can help you reach your goals. Whether your objectives are to build your business, brand, or career, or simply to learn and grow, there are groups that can help you.

Think strategically, not tactically, when you participate in LinkedIn groups. While it might seem on the surface that all you're doing is publishing quick discussion updates, there are actually many additional creative opportunities waiting for you.

Following are 10 examples of things you could be doing on LinkedIn to help you meet your growth goals:

- Connect with larger audiences since you can message and send connection requests to fellow group members.

- Leverage a new place to join targeted discussions that are seen by focused audiences.

- Promote your upcoming speaking engagements, sales, and so on, using the Promotions tab in a relevant group.

- Share and like discussions posted by other members to show that you're helping to spread their content.

- Share links to your best blog posts or other online content that adds value to the group discussion.

- Ask and answer questions in group discussions.

- Send an InMail to group members who are not in your existing network to introduce yourself formally. You can send InMails to fellow group members for free!

- Publish career discussions on a group's Jobs tab to have more targeted conversations about careers and working in a field related to the group.

- Go through the group member list and send connection requests to people who can help you reach your goals. Check out their profiles and be sure to follow them on Twitter and other social sites that they list in their profiles.

- Post a discussion in a large, popular group that you belong to and recommend a subgroup that's more closely targeted to your objectives. Mention that you are available to manage or moderate the subgroup's activity!

Across the top of each group page is a series of common tabs:

- **Discussions** Public discussions between group members appear in the discussions feed. Your activities in participating in discussions also appear through network updates to members who've configured their LinkedIn profiles to receive group updates.

- **Members** View a list of members, search for members, and view recently added members from this tab.

- **Promotions** People can post marketing promotions in discussions on this tab. Promotions don't expire.

- **Jobs** People can post career discussions and job openings from outside the LinkedIn Jobs tool discussed in Chapter 15. These posts appear on the Jobs tab within a group to target a focused audience. Job and career discussions expire after 14 days.

- **Search** Use the search tools on this tab to find specific discussions published to the group.

- **More...** Access member updates, updates from the group members you're following, your account settings, subgroups, and the group profile.

INSIDER SECRET

Group managers can add the **Promotions** and **Jobs** tabs to move these discussions off the main group discussion timeline. Depending on the group rules, managers and members can flag discussions as jobs or promotions, so they're moved to the appropriate tab.

Follow Group Members

If there are members of a group that you belong to whom you think offer particularly good content and conversations, you can follow them so their activities are easy for you to keep track of.

As you scroll through updates on a group's Discussion page, you'll see a link under each person's profile picture inviting you to follow that person. Just click the **Follow [Name]** link to start following them. You can follow or unfollow group members at any time.

You can view a full list of people you follow in groups, and people who are following you by clicking the **Groups** link in the LinkedIn top navigation bar and selecting the **Following** tab from the main Groups page that opens. Use the links in the left sidebar to view follower details.

You can view the update feed from any group member you follow by clicking the **More...** tab and selecting the **Updates** link. Choose the **People I'm Following** tab from the updates page to skim through updates from those important people. It's a great way to reduce clutter and hone in on the kind of information you need.

Join Discussions

The primary way to participate in LinkedIn groups is by starting and joining discussions. When you visit a group page that you belong to, the Discussions tab is where most of the action happens. Just as you start discussions on your LinkedIn profile by posting a text update (with or without a link), you can do the same in LinkedIn groups. Type your message into the status update text box, shown in Figure 7.5. When you're happy with your update, click the **Share** button to publish it to the group discussion tab. If you want to also tweet your group update to your Twitter profile, select the check box next to the Twitter bird icon before clicking **Share**.

The update automatically appears at the top of the Discussion page (if the group manager doesn't moderate comments first), in your activity feed, and in the group's activity feed. Other group members can choose to follow you; reply privately to you; or view, share, like, or comment on your update. This group manager can choose to feature specific discussions as "Manager Choice" discussions, pinning them to the top of the page.

> **WARNING**
>
> In groups that allow it, members can flag updates as inappropriate, as a job posting, or as a promotional posting using the links beneath each update, any of which could remove the update from the main discussion tab.

The key to group discussion success is adding value to the conversation. Don't self-promote. You have to give more than you receive by listening to other members, acknowledging them, and helping them. Indirect marketing of yourself, your brand, and your business will happen organically as your reputation and exposure grow through your valuable group participation. Group success doesn't happen overnight, but like all forms of networking, the relationships that you build through group interaction can be critical to reaching your long-term goals.

The Least You Need to Know

- Group membership can expand your LinkedIn network.
- You can join multiple groups to expand your reach.
- It takes just minutes to start a LinkedIn group.
- The more active you are in groups, the more exposure you can get.

Giving and Receiving Recommendations

Chapter

8

In This Chapter

- Introducing LinkedIn recommendations
- Recommendations as testimonials and referrals
- How to ask for and write recommendations
- Showing off your recommendations

LinkedIn offers a unique feature that can help you land a job, get new customers, and more. It's called LinkedIn Recommendations, and is one of the most important but frequently overlooked parts of your LinkedIn profile and your overall business, brand, or career story. When someone recommends your work, that recommendation adds credibility to your LinkedIn profile. It's important to understand that profile recommendations are different from the Company Page product and service recommendations discussed in Chapter 4.

Offline, customer testimonials and recommendations from previous employers can help you build your business or get a job, and they can do the same on LinkedIn. Research shows that most employers view an applicant's social website profile (including their LinkedIn profile) before hiring that person. Companies and customers do the same thing when they're looking for businesses to work with. Getting recommendations on your LinkedIn profile can make the difference between reaching your goals and falling short. This chapter teaches you how to get, give, and use recommendations.

What Are Recommendations?

LinkedIn recommendations are testimonials. They provide third-party verification of the information in your LinkedIn profile. You can ask any of your first-degree connections on LinkedIn to write a recommendation for you. Each recommendation is linked to a specific job you've held as listed in your LinkedIn profile. It's a good idea to try to get recommendations for all of your past jobs with particular focus on jobs that demonstrate you have skills and experience related to the type of work you want to do in the future.

LinkedIn members can recommend any of their connections at any time. Alternatively, LinkedIn offers a simple form that enables members to request recommendations from their connections. Don't wait around for recommendations. Instead, use that form and request recommendations as discussed in the "Requesting Recommendations" section later in this chapter.

Recommendations that you receive are displayed in your LinkedIn profile in the Experience and Recommendations sections. Recommendations that you write for your connections appear in the Experience and Recommendations sections of their profiles as well as on the right side of your own profile in the [Your Name Here] Recommends box as shown in Figure 8.1.

> **QUICK TIP**
>
> Recommendations that you receive will not display on your LinkedIn profile until you accept them as described in the next section.

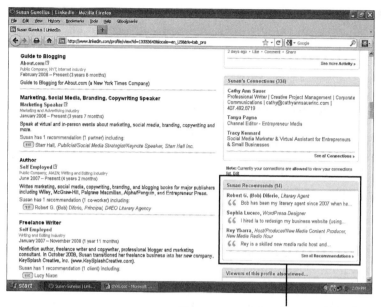

The recommendations box on a LinkedIn profile

Figure 8.1: *Recommendations you write for other people display on the right side of your LinkedIn profile.*

How Recommendations Can Help You

People trust opinions and recommendations from their friends, family, colleagues, and peers. Which would you believe: a résumé or a list of great referrals that you can actually validate by investigating who wrote them? Hopefully, you picked the second choice. Your LinkedIn profile reads somewhat like a résumé, but you can bring your story to life with recommendations.

Spend time building your list of quality recommendations so people you haven't worked with before truly understand the type of person you are and work you do. It's like walking into a job interview with your previous bosses and co-workers behind you to substantiate your claims and validate your experience and abilities. Recommendations are even more powerful when someone in your extended network sees that you have been recommended by a mutual connection.

Still not convinced that recommendations can help you meet your goals? Here are five common examples of ways that recommendations help LinkedIn users:

- A hiring manager has to choose between you and another applicant. Your LinkedIn profile has 20 positive recommendations that the hiring manager can verify, but the other applicant has none. All else being equal, guess who is more likely to get the job? You, of course!

- A potential investor is considering investing in your company. He reads dozens of recommendations on your LinkedIn profile and understands you are a safe risk based on credible past achievements.

- You're being considered for a leadership role in a new organization. The hiring executive sees that you have recommended many of your previous colleagues and subordinates on LinkedIn and understands that you actively recognize your team members and give them the praise, recognition, and motivation they deserve, which is an essential leadership skill.

- A person is looking for an individual or business to work with on a specific project. She searches LinkedIn profiles using related keywords. She also selects the industry and some other criteria and sorts the results by Relationship + Recommendations, bringing your profile with many recommendations closer to the top of the results list than profiles with few or no recommendations.

- You receive a recommendation. Once you have a recommendation, you can be included in the Service Provider Directory (discussed in Chapter 10), creating another way for people to find you on LinkedIn through Service Provider Directory searches.

Recommendations help validate your LinkedIn profile and create more opportunities for people to find you. Remember, recommendations make it easier for your profile to be found via profile searches, Service Provider Directory searches, and through other LinkedIn members' profiles who have recommended you. That's because when one of your connections recommends you, the activity appears in their update stream as well as in the Recommendations box on the right side of their profiles. There is no doubt that recommendations are a powerful part of LinkedIn.

Requesting Recommendations

It's important to request recommendations only from people you've actually worked with and who can give an honest testimonial about your experience and abilities. Recommendations are linked to specific jobs in your LinkedIn profile, so look for first-degree connections who can offer relevant testimonials. The quality of the recommendations you receive matters. Imagine a recommendation that says, "John was great to work with." This recommendation adds little value. Quality trumps quantity.

To request a recommendation from one of your first-degree connections, select the **Profile** link from the top navigation bar when you're logged in to your LinkedIn account. Next, click the **Recommendations** link in the drop-down list to open the Received Recommendations page. Click the **Request Recommendations** tab at the top of the page to open that page as shown in Figure 8.2.

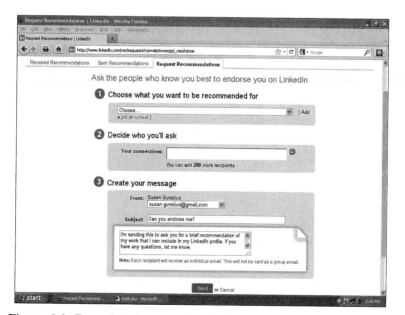

Figure 8.2: *Enter the information into the form to request a recommendation.*

Use the drop-down menu to choose the job or school you want to be recommended for. Next, enter the name of the person you want to recommend you in the **Your Connections** text box or click the **IN** icon to the right of the text box to choose from a sortable list of your connections.

> **QUICK TIP**
>
> Click the **Job** link or the **School** link to add a new job or school to your LinkedIn profile. It will then appear in the recommendations form.

Finally, choose the email address you want to send the request message from, enter a subject line for the email message, and enter your message body. When your message is done, click the **Send** button.

Always take time to write a personal message to increase the chances that the recipient will actually write the recommendation for you. This is particularly important for people you aren't in contact with all the time. While your close friends might not mind receiving the generic message that defaults in the message text box, people you don't know as well need to receive more information. Remind them of how you worked together, tell them why you want them to recommend you, and be sure to let them know if you're prepared to write a recommendation in return.

> **INSIDER SECRET**
>
> You can enter up to 200 names in the **Your Connections** text box to save time and send a mass recommendations request. However, it's always best to ask individuals to help you personally through individual requests.

When someone recommends you on LinkedIn, you should always send a personal thank you note, and be sure to thank them publicly via a LinkedIn profile update.

Writing Recommendations

Before you write a recommendation on LinkedIn, read recommendations that are published on other members' profiles. The best recommendations are specific. For example, the recommendations you write should include explanations of how you worked together, what impressed you about the other person, and what you know they're capable of doing. Try to keep your recommendations down to a paragraph or two. No one wants to read a novel. Be succinct. At the same time, you don't want your recommendation to sound like an ad or marketing pitch. Be honest and write a believable recommendation that validates the person's profile and experience.

To recommend a first-degree connection, click the **Recommend** link on the right side at the top of his or her LinkedIn profile to open the Make a Recommendation form. Alternatively, click the **Received Recommendations** or **Sent Recommendations** tab (shown in Figure 8.2), and scroll to the bottom of either page to see the Make a Recommendation form shown in Figure 8.3.

Figure 8.3: *Complete the form to recommend a first-degree connection.*

Enter the person's name and email address, and select the radio button next to the appropriate relationship, then click the **Continue** button to open the detailed Create Your Recommendation form. If you choose to recommend a person as a Service Provider, your form displays as seen in Figure 8.4. Figure 8.5 shows the form for Colleagues, Business Partners, and Students.

QUICK TIP

Click the **Select from Your Connections List** link beneath the name fields in the Make a Recommendation form to choose from a list of your connections.

Figure 8.4: *Enter the details requested in the Create Your Recommendation for a Service Provider form.*

Select the appropriate choices from the drop-down menus in the Create Your Recommendation form, and then enter your recommendation in the text box provided. You can also view or edit the email message that your connection automatically receives when you submit your recommendation. It's a good idea to personalize this message, particularly if you're writing the recommendation without being asked to do so first. Just click the **View** or **Edit** link to see how the email message looks and revise it if necessary. Finally, click the **Send** button to submit your recommendation.

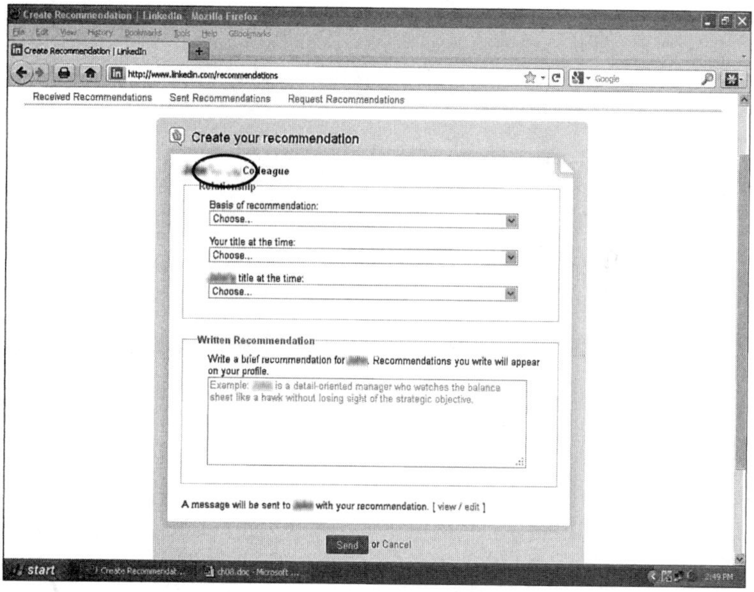

Figure 8.5: *The Create Your Recommendation form for Colleagues, Business Partners, and Students is similar.*

The recipient receives a message telling him that you wrote a recommendation and he can choose to accept, decline, or publish that recommendation as described in the next section of this chapter.

You can edit or withdraw a recommendation at any time by visiting the Sent Recommendations tab in your LinkedIn account and selecting the **Edit** link to the right of a recommendation as shown in Figure 8.6.

Figure 8.6: *Edit, withdraw, or hide recommendations from the Sent Recommendations page in your LinkedIn account.*

It is also possible to hide specific recommendations, so they are not visible on your LinkedIn profile. Click the drop-down menu under the **Display on My Profile To** column heading and select from the three options provided: show the recommendation to your connections only, to everyone, or to no one.

INSIDER SECRET

Scroll to the bottom of your list of recommendations to access a bulk modification option to change all recommendation display settings to the same setting at one time.

Recommendations are as much a reflection on you as they are on the people you write them for, so always take the time to write meaningful recommendations. However, there are times when people will send you recommendation requests that you aren't comfortable giving. When you receive such a request, be sure to click the **Reply** button and offer an explanation before you delete the request or archive it for later.

Displaying Recommendations on Your Profile

Recommendations that you receive are only visible on your LinkedIn profile (when you accept them) to your existing network. They are not visible on your public profile. However, as you learned earlier in this book, your extended LinkedIn network can include a lot of people, so it's important that you showcase your LinkedIn recommendations to add credibility to your online reputation.

When a new recommendation is submitted to your LinkedIn profile, you receive a message in your LinkedIn Inbox notifying you. You can review the recommendation and accept it, request a replacement, or archive it as follows:

- Select **Accept Recommendation** if you're happy with it. You can then choose to display it on your profile or hide it.

- Select **Request a Replacement** if there is an error in the recommendation that needs to be revised before you can accept it. The author will receive your message and has the option to revise the recommendation.

- Select **Archive** if you're not ready to accept the recommendation or request a replacement.

You can change the visibility of individual recommendations or request replacements at any time by visiting the Received Recommendations page in your LinkedIn account as shown in Figure 8.7.

QUICK TIP

You can request recommendations for any position in your LinkedIn profile by clicking the **Ask To Be Endorsed** link beside each job on the Received Recommendations page of your account.

Some people are very good at asking others to recommend them. To other people, asking for any type of self-promotion can be uncomfortable. Don't be shy. Recommendations are an important part of the LinkedIn user experience. What's the worst that could happen? Someone ignores your request or declines it. That just means they aren't the right person to endorse you. Move on to the next appropriate person, and send a new request. And don't forget that recommending another person first is a great way to encourage them to reciprocate and recommend you in return.

Figure 8.7: *Display, hide, or request revised recommendations from the Received Recommendations page.*

The Least You Need to Know

- LinkedIn recommendations can be written for any first-degree connection.
- LinkedIn recommendations can be visible or hidden.
- You can request and write recommendations from your connections, but both should be done only for people you've actually worked with and can honestly endorse.
- LinkedIn recommendations make your profile more credible, more searchable, and more visible.

Using LinkedIn Answers

In This Chapter

- Asking questions to all LinkedIn users
- Finding questions to answer and answering them well
- Gaining expert status
- Keeping up with hot topics

LinkedIn Answers offers another way that you can demonstrate your knowledge, meet new people, and get valuable information that you need from experts. Anyone can visit linkedin.com/answers to view questions that have been asked and answers to those questions, but the real power of LinkedIn Answers comes after you log in to your LinkedIn account and dive deeper.

This chapter teaches you how to ask and answer questions using LinkedIn Answers so you can reach your business, brand, and career goals. You also learn how to automate the process of finding questions to answer related to your area of expertise, so you can work smarter, not harder.

Asking Questions

Anyone with a LinkedIn profile can ask a question on LinkedIn Answers. Just click the **More** link in the top navigation bar when you're logged in to your account and select the **Answers** link from the drop-down menu to open the Answers Home page shown in Figure 9.1.

Figure 9.1: *You can access all parts of LinkedIn Answers from the Answers Home page of your LinkedIn account.*

The Answers Home page is divided into several sections. Across the top of the page are five tabs where you can quickly access pages to ...

- **Answers Home.** View your LinkedIn Answers Home page.

- **Advanced Answers Search.** Conduct an advanced answers search.

- **My Q&A.** View the questions and answers you've submitted.

- **Ask a Question.** Publish a question to LinkedIn Answers.

- **Answer Questions.** Find open questions asked by people within your LinkedIn network, closed questions, and people who have earned expert status (described later in this chapter).

Beneath the tabs on the Answers Home page, there is an area where you can ask a question by typing it into the text box, answer a question by selecting a category from the recommended list of links, scroll through a list of new questions submitted by people within your LinkedIn network, click to view questions in a category featured by an advertiser, click to view your open questions (or view all of your asked and answered questions), browse through categories to find questions to answer or simply learn from, and scroll through a list of this week's top experts.

INSIDER SECRET

There are many ways to find questions, so it's a good idea to conduct a search (as discussed in the next section, "Searching for Questions to Answer") for similar questions and read the answers provided before you publish your own question. It's possible that your question has been asked and answered many times before.

LinkedIn does have some guidelines about the types of questions that should be asked on LinkedIn Answers. Those guidelines are paraphrased as follows:

- Write your question as such, not as a comment, opinion, observation, or other statement.

- Your questions should be related to business and appropriate for the professional LinkedIn audience. If you wouldn't ask your boss or co-worker, don't ask it on LinkedIn.

- Don't try to fit every detail into the actual question. Use the separate Details text box to provide extra information that will help people give the best possible answers.

- Don't use bait-and-switch techniques. In other words, don't publish a question for the purpose of finding people to connect with on LinkedIn.

- Inappropriate questions can be flagged by other LinkedIn members. If you publish a question related to hiring for your company, looking for a job, or promoting yourself or your business, identify the question as such and share it only to your first-degree connections.

> **WARNING**
>
> Using the Report As feature, LinkedIn members can flag LinkedIn ques-
> tions as inappropriate. When several members flag the same question,
> that question is deleted. LinkedIn reviews all flagged questions and
> repeat offenders may find their ability to ask questions blocked in the
> future.

When you're ready to ask a question, click the **Ask a Question** tab
to open the full Ask a Question form shown in Figure 9.2.

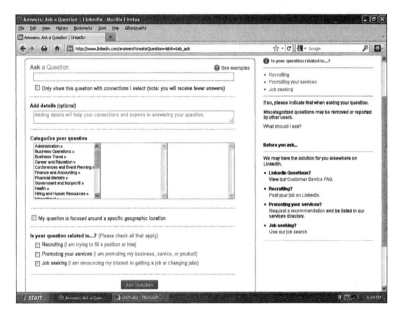

Figure 9.2: *Enter your question and details into the Ask a Question form.*

In the first text box, enter your question. Select the check box under
the question text box if you want to make your question visible only
to your first-degree connections (you'll be prompted to choose up to
200 connections and write a message to send the question to their
LinkedIn Inboxes). In the Add Details text box, you should enter any
details that will help people provide the best possible answers. You
can enter up to 1,996 characters in this text box, so be sure to provide enough details. However, don't get too verbose or no one will
read it all!

INSIDER SECRET

Use keywords in your question and details to increase the chances of people finding it through searches.

Next, select the appropriate categories for your question using the list provided. When you choose a category in the first column, a list of subcategories appears in the second column, and when you select a subcategory, a list of even more focused categories appears in the third column. Try to choose the most targeted categories possible to ensure the most qualified experts see your question. Keep in mind, not all categories have subcategories.

Once you select your question category, a link appears beneath the category boxes that says **Select Another Category**. If you'd like your question to be published in more than one category, click this link and add another category. You can select up to two categories.

It's also important that you select the **My question is focused around a specific geographic location** check box if yours is a localized question. Finally, select the appropriate check box to identify your question as related to Recruiting, Promoting Your Services, or Job Seeking, and click the **Ask Question** button to publish your question to LinkedIn Answers.

Your question is immediately published to the Open Questions page, where people can answer it (unless you checked the option to make your question visible only to your connections). That means it is open to all LinkedIn members to answer and remains open for seven days (you can reopen it later if you don't get the answers you need). Note that private questions sent only to your connections don't expire.

Your question also appears on your LinkedIn profile, and an update is published to your activity feed. Remember, public questions are exactly that: public. That means they appear in search engine results and can be viewed on LinkedIn Answers even to nonusers.

> **WARNING**
> You can ask no more than 10 questions per month. You can track how many questions you have asked each month on the My Q&A page of your account.

Think about how you can leverage the knowledge of your LinkedIn network to help you learn, grow, and develop your business, brand, or career. You have the potential to gain insight from a large audience of experts on LinkedIn, and most of them are using LinkedIn for that very reason: to share their expertise. To get your creative juices flowing, here are some ideas for types of questions that typically generate great answers, deeper relationship opportunities, and fantastic learning:

- **How To**   Is there an area of your industry or a career that you're trying to break into that is unclear to you? Ask a question!

- **Who**   Do you need to find contacts in a local area or experts in specific fields for a future business event? That's a great question to ask on LinkedIn Answers with the specific geographic location box selected.

- **Market Research**   Learn about your industry, customers, clients, vendors, and more by asking people in specific industries about their opinions.

- **Predictions and Trends**   Gain insight as to the predictions and trends experts believe are coming for their industries.

- **Interviews**   Looking for someone to interview for a story, book, or other purpose? There are experts waiting to volunteer on LinkedIn Answers.

As long as you follow the LinkedIn Answers guidelines related to asking questions, provided earlier in this chapter, you can be creative in using the tool to improve your knowledge and get help when you need it from other professionals and trusted experts.

Searching for Questions to Answer

Are you ready to start answering questions on LinkedIn Answers? It's a great way to further establish your expertise and reputation as an authority in your field. Answering questions also gets you in front of wider audiences of people who are looking for the exact type of knowledge and experience that you have.

Before you start answering questions, you need to know how to find questions that you're capable of answering with authority. Giving answers that aren't helpful is a LinkedIn *don't*. For example, never answer a question if you feel compelled to include the phrase, "I'm not an expert, but ..." or "I've never actually done this, but ...." The last thing you want to do is clutter questions with answers that don't add value to the conversation. If you can't answer with conviction, don't answer at all.

There are a lot of questions asked on LinkedIn Answers every day, and as your connections and network grow, the lists of questions asked from your network that appears on your Answers Home page will get cluttered. Fortunately, you can bypass the clutter by going directly to the Advanced Answers Search tab shown in Figure 9.3.

Enter your chosen keywords into the search form, select a category (if subcategories are provided, select one to get the most targeted results), and select the check box next to Show Only Unanswered Questions if you want to limit your results to questions that have yet to be answered (giving you an opportunity to jump in and save the day with a great answer). Click the **Search** button, and a list of results is provided as shown in Figure 9.4.

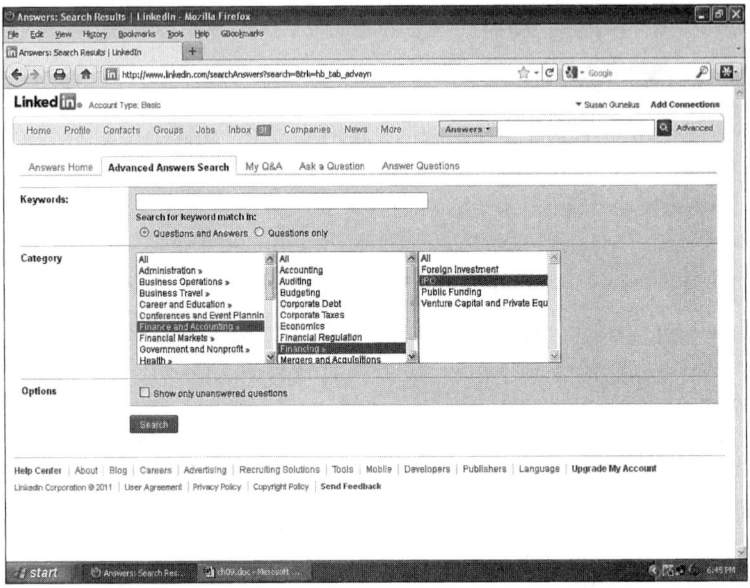

Figure 9.3: *Find questions about specific topics within your area of expertise quickly using the Advanced Answers Search tool.*

Figure 9.4: *You can sort search results by degrees of separation, relevance, or date.*

You can refine your search using the tools in the box on the right side of the results screen. Use the links at the top of the results list to sort your results by Degrees Away From You, Relevance, or Date. If you want to see only open questions, click the **Open Questions** tab at the top of the page.

Browse through the questions in your results list and look for ones that are highly relevant to your expertise. Be sure to read through any other answers that have already been submitted before you write your own response. You want to add to the conversation, not duplicate content.

If you don't have a specific area that you want to answer questions for, you can choose the **Answer Questions** tab at the top of the page. Here you can browse through Open Questions, Closed Questions, and Experts (discussed later in this chapter), and narrow your search by question category. It's typically more time consuming to find the best questions for you to answer this way, but it can give you a better understanding of the types of questions people are asking in your industry.

As you search questions and read answers, take the time to flag those questions and answers that you come across which are inappropriate based on the LinkedIn Answers guidelines. When you see an ad, a recruitment message, a job-seeking message, or a similar message disguised as a question or answer, flag it as inappropriate by clicking the **Report As** link under the question. Do the same if you become aware of a question that is intended for connection building only, includes inappropriate content for the LinkedIn audience, or is a duplicate question or answer. Doing so helps to keep the LinkedIn Answers tool truly useful and free of clutter that appears on so many other social sites and online forums.

How to Answer Questions

As you learned earlier in this chapter, it's important to write useful answers that add value to the conversation and actually help the people who ask questions on LinkedIn. Your answers should not be used as a place for you to promote yourself or your business. However, self-promotion is absolutely an indirect benefit of answering questions on LinkedIn, particularly when you include a useful link to your own content off of LinkedIn, where you can provide additional details that support your answers.

QUICK TIP

You can answer up to 50 questions within a 24-hour period, so get involved! However, if you don't have any first-degree connections yet, you can only answer up to 5 questions within a 24-hour period.

Read questions thoroughly before you answer, and ask for more details if you need them in order to give a good answer. Remember, your answers appear in your own LinkedIn profile, appear in your network updates, are visible to your entire LinkedIn network, and appear in search engine results. You need to put your best foot forward at all times because the answers you provide through LinkedIn Answers can have a direct and significant effect on your online reputation.

When you find a question you want to answer, click the **Answer** button beneath the question and complete the form shown in Figure 9.5.

Figure 9.5: *Complete the form to submit your answer to a question.*

In the Your Answer text box, enter your complete answer to the question that you want to be visible to all LinkedIn users (unless you're answering a private question). Remember to use keywords so your answers have a better chance at appearing in search results.

Next, provide links to additional resources that support your answer and offer additional help. For example, this is a great place to provide links to one of your articles or videos that give more information. If you know another person on LinkedIn who could provide a great answer to the question, click the **Select Experts** button to choose up to three people from your LinkedIn network list. Each person will be notified that they've been suggested as an expert to answer a question on LinkedIn Answers via a message to their LinkedIn Inboxes.

> **QUICK TIP**
>
> If you find a question you can't answer, but know an expert in your network who can, save time by clicking the **Suggest an Expert** button beneath the question instead of the **Answer** button.

Select the check box next to Write a Note to [Person] (Optional) if you want to add a private note that only the person who asked the question can see. Next, click the **Submit** button and your answer immediately appears at the bottom of the list of submitted answers. For public questions, your update appears in your activity feed and appears on your LinkedIn profile in the questions and answers box.

Finding appropriate questions to answer in order to build your reputation as an expert in your field takes time, however, it's worth it when people start to recognize you as a go-to person in your field.

Earning Expertise

At the bottom of the Answers Home page in your LinkedIn account is a list of top experts, which is updated each week. In order to earn expert status, your answer to a question must be rated as *Best* by the person who originally asked it.

For each Best rating you get, you earn a point, which is added to your expert score. The higher your score, the higher you appear in the weekly list of top experts on the Answers Home page. This provides another way that people can find you on LinkedIn and recognize you as a trustworthy authority in your field.

It's important to understand that the expert rating process in LinkedIn Answers is far from perfect. It is possible for people to team up and artificially boost their expert status by answering each other's questions and rating those answers as best. Furthermore, there are many experts on LinkedIn who simply don't answer questions frequently enough to earn a lot of best ratings and points. Finally, many people who ask questions never take the time to rate the best answers to those questions. Therefore, although the LinkedIn Answers experts list provides another way to find people on LinkedIn, do your due diligence and confirm that person's real-world expertise by viewing his or her LinkedIn profile.

Subscribing to Q&A Category Feeds

You can save time and make sure you don't miss questions published in specific categories on LinkedIn Answers by subscribing to individual question category RSS feeds.

To subscribe to receive new questions in a LinkedIn Answers category via feed reader, click the **Answer Questions** tab and select a category from the list in the Browse box on the right side of your screen as shown in Figure 9.6.

Drill down to the most targeted and appropriate categories for you, and click the link for your chosen category. A list of questions appears on the left side of your screen, but in order to subscribe to receive the questions in this category via your feed reader in the future, you need to scroll down to the bottom of the Browse box on the right side of your screen. Here you can find a message that says "Subscribe to new questions in:," as shown in Figure 9.6.

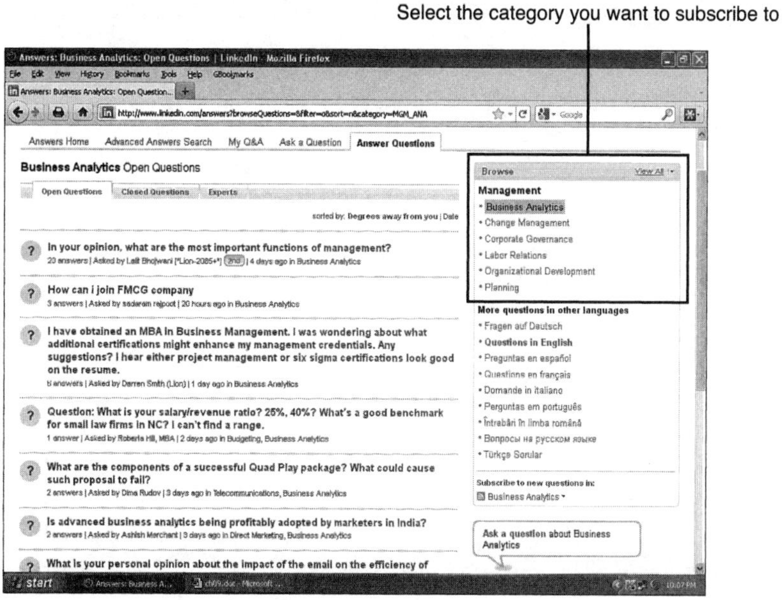

Select the category you want to subscribe to

Figure 9.6: *Use links in the Browse box to find questions to answer by topic.*

Beneath that message is the RSS icon followed by the name of the category as a link. Click the category link next to the RSS icon to open the Subscribe Now pop-up window shown in Figure 9.7.

Just choose your preferred feed reader from the list provided, and follow the instructions to add the feed subscription to your feed reader account. From now on, you can see new questions, along with all other feeds you subscribe to, without even logging in to LinkedIn. When you see a question in your feed reader that you can answer, log in to your LinkedIn account and submit your answer. It's a great time saver!

You can subscribe to the feeds of as many question categories as you want. This is particularly useful if you use LinkedIn for multiple purposes and to connect with varied audiences such as clients, investors, recruiters, and more. Just make sure you keep your questions and answers focused on activities that can help you reach your goals, so your time is invested wisely and your reputation and exposure grow in the best possible ways.

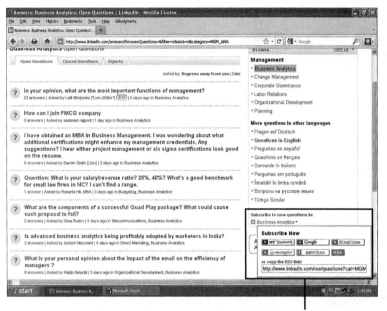

Subscribe to question topic feeds here

Figure 9.7: *Subscribe to question topic feeds here. Choose your preferred feed reader to subscribe to a question category.*

The Least You Need to Know

- You can use LinkedIn Answers to ask public questions that everyone on LinkedIn can see or private questions that only your selected connections can see.

- Answering questions is a great way to demonstrate your expertise, boost your reputation, and get exposure to new audiences.

- If you know someone who can answer a question on LinkedIn Answers, suggest him or her as an expert. Both the person who asked the question and the expert are sure to appreciate the help and exposure opportunity.

- You can subscribe to the RSS feeds of question categories in LinkedIn Answers, so you receive new questions via your preferred feed reader.

Marketing Yourself Through LinkedIn

It's time to promote yourself, your brand, or your business on LinkedIn! While continual self-promotion is a guaranteed way to fail on LinkedIn, there are many opportunities for indirect promotion and some acceptable self-promotion opportunities (as long as they're not overused).

In Part 3, you learn how to use LinkedIn features and apps to demonstrate your expertise and abilities as well as for direct promotion. Get introduced to advertising on LinkedIn through LinkedIn Ads and learn how to integrate your LinkedIn efforts into your overall marketing plan. Finally, read through the tips and suggestions provided to use LinkedIn as a market research tool.

Marketing Tools, Features, and Apps

In This Chapter

- Getting listed in the Service Provider Directory
- Promoting and finding events
- Showing off your portfolio
- Making it easy for others to promote you

In Chapter 6, I introduced you to a variety of LinkedIn applications (apps) that you can use to enhance your profile. Each of those apps can indirectly promote you and your business, but this chapter introduces you to tools, features, and apps that enable you to directly market you and your business.

Whether you want to invite people to an online or offline event, show off your portfolio, or share company news and information, there is a tool or app that makes it easy to do so. Using plugins from the LinkedIn Developer Community can also make it easy for your audience to help promote you and your business.

Service Provider Directory

The LinkedIn Service Provider Directory is accessible from the link in the footer of the LinkedIn home page when you're not logged in to your LinkedIn account, or you can visit linkedin.com/directory/sp/ at any time to open the directory home page as shown in Figure 10.1.

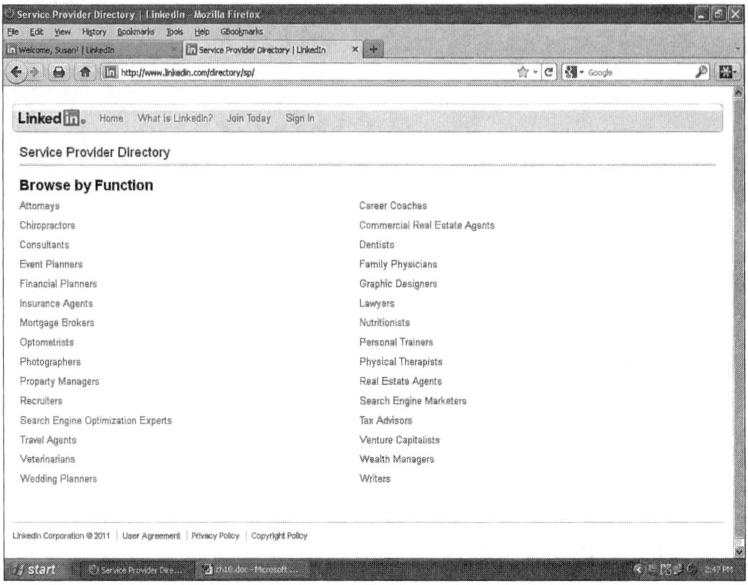

Figure 10.1: *Browse the Service Provider Directory by category.*

You cannot add yourself to the Service Provider Directory. Instead, other LinkedIn members must first recommend you by using the profile recommendation form discussed in Chapter 8 and selecting the **Service Provider** option at the bottom of the form. They also must choose the appropriate service provider category in the recommendation form, so your profile is attributed to the correct category in the Service Provider Directory. You are automatically added to the directory when you receive a predetermined number of service recommendations in the same category (your listing appears in that category in the directory). Most recently, the magic number was reported as six recommendations.

> **WARNING**
>
> The service provider recommendation submitted to a person's profile for work they've done in a specific job is different from recommendations of products and services that people can submit to Company Pages on LinkedIn. Make sure you're submitting the appropriate recommendation in the correct place. Personal recommendations go on individual profiles; product and service recommendations go on Company Pages.

The Service Provider Directory is difficult to navigate and does not always load correctly or fully. However, it does offer one more way for people to find you on LinkedIn. Don't spend a large amount of time trying to get listed in the directory. If you do great work and ask for recommendations from the right people, your listing will happen naturally. Instead, spend time interacting, building relationships, and demonstrating your expertise, which can help you reach your LinkedIn goals.

Events

Do you hold online and offline events? For example, do you host web-based seminars or training classes? If you hold events that your LinkedIn network might be interested in, then you can spread the word—and even find events that you want to attend—using the LinkedIn Events app.

When you add your events to the Events app, they are listed in the app directory and in a special Events section in your LinkedIn profile as shown in Figure 10.2.

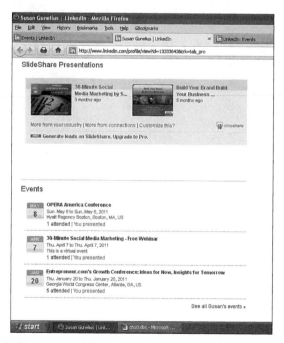

Figure 10.2: *Your past and future events are displayed in your LinkedIn profile.*

To add the Events app to your LinkedIn profile, click the **More** link from the top navigation bar when you're logged in to your LinkedIn account, and then select the **Get More Applications** link from the drop-down menu. The Application Directory opens, which you can scroll through to find the Events app listing. Click the **Events** link to open the app page, and then click the **Add Application** button. The app is immediately added to your profile, and you can start listing your events and browsing events listed by other LinkedIn members.

> **QUICK TIP**
>
> If the Events app isn't included on the Applications Directory page, click the **Browse More Applications** link in the upper-right corner of the page.

Once you've added the Events app, you can visit the Events Home page at any time by selecting the **Events** link from the **More** drop-down menu in the top navigation bar. This page is shown in Figure 10.3.

Figure 10.3: *On the Events Home page, you can find and add events.*

From the Events Home page, you can find events that your LinkedIn network is attending or hosting, find events recommended to you by LinkedIn based on your industry and job function, add your own events, see who is attending events, identify events that you're attending, and publish comments on event listings. Get started by scrolling through the events listed under the Browse Events heading shown in Figure 10.3. There are two tabs available, which enable you to browse events that your connections are hosting or attending (the My Connections tab) and browse the most popular events (the Most Popular tab).

Click the **Find Events** tab or click the **Advanced Search** link on the right side of the Events Home page to open the Find Events page shown in Figure 10.4.

QUICK TIP

To perform a quick search from the Events Home page, enter keywords in the Find an Event search box on the right side of the Events Home page and click the **Search** button.

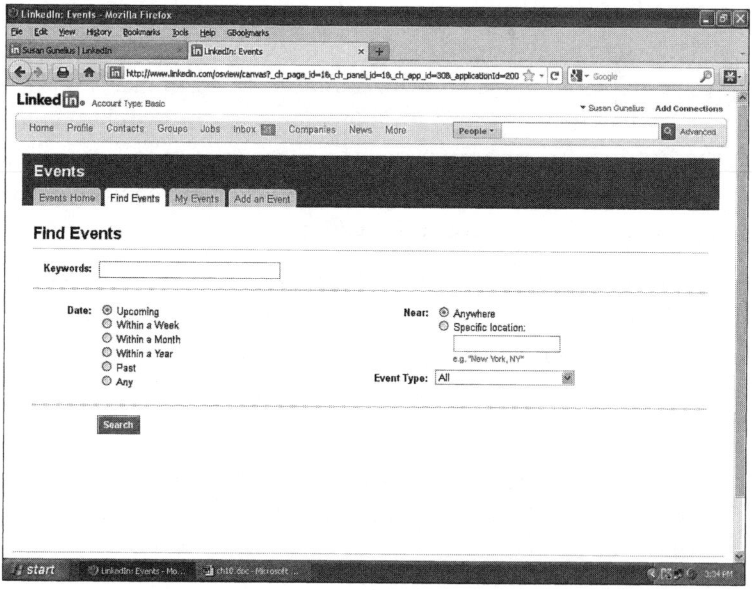

Figure 10.4: *Enter search criteria to find events that you might want to attend.*

Click the **My Events** tab to view your upcoming and past events, and click the **Add an Event** tab to open the Add an Event form shown in Figure 10.5.

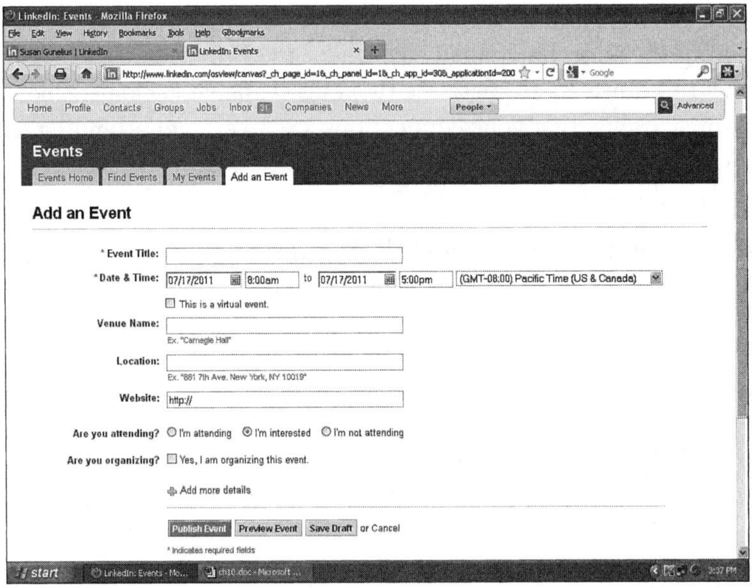

Figure 10.5: *Complete the form to add an event to the Event directory.*

Simply enter the requested information into the form (use keywords to boost the chances of people finding your event in searches) and click the **Publish Event** button to add your event to the Event directory and display it on your LinkedIn profile. The action also appears as an update in your network activity feed.

Once you've published an event, you can share it with your connections, mention it in groups, invite people to attend, publish questions to strike up conversations using the comment feature, and collect information about people who indicate they are attending, or are interested in, the event.

This is a great way to spread the word about any kind of event, but don't spam the Event directory. Only add events that are relevant to your LinkedIn audience.

Portfolio Display

If you're a designer, artist, or photographer, then the Creative Portfolio Display app is perfect for you to bring your story to life on your LinkedIn profile. However, the app can work for anyone who has samples or documents that they want to display on their profiles. Don't be afraid to get creative with how you use this app.

To add the app to your profile, click the **More** link in the top navigation bar when you're logged in to your LinkedIn profile and select the **Get More Applications** link from the drop-down menu. Scroll through the list of available apps, and click on the **Creative Portfolio Display** listing, which brings you to the page shown in Figure 10.6.

Figure 10.6: *Scroll through the Creative Portfolio Display Application Preview images to see creative ways the app is used.*

Simply click the **Add Application** button (lower-right corner of Figure 10.6) to add the app to your LinkedIn profile. Make sure the check box that says **Display on My Profile** is selected, so your portfolio is visible to people who view your LinkedIn profile.

You'll be prompted to upload your portfolio to the Behance Network (behance.com), which is a site that enables people to create online multimedia portfolios that can be displayed on Behance partner sites like LinkedIn. You can upload as many multimedia projects to the Behance Network as you want and pick and choose the ones you want to show on your LinkedIn profile via the Creative Portfolio Display app.

By showing off your portfolio of work, you can demonstrate your skills, attract new customers, and land a new job. You never know who might see your portfolio on LinkedIn, so use the Creative Portfolio Display app to show what you can do.

My Travel

If you are a frequent traveler who likes to meet up with LinkedIn connections at your travel destinations, then you should try the My Travel app from TripIt. This app lets you display your upcoming trips, your current location, and your travel stats to your LinkedIn network. It's a great way to connect with people in specific cities to schedule meetings or informal gatherings when you'll be in town, and for other users to find out where you're going in the future.

To add the My Travel app to your LinkedIn account, visit the Applications Directory page and click the **My Travel** listing to open the app page shown in Figure 10.7, and click the **Add Application** button.

Nothing helps make an online relationship stronger than getting a chance to meet face to face. My Travel is the perfect example of how LinkedIn can lead to offline opportunities!

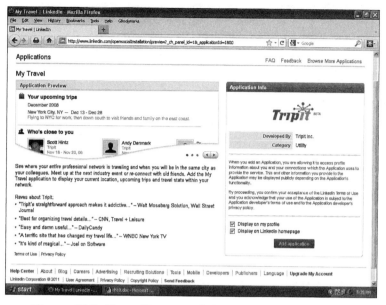

Figure 10.7: *Show off your travel plans with the My Travel app.*

Plugins

In Chapter 4, you learned about LinkedIn plugins that help you promote your Company Page. In this chapter, you learn about LinkedIn plugins available through the LinkedIn Developer Community that help you indirectly promote your LinkedIn profile. To view the available LinkedIn plugins, log in to your LinkedIn account and visit: developer.linkedin.com/plugins.

The following plugins are recommended to quickly and easily give your LinkedIn profile, your website, and your blog more exposure.

Share on LinkedIn: Add a Share on LinkedIn button to your website or blog. This plugin allows visitors to share the link to that content with their LinkedIn networks with a click of the mouse. A share count can be included to show off how popular your content is! You can choose to embed the plugin in the three formats shown in Figure 10.8.

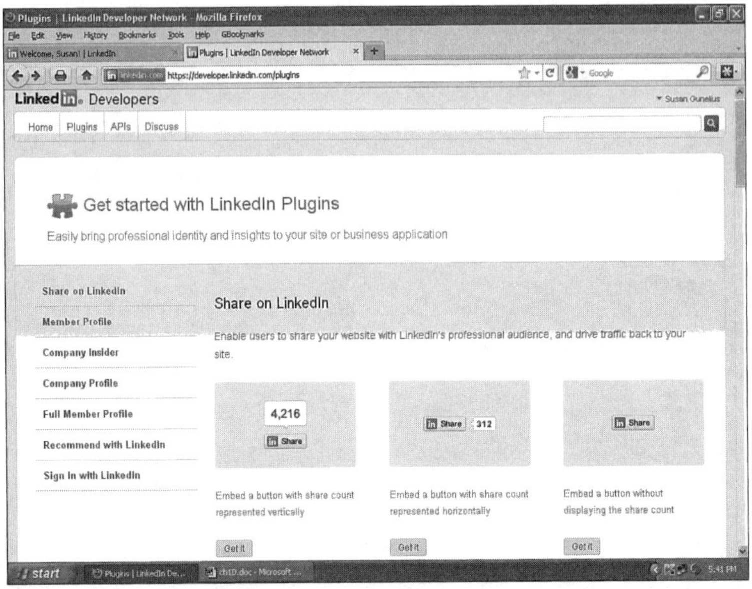

Figure 10.8: *The Share on LinkedIn plugin makes it easy for people to share your website and blog with their LinkedIn networks.*

Member Profile: Show off your LinkedIn profile on your website or blog with the Member Profile plugin. When this plugin is embedded in your website or blog, visitors can see your profile summary and common connections (if they're logged in to LinkedIn). The amount of information visible depends on the format of the plugin that you choose to use.

When it comes to building your personal or business brand and your career using LinkedIn, you can't operate in a silo. Instead, you need to spread your wings and find ways to surround people with your experience, content, knowledge, and expertise. Making it easy to find you through your varied online profiles, websites, and blogs by displaying your LinkedIn Member profile is one way to do it. At the same time, make it easy for people to share your blog and website with the Share on LinkedIn plugin so people can learn more about you, see more of your work, and deepen their relationships with you.

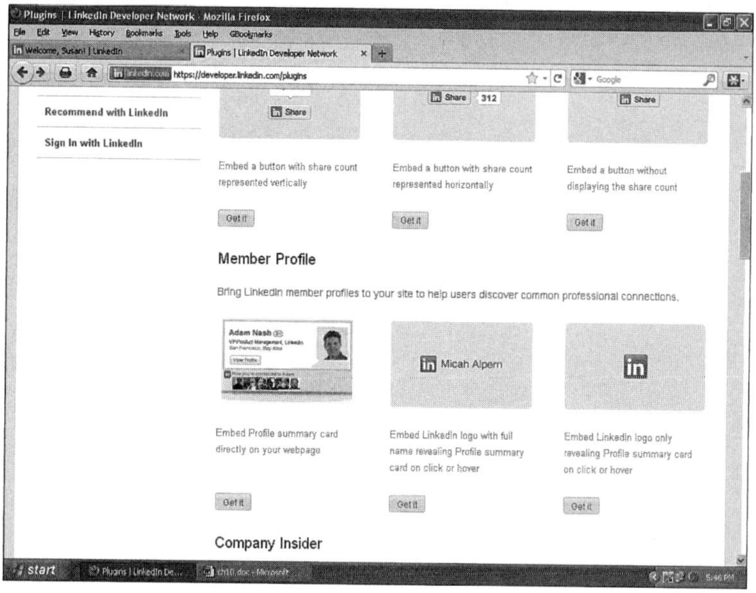

Figure 10.9: *Show off your LinkedIn profile on your blog or website with the Member Profile plugin.*

If you only hang out in your own home and never leave, you'll only make so many friends. You have to put yourself out there, but always lead people back to your home base (in this case, your LinkedIn profile) where the bulk of your connections, conversations, and content live.

The Least You Need to Know

- If you're a service provider, you must get recommended as a service provider in a specific category multiple times before you can appear in the LinkedIn Service Provider Directory.
- With the LinkedIn Events app, you can promote your own events and find events to attend that interest you.
- Use LinkedIn apps to share your portfolio and coordinate meetups with other LinkedIn members while you're traveling.
- LinkedIn plugins are easy to embed in your website or blog and offer reciprocal promotion between your online profiles and destinations.

LinkedIn Ads

In This Chapter

- Reviewing LinkedIn advertising options
- Creating your LinkedIn ad the right way
- Following the rules
- Understanding budgets and results

LinkedIn Ads is a tool that anyone with a LinkedIn account and a credit card can use to advertise a product, service, company, brand, and so on, to the LinkedIn user community. You create your own ad, choose your budget, and select targeting criteria to ensure your ad is displayed to the most appropriate LinkedIn members.

All LinkedIn ads lead to specific URLs chosen by the advertisers who pay for those ads based on clicks or impressions, which is the number of times the ad is displayed on the site. This chapter teaches you how to create your own LinkedIn ads for optimum results. You also learn how to set your budget, so you aren't surprised with a huge bill, and how to track the performance of your ads.

Types of LinkedIn Ads

You can set up your own LinkedIn ad within a few minutes. All you need is your credit card, some text, a URL to send people to when they click on your ad, and an image. The more time you spend developing a great message, choosing the best URL to send consumers to, and creating targeting criteria to ensure the most appropriate people see your ad, the better your results will be.

LinkedIn ads typically look like the ads shown in Figure 11.1. They include a headline, image, and description. When you click on the ad, you are taken to the URL specified by the advertiser.

Figure 11.1: *LinkedIn ads usually include a headline, image, and description.*

In some instances, an image will not appear with your ad. For example, Figure 11.2 shows a text-only ad at the top of a LinkedIn member profile page. Ads in this location are typically paid for based on the number of clicks they get, which is discussed in more detail later in this section.

QUICK TIP

If your LinkedIn advertising budget is over $25,000, contact a LinkedIn Marketing Solutions salesperson using the form at http://marketing. linkedin.com/contact to discuss display advertising options.

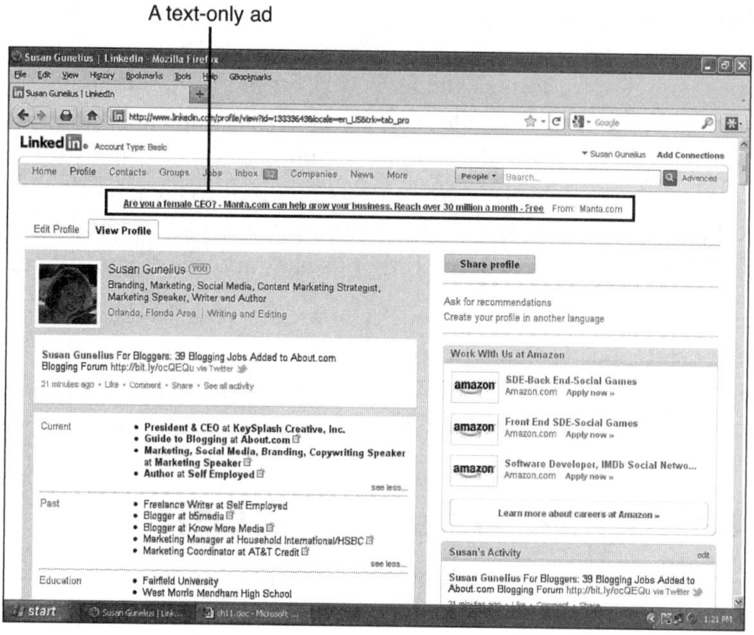

A text-only ad

Figure 11.2: *On some LinkedIn pages, images do not appear with ads.*

LinkedIn ads are displayed on prominent pages such as profile pages, the Home page, InBox, search results page, and group pages. Depending on where your ad is displayed, it could appear along with up to two additional ads. Furthermore, when you create a LinkedIn ad, you have the option to allow your ad to be displayed on other websites. These sites are LinkedIn partners and are part of the LinkedIn Audience Network, which gives your ads more exposure.

LinkedIn provides two payment models that you can choose from for your ads.

Cost-per-click (CPC): You pay based on how many times people actually clicked on your ad. Generally, the cost-per-click payment model is best for direct marketing purposes such as lead generation, making sales, and so on, within specific audiences. For example, if you're offering a discount on a specific product on your website, a cost-per-click ad is a good choice because you don't just want to raise awareness, you want to drive sales.

Cost-per-impression (CPM): You pay based on how many times your ad was actually displayed onscreen to visitors. Typically, the cost-per-impression payment model is best for brand-building and raising awareness across broader audiences. For example, if you're trying to spread the word about a new brand, a cost-per-impression ad is a good choice, because people aren't required to click on the ad for you to achieve your goal. As long as they see the ad and understand what it's for, you've successfully raised awareness of your brand.

Regardless of which payment model you use for your LinkedIn ads, you can create a daily budget threshold to control your costs. Read the budgeting section later in this chapter ("Budgeting, Bidding, and Payment") to learn more about advertising costs and budgets.

Creating an Ad on LinkedIn

When you're ready to start advertising on LinkedIn, just log in to your account and click the **Advertising** link in the footer or click the **Home** link in the top navigation bar followed by the **Advertise on LinkedIn** link that appears in the drop-down menu. This takes you to the Home page of LinkedIn Ads where you can simply click the **Start Now** button to open the Create Your Ad Campaign form shown in Figure 11.3.

In the Ad Campaign Name field, enter a name for your ad that will help you easily remember the ad in the future. You're the only person who will see this name. It can be confusing to remember specific ads if you create many, so be descriptive with the name you enter in this field. When you want to manage your campaign in the future, track performance, adjust your budget, and so on, you'll save a lot of time by giving your ad a recognizable name now.

Next, create your ad! If you want people to be taken to a website outside of LinkedIn.com when they click on your ad, select the radio button next to Your Web Page, then click on the **example URL** to open a text box where you can type in the URL of your choosing. If you want people who click on your ad to be taken to your profile or

Company Page on LinkedIn, select the radio button next to **A Page on LinkedIn** and choose the appropriate destination from the drop-down menu that appears.

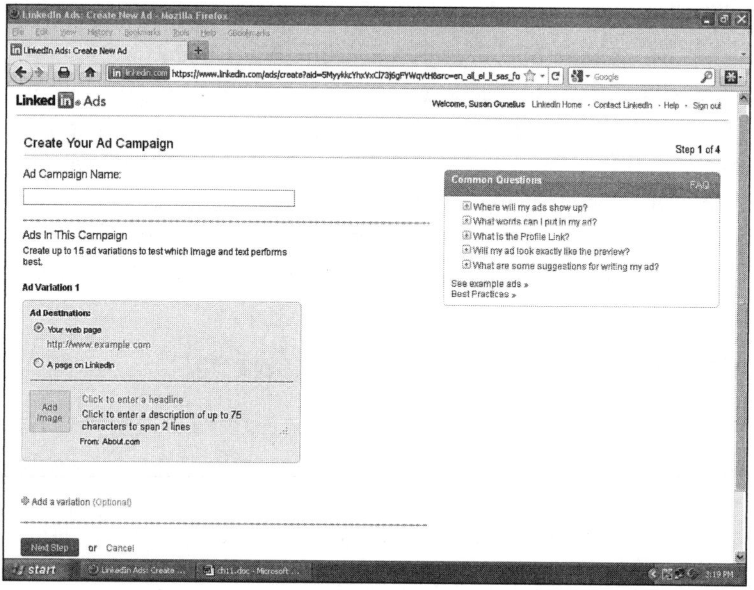

Figure 11.3: *Complete the form to create your ad campaign.*

Add an image by clicking on the **Add Image** link. A pop-up window appears where you can browse your hard drive and upload your image. Keep in mind, your image must be in .png, .jpeg, or .gif format and under 2 MB. Also, it will be resized to 50×50 pixels, so make sure it's in a usable format and size before you upload it.

Input your ad headline and description by selecting the **Click to Enter a Headline** and **Click to Enter a Description** links, respectively.

WARNING

You can only enter up to 25 characters for your ad headline and up to 75 characters for your ad description.

Finally, you can enter up to 15 variations of your ad, so you can test images, headlines, descriptions, and landing page URLs. Track the performance of each ad version to learn which is most successful. You can use the information you gather to create even better ads in the future.

Once you've completed the form, click the **Next Step** button. You'll have an opportunity to select targeting criteria and set your budget before you are required to provide your credit card information and submit your ad for review. If your ad meets the LinkedIn Ads standards, it will be approved and begin displaying on LinkedIn. The remainder of this chapter provides details about targeting, budgeting, advertising guidelines, best practices, and tracking performance.

Targeting Your Audience

The second step in creating your own LinkedIn ad is choosing the audience targeting criteria. Every ad has a specific type of audience who is most likely to respond to it. For example, a high-end women's clothing brand is more likely to get better results and a higher Return On Investment (ROI) if it targets women with executive and upper-management job titles. That's because women are more likely to purchase these clothes than men, and women with higher incomes are more likely to purchase high-priced clothing than women with lower incomes and less discretionary income. There are always exceptions, but the key is targeting people who are most likely to actually make a purchase, thereby making your investment in the ad worthwhile.

Figure 11.4 shows you what the Targeting page looks like when you create your LinkedIn ad.

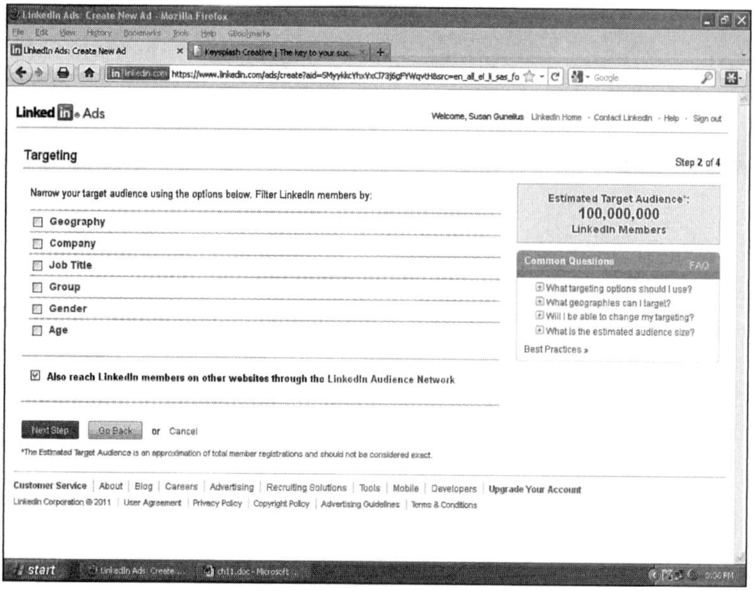

Figure 11.4: *The Targeting page.*

You can target your ad using criteria in six primary categories. The primary targeting categories are …

- **Geography.** Narrow your search down to specific regions within the United States and around the world.

- **Company.** Select specific companies or categories of companies, including industries and company size.

- **Job Title.** Choose specific job titles or categories of job titles, including job function or seniority level.

- **Group.** Enter specific LinkedIn group names to target members of those groups.

- **Gender.** Narrow your results to only men or women.

- **Age.** Select the age ranges of your target audience.

Click on each category to expand it and select the specific criteria of the audience you want to see your ad. As shown in Figure 11.5, you can continue to click on subheadings to narrow your criteria more and more. As you narrow your selections, the estimated target audience of matching LinkedIn members is displayed on the right side of the screen.

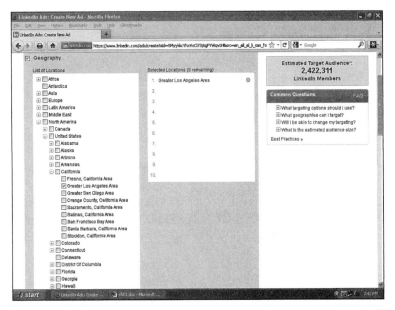

Figure 11.5: *Narrow your targeting criteria using the options provided within each category.*

The information used to identify people in your target audience in order to display your ad to the right people is gathered from data that LinkedIn members enter into their profiles, groups, Company Pages, and other LinkedIn activities. You cannot choose specific individuals to serve your ad to, nor can you identify specific individuals who actually saw your ad after the fact.

You're not required to choose targeting criteria for your ads, but it does help boost the return on your advertising investment. When the right people see your ad, your results should improve. Following are a few suggestions for how you can use LinkedIn Ads targeting to improve the performance of your ads:

- A brick-and-mortar training facility can choose specific geographic areas for local advertising to increase class attendance.

- An executive recruiting firm can target common leadership job titles and seniority levels to increase response rates from qualified leads.

- A financial planner can target by age range to attract a young audience just starting their careers or an older audience looking to quickly grow their retirement savings.

Depending on your ad and your goals for that ad, you can use the targeting criteria available as part of LinkedIn Ads to place your ads in front of varied specific audiences. Because you pay for your ads by the click or by the impression, it's essential that the best audience sees your ad and clicks on it. Don't waste your money on broad audience clicks and impressions. Instead, invest wisely on delivering your messages to focused audiences.

Budgeting, Bidding, and Payment

After you select your ad-targeting criteria, select the **Next Step** button to set up your payment method and budget on the Campaign Options page shown in Figure 11.6.

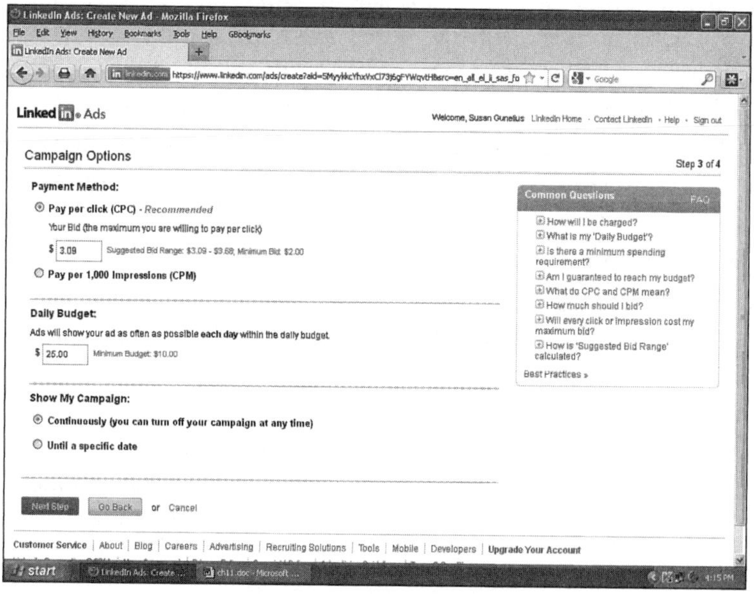

Figure 11.6: *The Campaign Options page.*

You must configure your payment options and budget before your ad goes live. First, you need to choose your payment options. You have two choices:

- **Pay-per-click** Enter the maximum amount you're willing to pay for each click on your ad.

- **Pay-per-impression** Enter the maximum amount you're willing to pay per 1,000 impressions of your ad.

Based on the content of your ad and the targeting criteria you selected in the previous step, LinkedIn offers recommendations for the payment option and bid amount. LinkedIn advertising works by using a bidding process. Advertisers place bids on ad-unit space. That means ad space is sold on an auction basis with many advertisers bidding on the same spaces. When a user matches your selected targeting, your ad will be placed in an auction for ad space that the user sees, along with other ads matching the same targeting criteria. The high bidder for the same ad space wins and his ad appears in that space.

LinkedIn offers suggested bid prices based on competitive bids, so it's a good idea to start your foray into LinkedIn advertising by placing a maximum bid within that range. Bidding starts at $2 per click or per 1,000 impressions. It's important to understand that you won't always have to spend your maximum bid on your ads. Your maximum bid represents how much you're willing to pay for ad space for your target audience, but your actual costs will be discounted based on the next highest bid. In other words, you'll never pay more than the minimum amount necessary to beat the next highest bidder below your maximum bid.

Once you choose your maximum bid, you need to enter your maximum daily budget in the text box shown in Figure 11.6. The dollar amount you enter should represent the most you're willing to spend each day on LinkedIn advertising for this specific ad unit. It's not guaranteed that your ad will be displayed frequently enough to reach your maximum daily budget every day, but you'll never spend more than 20 percent above your maximum daily budget on a single day.

That overage happens occasionally when there is a delay between the time you reach your maximum budget and the time that ads stop automatically displaying for you. If you can't afford to pay the additional 20 percent, reduce your daily budget to ensure there are no unpleasant surprises for you. The minimum daily budget is $10.

The last step on the Campaign Options page is to choose how long you want your ad to run. If you want your ad to run until you manually turn it off, select the radio button next to **Continuously** (see Figure 11.6). If you know there is a specific end date for your campaign, such as the expiration date for a discount, choose the radio button next to **Until a Specific Date** and enter the date you want your campaign to stop running.

When you're satisfied with your campaign options, select the **Next Step** button. The Billing Information page opens where you can enter your credit card details and click the **Buy Now** button to agree to the LinkedIn Ads Guidelines (see the next section for details) and Ads Agreement (linkedin.com/static?key=pop%2Fpop_sas_terms), and submit your ad for review and approval by LinkedIn.

LinkedIn Ads Guidelines

Your ad will be listed as *under review* in your account until it is approved by LinkedIn. At that time, it will be switched to *on* and bidding will begin! For quick approval, follow the LinkedIn Ads Guidelines (linkedin.com/static?key=pop%2Fpop_sas_ guidelines).

Some of the basic rules of LinkedIn advertising are the following:

- Don't be dishonest or use deceptive links in your ad.

- Don't use excessive or inappropriate capitalization, punctuation, symbols, spelling, or grammar in your ads.

- Don't repeat words or phrases in your ads.

- Don't use unprofessional or offensive language in your ads.

- Don't violate trademark and copyright laws in your ads.

- Don't refer to LinkedIn in your ads.

- Don't use any type of affiliate advertising in your ads.

- Don't collect members' information or data through your ads.

- Don't advertise any of the items on the "not allowed" list in the LinkedIn Ads Guidelines document such as tobacco, firearms, drugs, ringtones, dating sites, and more.

Users who don't meet the LinkedIn Ads Guidelines could be removed from the site and restricted from advertising on LinkedIn in the future. Err on the side of caution to ensure your ads are approved and your account remains in good standing with LinkedIn.

LinkedIn Advertising Best Practices

Everything from your targeting criteria to your ad content and your landing page could affect your ad's performance, that's why it's such a good idea to create different versions of your ad to compare performance and determine what's working and what's not. Use that data with the following suggestions to improve your overall LinkedIn Ads results.

Budget and bidding: It's important that you set a daily budget that's high enough to give your ad a chance to be seen. If your budget is expended too quickly, you might not get the number of clicks or impressions that you need. Similarly, if your bid is too low, you might be losing excellent opportunities to get your ad in front of your best audience. Analyze your ad's performance over the period of a week or two and determine if your daily budget and bid need to be increased to get more clicks or impressions. Without exposure, your ad has no chance of delivering positive results.

Ad content: The content of your ad matters. If your ads aren't delivering a click-through rate (the number of times an ad is clicked divided by the number of impressions the ad received) of at least 0.025 percent (learn more about ad tracking at the end of this chapter), then it's time to start testing different images, headlines, and descriptions. Make sure your ad is clear, concise, action-oriented, and includes a message that addresses the target audience's wants, needs, problems, and concerns.

Targeting: A low click-through rate could also be an indication of poor targeting. Modify your ad's targeting criteria to make it more focused and see if you get more clicks.

Landing page: Of course, your ad needs to get clicks first, but if you're not sending people to the right landing page when they do click on your ad, then your advertising efforts and investments are wasted. Make sure you do the work outside of LinkedIn to create a successful campaign. Create a landing page that speaks directly to the ad's audience and motivates them to complete your call to action.

LinkedIn Ads are not an exact science because you don't have complete control. However, the more data you can gather about your target audience and what they respond to, the better you can make your ads. That's where performance tracking comes into the picture!

Tracking Results

LinkedIn offers a variety of reports that you can use to track the performance of your LinkedIn ads. In fact, you can track down to specific ad-unit variations, and tweak targeting criteria and ad content to exploit opportunities. On the flip side, you can turn off ads that are underperforming at any time.

LinkedIn cannot predict click-through rates on your ads and makes no guarantees for ad performance. Furthermore, LinkedIn cannot serve your ads on specific days or at specific times, so in many ways, you're at the mercy of LinkedIn. Because there is no way to know exactly who you're competing against for ad space and what competitor bids are for that space, all you can do is monitor what appears to be working in your ads and do more of it.

LinkedIn displays ads based on bids and ad performance. Therefore, you need to invest in your bids but also in improving your ads. You can access reports about your ad clicks, impressions, click-through rate, average cost per click, budget, and the total amount of money you've spent by campaign and within date ranges that you select. You can also compare campaigns and download reports.

Be patient and don't get discouraged. It takes time to learn what works and what doesn't for each ad and advertiser. What works for one company might not work for the next. Your budget, ad content, and target audience have a significant effect on your LinkedIn advertising success, so commit to testing, learning, tweaking, and trying again. In time, you'll learn what works best for your product and audience and you'll see your click-through rates rise!

The Least You Need to Know

- Anyone with a LinkedIn account and a credit card can advertise on LinkedIn.
- LinkedIn ads are displayed using a bidding system and an auction for ad space with bids starting at $2.
- You can develop up to 15 versions of each ad campaign you create and track them individually.
- LinkedIn ads can be turned off or on at any time.

Integrating Your Marketing Efforts

Chapter 12

In This Chapter

- Using handy LinkedIn tools for marketing integration
- Cross-promoting offline and online
- Considering search engine optimization
- Diving into the daily grind and going mobile

You've created your LinkedIn profile and Company Page. You've joined groups, made connections, written recommendations, answered questions, and even published ads. Now what?

This chapter teaches you how to integrate your varied marketing efforts on LinkedIn, across the web, and offline. You learn how to streamline processes, manage daily activities, and effectively use LinkedIn on the go. It's time to put everything you learned in Chapters 1–11 into action as a fully integrated marketing plan to build your business, brand, or career!

Using Toolbars and Widgets

In Chapters 6 and 10, you learned about a variety of LinkedIn applications and plugins that can help you enhance your LinkedIn profile and offer additional exposure. Now it's time to use some handy LinkedIn toolbars and widgets to make your daily LinkedIn activities more efficient and more effective.

Depending on how you use LinkedIn and your LinkedIn goals, some or all of the toolbars and widgets mentioned in this chapter could be useful to you. They're all free, so give them a try and see which ones make your LinkedIn life easier to manage.

Browser Toolbar

If you use Mozilla Firefox for PC or Mac, or Microsoft Internet Explorer as your web browser; then you can download the corresponding LinkedIn toolbar. Click the **Tools** link in the LinkedIn footer to open the LinkedIn Tools Overview page shown in Figure 12.1. Click the **Download It Now** button in the browser toolbar box on the right side of the screen, and then select Internet Explorer or Firefox from the drop-down menu.

Figure 12.1: *Click the **Download It Now** button in the browser toolbar box to download the Internet Explorer or Firefox toolbar for LinkedIn.*

The LinkedIn browser toolbar makes it easy and quick to bookmark profiles, jobs, and searches on LinkedIn so you can access them at a later date. Simply click the bookmark button in the toolbar and the page is saved.

> **QUICK TIP**
>
> The browser toolbar also comes with the LinkedIn JobsInsider feature, which is discussed in detail in Chapter 14.

Outlook Social Connector

The LinkedIn Outlook Social Connector tool connects your LinkedIn account with your Microsoft Outlook email account. Just click the **Outlook Social Connector** tab at the top of the LinkedIn Tools Overview page shown in Figure 12.1 to open the LinkedIn for Outlook page shown in Figure 12.2.

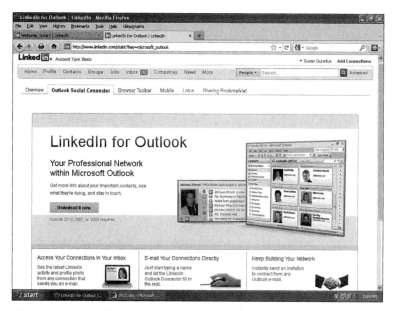

Figure 12.2: *Link your Outlook email account and your LinkedIn account with the Outlook Social Connector tool.*

Click the **Download It Now** button to download the Outlook Social Connector tool and start using it right away. You can email your LinkedIn connections directly from your Outlook account when you use this tool, and you can see the latest LinkedIn activities and photos from your LinkedIn connections who email you. The tool also helps you save time by allowing you to send LinkedIn connection requests without leaving your Outlook inbox!

Lotus Notes Widget

If you use Lotus Notes as your email tool, then the LinkedIn Widget for Lotus Notes is a great option for you. Click the **Lotus** tab on the LinkedIn Tools Overview page shown in Figure 12.1 to open the LinkedIn Widget for Lotus Notes page in Figure 12.3.

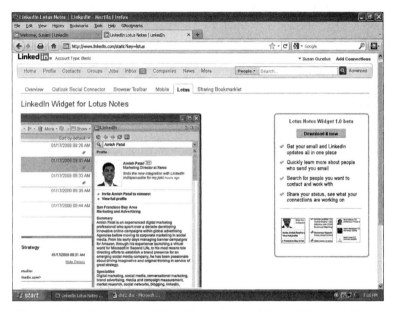

Figure 12.3: *Connect your LinkedIn account with Lotus Notes email with the Lotus Notes Widget.*

Just click the **Download It Now** button to start using the widget. You can access your LinkedIn updates without leaving your Lotus Notes account, get additional information about people who send you email to your Lotus Notes account, share updates, read your connections' updates, and more. It's a great time saver!

Email Signature Tool

Adding your LinkedIn profile and details to your email signature is an excellent way to cross-promote your content and brand. It's also an unobtrusive way to build your LinkedIn network because it makes it easy for anyone who gets an email from you to find and connect with you on LinkedIn.

To access the LinkedIn Email Signature tool, click the **Try It Now** button to the right of the Email Signature listing shown in Figure 12.1.

> **WARNING**
>
> The LinkedIn Email Signature tool only works in Outlook, Outlook Express, and Thunderbird.

The Create Email Signature page shown in Figure 12.4 and Figure 12.5 opens. Enter the requested information to create your personal signature, which will be appended to the end of your email messages.

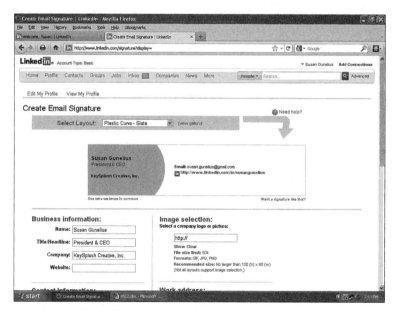

Figure 12.4: *Choose your email signature layout from the gallery.*

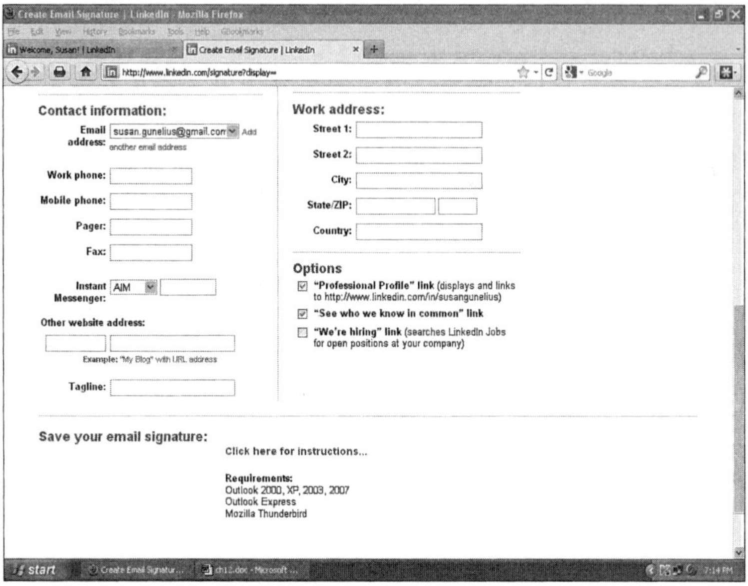

Figure 12.5: *Enter your contact information to complete your email signature.*

To personalize your email signature, click the **Select Layout** drop-down menu shown in Figure 12.4 and choose your preferred style from the list. To view all choices, click the **View Gallery** link. The design you select appears with your information included beneath the Select Layout box.

Next, enter your personal information into the form provided (see Figure 12.5). You can enter your business and contact details, and upload a logo to include with your signature. In the Options section of the form, you can choose to remove the **"Professional Profile" link** that leads to your personal LinkedIn profile and the **"See who we know in common" link** by deselecting the corresponding check boxes. You can also add a **"We're hiring" link** to display open positions at your company as advertised on your Company Page through LinkedIn Jobs by selecting the corresponding checkbox.

When you're satisfied with how your email signature looks, select the **Click Here for Instructions** link at the bottom of the form to get the necessary code and instructions to add the link to your email signature as shown in Figure 12.6.

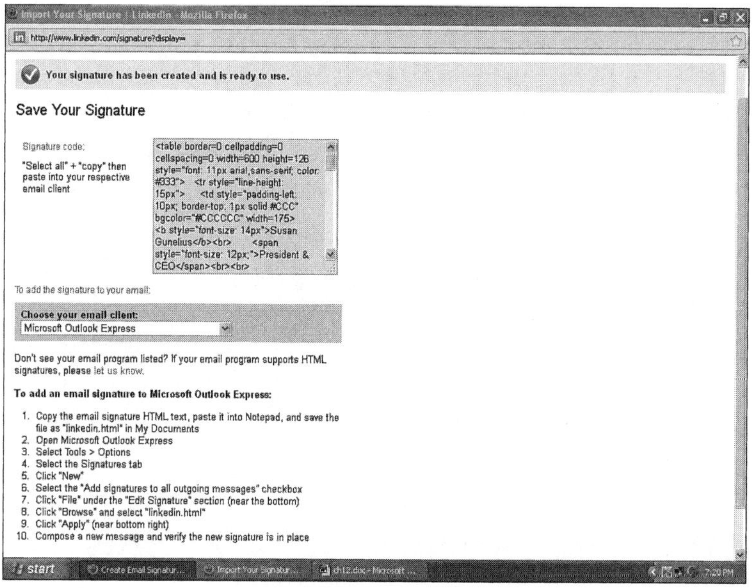

Figure 12.6: *Copy the code and follow the instructions to add your signature to your email messages.*

Be sure to select the right email client from the drop-down menu.

Mac Search Widget

The Mac Search Widget is very handy for people who use Macs. Simply click the **Download It Now** button to the right of the Mac Search Widget listing shown in Figure 12.1 to instantly download and use the widget.

> **WARNING**
>
> At the time of this book's writing, the Mac Search Widget worked with Mac OS 10.4 (Tiger) only. Check LinkedIn to see if the widget works with your operating system before you try to use it.

Once you've installed the Mac Search Widget, you can use it to quickly search LinkedIn from your Mac dashboard for people, groups, answers, or jobs.

Google Toolbar Assistant

Google is the most popular search engine, and many people already have Google search toolbars displayed in their web browsers. The Google Toolbar Assistant adds a LinkedIn search icon to your Google Toolbar, so you can quickly search for people on LinkedIn at any time.

To add the LinkedIn search icon to your Google search toolbar, you need to have the Google toolbar installed first. Just click the **Download It Now** button to the right of the Google Toolbar Assistant listing shown in Figure 12.1 to download the LinkedIn icon. If you don't already have the correct Google toolbar installed, you'll be prompted to download it first.

Offline Marketing Integration

LinkedIn marketing doesn't stop offline. You should look for any opportunities to build your LinkedIn network and reach your goals. Whether you're trying to grow your business or build your career, LinkedIn is an important tool in your efforts. It's your online professional profile and Company Page that you control and use to tell your story. Don't miss opportunities to spread that story!

For example, include your LinkedIn profile URL on your business cards and in your résumé. Invite people to connect with you. Ask customers to recommend your products and services on your Company Page, and ask former and current colleagues and business partners to recommend you via your personal profile.

If you manage a LinkedIn group or are an active member of a group, invite your offline business connections to join LinkedIn and the group. Add your offline events to LinkedIn using the Events app discussed in Chapter 10, and share your offline presentations via the SlideShare app discussed in Chapter 6. If you are an author or write for a print publication, add the Publications section to your LinkedIn profile and list your books and articles.

There are many ways to integrate your online and offline activities through LinkedIn. As long as you don't spend all of your time self-promoting, there is nothing wrong with sharing useful information or demonstrating your expertise via LinkedIn. It's all part of telling your story and opening doors for conversations, connections, and deeper relationships.

Online Marketing Integration

Throughout this book, I've mentioned a wide variety of ways that you can integrate your LinkedIn efforts with your overall online marketing efforts. For example, in Chapters 6 and 10, you learn about a number of tools, applications, and plugins that you can use to spread your content and broaden your online exposure. If you haven't read those chapters, read them now, and then add the suggestions included in this chapter to make your online marketing integration efforts even more powerful.

Your goal should be to surround your audience with opportunities to connect with you, learn from and about you, and build relationships with you on the online destinations that they prefer. However, you can't be everywhere all the time, so you should choose a single online destination to act as your central hub. Your LinkedIn profile and activities could be that central hub where all roads lead to.

Social Sharing Buttons and Links

In Chapters 6 and 10, you learned about the various LinkedIn plugins that make it easy for you to share your LinkedIn profile and Company Page on your website and blog. You also learned about plugins that enable visitors to your website and blog to share your content and recommend it on LinkedIn with the click of a button. These plugins are incredibly useful and should absolutely be used.

LinkedIn also offers a Sharing Bookmarklet that makes it easy for you to share on LinkedIn any content you stumble upon across the web. You can get the Sharing Bookmarklet by clicking the **Sharing Bookmarklet** tab shown in Figure 12.1 to open the Easily Share from Anywhere page shown in Figure 12.7.

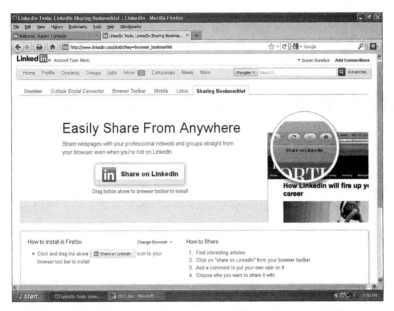

Figure 12.7: *Share any online content via LinkedIn using the Sharing Bookmarklet.*

If you use Firefox as your web browser, just click and drag the **Share on LinkedIn** button to your browser toolbar, or click the **Change Browser** link at the bottom of the page to choose a different web browser and follow the installation instructions provided. Once the bookmarklet is added to your toolbar, you can click the Share on LinkedIn button at any time. You can add a comment, choose who you want to share the link and comment with from your LinkedIn network, and publish the comment to your activity updates on LinkedIn.

INSIDER SECRET

Sharing works both ways. You can't expect people to share your content if you don't reciprocate and share their content as well.

By sharing content published by other people, you acknowledge that you like what they've done and get on their radar screens. This gives you opportunities to expand your network and connect with interesting people. You never know where new connections can take you!

Social Media Icons

In addition to the social plugins discussed in Chapters 6 and 10, there are many free social media icons available online that you can add to your website or blog to encourage people to connect with you on LinkedIn. Social media icons are images that lead directly to a social profile or page. An example of a blog with social media icons is shown in Figure 12.8. When visitors click on those icons, they are taken directly to the owner's profiles where they can connect with them.

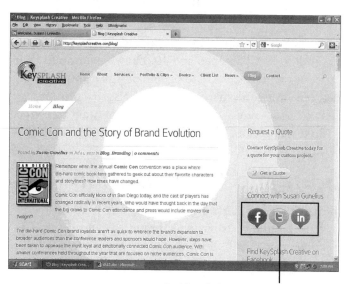

Social media icons are commonly found in blog sidebars.

Figure 12.8: *Social media icons offer unobtrusive invitations to connect with a person or company on social sites.*

You can find social media icons through a simple online search. Two excellent resources to find a wide variety of social media icons are About.com Blogging (weblogs.about.com/od/Social-Media-Icons/Social-Media-Icons.htm) and Wpmods.com (wpmods.com/ultimate-social-media-icon-list/).

Many social media icons are offered in sets, so you can get matching icons for your LinkedIn profile, Twitter profile, Facebook profile, and more. They might come in different sizes and colors, or you can change the sizes to make them fit into your website or blog design. Whether you want to find social media icons shaped like panda bears or bottle caps, you can probably find it for free online!

Cross-Promotion Opportunities

There is rarely a bad time to look for cross-promotional opportunities. Every day, I see more television commercials and table cards at restaurants with links to social media profiles and pages for brands and companies. What might seem like a strange place to draw attention to your LinkedIn profile, page, or group today might be common practice tomorrow.

Pursue the cross-promotion opportunities already mentioned in this chapter as well as in Chapters 6 and 10. Draw attention to your LinkedIn activities on your website, blog, email signature, other online profiles, business card, marketing materials, ads, résumé, invoices, and so on. Let your audience decide if they want to connect with you on LinkedIn or not. The key is to give them the option.

Search Engine Optimization

An important part of using LinkedIn for marketing purposes— whether you want to build your business, brand, or your career—is *search engine optimization* (*SEO*). Both the use of keywords and links can help make your LinkedIn efforts more successful.

DEFINITION

Search engine optimization (SEO) is the process of creating content to boost your content's search results for specific keyword phrases on popular search engines like Google, Bing, and Yahoo!.

I've mentioned a number of SEO tips for LinkedIn throughout this book, but it's important to offer a list of suggestions in one place so you can start implementing these useful tactics right away. The following sections help you better understand how to use SEO techniques as you go about your daily LinkedIn activities.

The Importance of Keywords

As people search for individuals, businesses, products, services, groups, companies, and so on, through search engines, LinkedIn profiles and Company Pages often appear within the results. At the same time, people conduct these types of searches using the search tools built into LinkedIn. It's imperative that your profile, Company Page, groups, questions, and answers appear in relevant searches.

The first step to using keywords within your LinkedIn content is identifying the types of keywords people use to find profiles, businesses, groups, and so on, like yours. Conduct some searches to try to find profiles, companies, and groups like yours. Use the keywords you would type in to find someone with your skills and experience. Do you appear in the results? Does your company?

You need to use the keywords related to you and your business within your profile, in your Company Page, in your LinkedIn Answers, and in your updates. Make sure your profile heading includes those keywords. A heading that simply says "author" says very little and is unlikely to appear in many searches. It's too broad. Instead, identify your areas of expertise so your profile attracts the right type of audience.

The LinkedIn search tools are far from perfect. You need to feed them with as much information as possible, and using keywords is an essential part of creating useful information. You could have the most useful LinkedIn profile and content in the world, but if no one can find it, it doesn't do you or anyone else any good. Keywords are very important to enabling people to find you and your useful content.

The Power of Link Building

Google and other search engines deliver search results using proprietary algorithms. It is generally accepted that these algorithms take incoming links into account when ranking search results under the assumption that pages with a lot of incoming links must have great content or no one would link to them.

You can use your LinkedIn profile and activities as a way to increase incoming links to your online content on your blog, website, and other online destinations by sharing links to your great content and inviting your LinkedIn connections to further share your content with their own audiences. This tactic also works in reverse. You can share your LinkedIn content on your other online profiles, website, and blog to increase links to it.

Here are five simple examples of how this tactic can work:

- When you answer questions using LinkedIn Answers, include links to your related blog posts to further support and explain your answer.

- Share links to your blog posts in your LinkedIn profile updates and related group updates.

- On your website, include links so visitors can easily recommend your products and services on your LinkedIn Company Page.

- Feed your LinkedIn updates to your Twitter profile so they automatically publish on your Twitter timeline in addition to your LinkedIn activity stream.

- Include Share on LinkedIn and Recommend on LinkedIn buttons and plugins on your blog posts.

As you cross-promote your online activities and integrate your online marketing efforts, link building will happen organically. I call this the compounding effect of social media and it's a powerful thing. The more quality content you publish and quality connections you make online, the more your content will spread and your search results and traffic will increase. Every effort you make to increase those links helps even more!

Prioritizing and Executing Activities

Where do you begin with implementing your LinkedIn marketing plan? It can feel overwhelming, but the trick is to remember that every additional minute you can spend on your social media activities, in this case your LinkedIn efforts, can only help you get closer to reaching your goals. Inaction is the worst thing you can do, so dive in and get going!

You can create a daily plan to keep yourself organized, or you can set weekly or monthly goals to stay on track. If your goals allow it, you can take a more casual approach to using LinkedIn and participate as your schedule allows. The choice is yours and truly depends on your objectives.

Jump-Starting Your LinkedIn Efforts

If you want to get going quickly and become an active member of the LinkedIn community sooner rather than later, then there are some specific steps you can take to jump-start your LinkedIn efforts. These steps aren't written in stone, and you can modify them to best meet your own goals and preferences. However, they provide a great framework for developing your LinkedIn presence and network quickly.

Following is my 10-step LinkedIn jump-start plan:

1. Create a comprehensive LinkedIn profile and make it public.

2. Connect with people you already know on LinkedIn, including former and current classmates, colleagues, and friends.

3. Add useful applications to further tell your story. Link your varied online profiles such as your blog, Twitter, SlideShare, and other accounts to your LinkedIn profile and automatically update and cross-promote your activities.

4. Add LinkedIn Share and Recommend buttons to your blog and website, as well as social media icons or LinkedIn plugins, to invite people who visit your blog and website to connect with you on LinkedIn. Also add an invitation to your email signature.

5. Start publishing useful updates on your LinkedIn profile activity stream. Comment on and share updates published by your connections.

6. Write and request recommendations from appropriate people within your LinkedIn network.

7. Join groups related to your area of expertise or the industry where you want your career to grow. Actively participate in those groups.

8. Search for questions related to your area of expertise and answer them. Be sure to include links to your related content on your blog or website.

9. Expand your LinkedIn network by searching through your second- and third-degree connections, and through the members of groups that you belong to. Send connection requests to people who share your interests or whom you can learn from.

10. Use InMail or request introductions from your connections to meet people who aren't in your network whom you want to connect with on LinkedIn.

These are just 10 easy steps that you can implement quickly. Within a week or two, you'll be amazed by how much progress you can make in terms of building your network and establishing your expertise on LinkedIn if you follow these 10 steps.

Sample Activity Checklists

Once you've ramped up your LinkedIn profile and connections, what should you do each day to stay active? It's hard to prioritize tasks, but if you use one of the checklists offered below (or a version of it based on your personal LinkedIn goals), it will be easier to stay focused.

It's easy to get lost on LinkedIn. You might sit down at your computer expecting to answer a few questions, and the next thing you know, two hours have passed! There are simply so many interesting things to see and links to follow. Here is a daily checklist to make sure you don't lose two hours without first accomplishing your goals for the day:

- Update your status.

- Read through recent updates by your connections and comment on at least two updates.

- Share a blog post or interesting content that you find online related to your area of expertise.

- Read through recent updates in at least one group that you belong to and post your own update or comment on another member's update.

- Review your Inbox and respond to any messages or invitations.

For some people, using LinkedIn every day isn't reasonable. If you fall into that category, then use the following weekly checklist to organize your efforts:

- Do all of the activities listed in the preceding daily checklist at least once. The more frequently you can do those activities, the better.

- Search for questions related to your area of expertise and answer at least two.

- Send connection requests to new people of interest using the People You May Know feature.

In addition to the daily and weekly activities suggested in the preceding checklists, use the following checklist monthly to make sure you don't forget to do these less common activities:

- Review your profile and make sure it's up to date. This includes updating the information in all sections and through applications you use.

- Write at least one recommendation and request at least one recommendation.

- Search for groups to join.

- Search for companies to follow.

- Ask and answer questions.

- Search for people to connect with.

- Update the information on your Company Page as necessary.

Again, you can modify these activities to meet your own needs. The intent is to make using LinkedIn seem less overwhelming by breaking it down into smaller activities.

Going Mobile

LinkedIn offers a mobile-optimized site at http://touch.linkedin.com. It's also very easy to use LinkedIn on the go thanks to handy mobile apps. Just click the **Mobile** link in the LinkedIn footer to open the LinkedIn Mobile page shown in Figure 12.9.

Figure 12.9: *You can download LinkedIn mobile apps for a variety of mobile devices.*

Just choose your phone from the list provided to download a mobile version of LinkedIn. At the time of this book's writing, free LinkedIn mobile apps were available for the iPhone, iPod touch, iPad, Android devices, BlackBerry devices, Palm devices, and the HP TouchPad. Be sure to check the LinkedIn Mobile page for a current list of compatible devices and mobile applications. You can also search the Apple App store, Android Marketplace, or corresponding app download center for your device to access mobile LinkedIn apps.

With mobile versions of LinkedIn, you can update your status, answer questions, participate in groups, and send messages anytime and from anywhere. It's easier than ever to use LinkedIn to reach your business, brand, and career growth goals.

The Least You Need to Know

- LinkedIn tools and widgets save you time and help you more efficiently reach your goals.

- It's important to integrate your online and offline marketing efforts to effectively build your business, brand, and career using LinkedIn.

- Search engine optimization can make your LinkedIn profile and Company Page easier to find, giving you more exposure to larger audiences.

- Break your LinkedIn activities down into manageable chunks using daily, weekly, and monthly checklists.

LinkedIn as a Market Research Tool

In This Chapter

* Gathering information from Company Pages
* Keeping up with hot topics
* Using polls and apps to conduct research
* Special tools for law and real estate research

One of the most useful aspects of LinkedIn that you might not realize is available to you is the ability to use LinkedIn to conduct informal market research. You can learn about companies, individuals, products, services, and issues by logging in to your LinkedIn account and poking around the freely available information that people around the world publish and share.

This chapter teaches you some of the easiest and most effective ways to do your own market research. Whether you want to learn about your competitors, learn about a company you're considering working with, or learn about the topics that matter to professionals in your industry, you can do it on LinkedIn. The data is there and waiting for you to tap into.

Follow Company Pages

In Chapter 4, you learned how to create a Company Page on LinkedIn. You also learned how to make your Company Page more visible on LinkedIn by making it more search-friendly, asking for product and service recommendations, and publishing ads. Guess what? Other companies, including your competitors, are doing the same thing! That means you can find their Company Pages, too.

By finding and viewing Company Pages, you can gather a great deal of market intelligence. For example, the following situations are perfect for using LinkedIn Company Pages to conduct research.

Competitor research: Learn what your competitors are up to, what products they're featuring, what job openings they're looking to fill, and who is working for them. You can use that data to predict their plans for the future, keep tabs on their updates and conversations, and more.

Investor research: If you need to gather investors for your company, LinkedIn Company Pages provide a great way to find and learn about potential investors. You can gain insights about employees and their activities from their LinkedIn page.

Hiring research: If you're looking for new employees, you can visit Company Pages in your industry or related industries and look for the talent you need on your team. It never hurts to reach out to people who fit the role and ask them if they're interested in changing jobs or know someone who is.

Job research: Company Pages offer huge opportunities for you to learn about companies that you're considering working for. Not only can you see who already works for the company, but you can follow conversations and updates, read recommendations, and more.

Industry research: What's happening in your industry? It's easy to keep up with news, events, and so on, by following Company Pages of industry-related organizations and associations.

QUICK TIP

Visit Company Pages and follow the links to read public employee profiles. Look for people within your network and connect with them or join groups that people belong to in order to add them to your network. You can learn a lot about a company from its employees!

Company Pages have activity feeds that are updated similarly to the way that LinkedIn Profile Activity feeds are updated. Company Pages can also include updates from associated Twitter feeds. That means active Company Pages can provide you with a lot of information for research purposes.

Fortunately, LinkedIn makes it easy to keep up with Company Page Activity Feeds with the Follow feature. If you have a LinkedIn account, you can follow any Company Page on LinkedIn, so it's easy to get updates from that company. When you follow a Company Page, you have the opportunity to receive notifications when that page's activity stream is updated.

When you find a Company Page that you want to follow, you can do so with a single click of the mouse. Figure 13.1 shows the Newstex Company Page on LinkedIn. Notice the **Follow Company** button in the upper-right of the page? Just click that button on any Company Page that you want to follow. That's all there is to it.

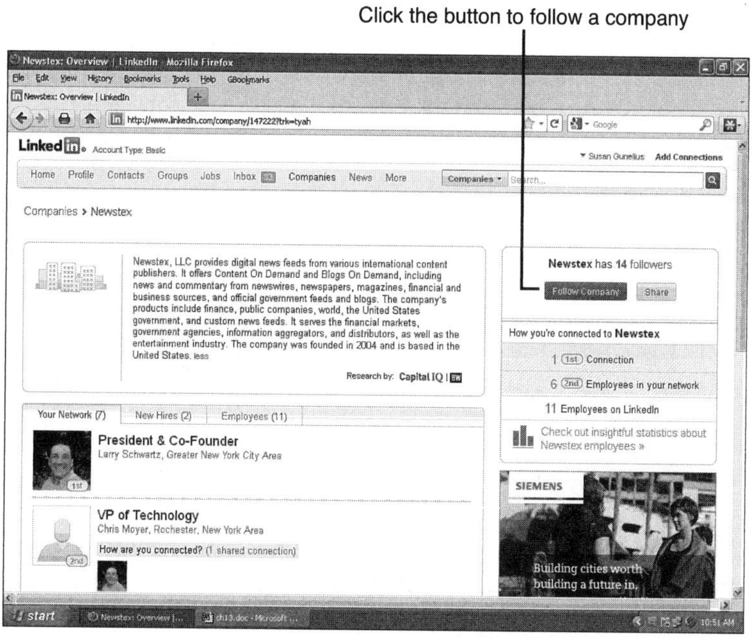

Click the button to follow a company

Figure 13.1: *Click the **Follow Company** button on any Company Page to instantly follow that company.*

Once you click on the **Follow Company** button, that button changes
to show a check mark and Following label along with a drop-down
arrow on the right side of the button. As shown in Figure 13.2, when
you click on the drop-down arrow, a drop-down menu appears with
two options: **Stop Following** and **Settings**.

QUICK TIP

You can stop following a Company Page at any time by clicking the
Following button on the Company Page and selecting **Stop Following**
from the drop-down menu that appears.

Click the button to stop following a company or edit settings

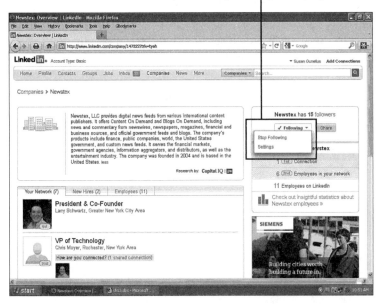

Figure 13.2: *When you click the* **Following** *button's drop-down arrow, a menu
appears showing two options:* **Stop Following** *and* **Settings**.

Click the **Settings** link to open the Change Following Settings
pop-up shown in Figure 13.3 and modify when you're notified about
updates to the Company Page activity stream.

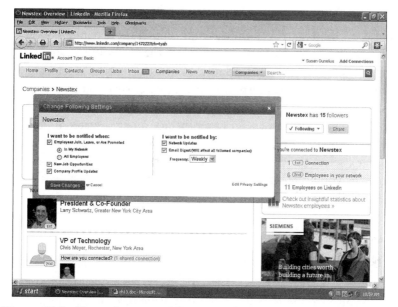

Figure 13.3: *Choose the types and frequency of Company Page notifications that you want to receive automatically.*

The **Change Following Settings** box is where you can choose the types of notifications you want to receive and how often you want to receive them. On the left side of the box, select the check boxes next to each notification you want to receive. Your choices are:

- **Employee updates.** Check the box to be notified when employees are promoted, or join or leave the company. If you want to limit these notifications to people in your network only, make sure the radio button next to **In My Network** is selected. To receive updates about employees outside of your network, too, select the radio button next to **All Employees**.

- **Job updates.** Check the box next to **New Job Opportunities** to be notified when the company publishes an open job posting.

- **Company updates.** Check the box next to **Company Profile Updates** to be notified anytime the Company Page activity stream is updated in any way.

Next, you can choose how frequently you want to receive updates from the Company Page. On the right side of the Change Following Settings box shown in Figure 13.3, select the check box if you want to receive **Network Updates**. When this option is selected, Company Page updates display in the Updates section of your LinkedIn Home page (when you're logged in to your account). If you want to receive email messages that include an aggregated digest of updates from all Company Pages that you follow (in a single email message), select the check box next to **Email Digest** and choose the frequency you prefer from the drop-down menu. Your choices are to receive daily email digests or weekly email digests.

QUICK TIP

You can follow up to 1,000 Company Pages at the same time.

You can also stop following a Company Page or change Company Page notifications by selecting the **Companies** link in the top navigation bar when you're logged in to your LinkedIn account. Next, choose the **Following** tab from the Companies Home page. A list of the Company Pages you're following is displayed as shown in Figure 13.4.

Click the **Notification Settings** link next to any Company Page you're following to open the Change Following Settings box shown in Figure 13.3. When you're done modifying your notification set-tings for each Company Page, be sure to click the **Save Changes** button.

When you follow a Company Page, it's considered an activity update and it will appear in your LinkedIn profile activity stream. If you don't want your activity updates to display on your LinkedIn profile, click your name in the top-right corner of your screen (when you're logged in to your LinkedIn account) and choose the **Settings** link from the drop-down menu.

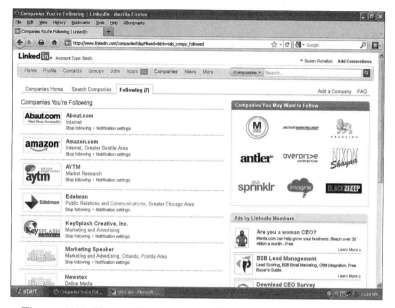

Figure 13.4: *You can change your notification settings or stop following any Company Page at any time.*

Your account settings page opens with the Profile tab already selected in the lower half of the page. Click the **Turn On/Off Your Activity Broadcasts** link to open the Activity Broadcasts pop-up shown in Figure 13.5.

This is where you turn on or turn off your activity updates that are published on your LinkedIn profile, including when you update your profile, when you write a recommendation, or when you follow a company. If you don't want your activities to display in your LinkedIn activity stream, make sure the box in the Activity Broadcasts pop-up is not checked. If you do want to display these activities, check the box. Of course, be sure to click the **Save Changes** button.

You'd be amazed by how much information you can gather about a company, industry, or consumers simply by following Company Pages on LinkedIn. Keep in mind, if you have a Company Page for your organization, other people can do the same kind of research by following your Company Page. Therefore, keep your Company Page content professional and relevant. You never know who might see it!

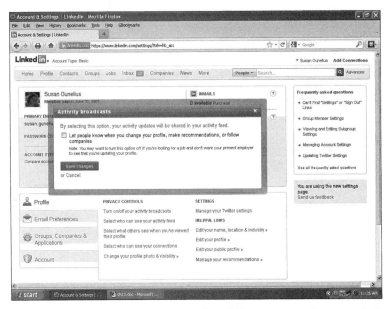

Figure 13.5: *To share your activities such as following companies and updating your profile, make sure the check box is selected.*

View Company Page Statistics

A great repository of data related to Company Pages can be found with a single mouse click. If charts, graphs, and statistics are what you're after, then visit the Company Page you want to learn about and click the **Check Out Insightful Statistics About [Insert Company Name] Employees** on the right side of the page as shown in Figure 13.1. The Statistics Overview page shown in Figure 13.6 opens.

The Job Functions tab is automatically selected. Scroll through the page to see charts about job function composition, annual company growth, employees who have changed their titles, employees with new titles, and a graphical representation of your LinkedIn connections at that company. The charts provide information culled from employee profiles on LinkedIn and include comparison data to similar companies based on industry and size. Some charts include a Filter button in the upper-right corner of the chart that enables you to drill down and see the data in different ways.

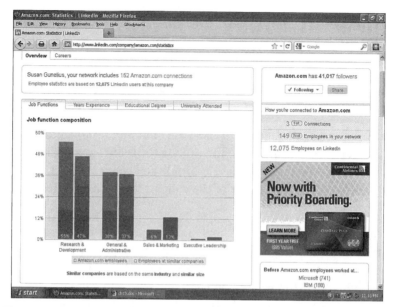

Figure 13.6: *Gather data on any Company Page by viewing employee statistics.*

Click through the tabs at the top of the Statistics Overview page shown in Figure 13.6 to view additional information. For example, you can see charts detailing Years Experience, Educational Degree, and University Attended for company employees.

WARNING

The only chart that changes between the tabs at the top of the Statistics Overview page is the first chart listed. All other charts stay the same on all tabs, so don't waste your time analyzing them in multiple places or worry that they aren't updating correctly.

It's important to remember that these statistics come from employee profiles and updates. They're great for directional thinking, but don't rely on them as 100 percent accurate representations of a company's performance or employee makeup.

LinkedIn Today

LinkedIn Today is an excellent feature that enables you to keep track of news that matters in your industry. In simplest terms, LinkedIn Today offers an aggregated view of the news and content people and companies are sharing on LinkedIn and via their Twitter updates.

Content featured on LinkedIn Today isn't curated by an editor. Instead, updates on LinkedIn Today are gathered from all LinkedIn members. Based on your LinkedIn profile and connections, LinkedIn Today offers you a quick view of the content that's making headlines and that people are talking about.

LinkedIn Today enables the people in your network to determine what news you see because the top headlines are pulled from your activities and their activities. To access LinkedIn Today, click the **News** link in the top navigation bar when you're logged in to your LinkedIn account. Your LinkedIn Today front page opens as shown in Figure 13.7.

Figure 13.7: *The LinkedIn Today front page is customized to each member.*

Scroll through your LinkedIn Today front page and you'll find the top articles shared on both LinkedIn and Twitter by the people in your extended LinkedIn network. You can also see what those people said about the articles as well as their names, titles, and companies as provided through their LinkedIn profiles. To make LinkedIn Today even more useful, you can set up notifications and digest emails, conduct searches, and save content to view at a later date.

INSIDER SECRET

The LinkedIn Today module automatically appears at the top of your LinkedIn Home page when you're logged in to your account. To remove it, click the **X** in the upper-right corner of the module and select the **Yes, Remove It** link. You can add the module back at any time by refreshing or reloading your web browser.

You can follow specific industries or sources on LinkedIn Today by clicking the **?** icon in the upper-right corner of your LinkedIn Today front page as shown in Figure 13.7. A drop-down menu appears. Click the **Follow/Unfollow** link from the menu to open the Browse All, Industries or Sources, pop-up shown in Figure 13.8.

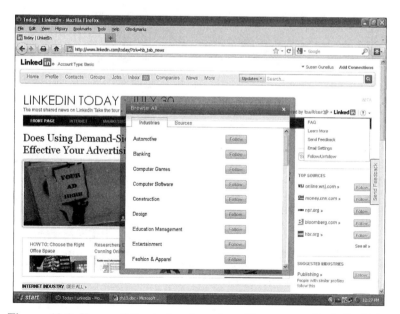

Figure 13.8: *You can follow industries and specific sources on LinkedIn Today.*

Click the **Industries** or **Sources** tab to scroll through the options available to you, and click the **Follow** button next to each listed industry or source that you want to follow. You can also follow or unfollow industries by visiting that industry's page on LinkedIn Today (through the links in the top navigation bar of LinkedIn Today) and clicking the **Follow** button on the right side of the page as shown in Figure 13.9.

Click the button to follow a topic

Figure 13.9: *Click the **Follow** button on the LinkedIn Today page of the industry you want to follow.*

You can modify the LinkedIn Today top news that you see on your LinkedIn Home page and that you receive via email, by changing some simple settings in your LinkedIn account. Click your name in the top-right corner of your screen and choose **Settings** from the drop-down menu. Scroll down and select the **Email Preferences** tab, and then select the **Set the Frequency of Emails** link to open the Frequency of Emails pop-up shown in Figure 13.10.

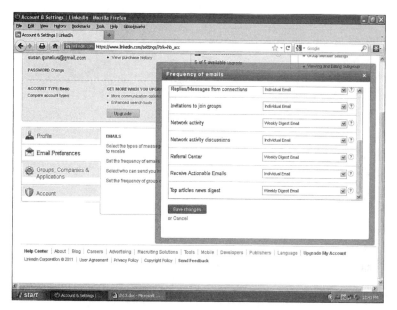

Figure 13.10: *Set the frequency with which you receive news updates to daily, weekly, or none.*

Scroll down the list to find the Top Articles News Digest listing. Click the drop-down arrow to the right and choose the frequency with which you want to receive Top News Update emails. Finally, click the **Save Changes** button to immediately put your changes into effect.

To modify the news updates you see on your LinkedIn Home page, click the **Account** tab shown in the settings window in the background of Figure 13.10 and then select the **Customize the Updates You See on Your Home Page** link to open The Updates You See on Your Home Page pop-up shown in Figure 13.11.

Scroll to the bottom of the pop-up and check the box next to **When Connections Follow News** under the News heading. You will be updated on your LinkedIn Home page when any of your LinkedIn connections follow news on LinkedIn Today. If you don't want to see these updates on your home page, make sure this box is not checked. Finally, click the **Save Changes** button to make your settings go live.

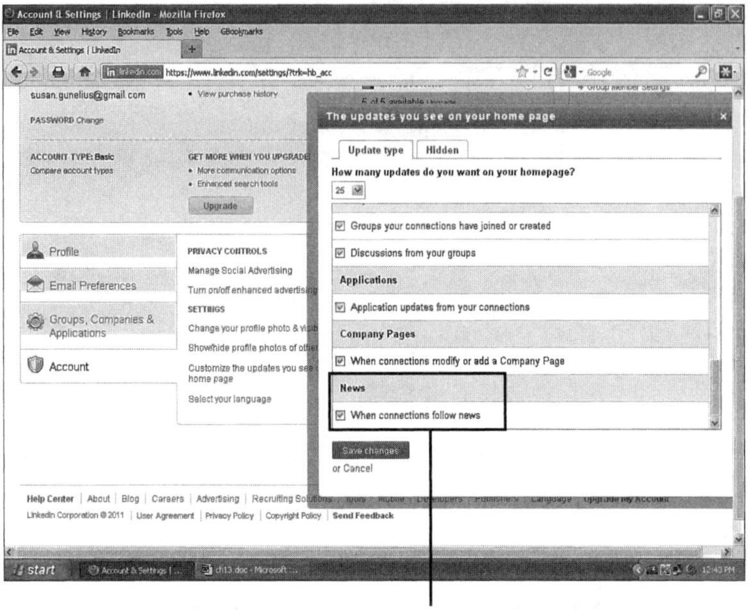

Select the checkbox to see updates when your connections follow news

Figure 13.11: *Choose **When Connections Follow News** to view, on your home page, updates about the news your connections are following.*

INSIDER SECRET

Any link that you share on LinkedIn which is set as visible to everyone could appear with your picture on LinkedIn Today, giving you more exposure. Share wisely!

LinkedIn Today offers real-time, targeted information about current hot topics in the industries, and from the news sources, you choose, as well as those that are directly related to you based on your LinkedIn profile and connections. It's easy to check in once or twice a day, or read a daily digest email, to get up to speed on the topics that matter to people in your industry. When you find an article you want to save for later, just click the **Save** icon next to that article. You can also share articles with your own LinkedIn connections by clicking on the **Share** icon. You can use LinkedIn Today from your computer and from many mobile devices.

LinkedIn Signal

LinkedIn offers a handy search feature called Signal that can help you find relevant news and updates. You can access Signal from the **News** drop-down menu in the top navigation bar when you're logged in to your LinkedIn account, or you can scroll to the updates section on your LinkedIn Home page to view and filter updates and tweets using Signal search features.

For example, click the **Signal** link under the News drop-down menu to open the main Signal search page shown in Figure 13.12.

Figure 13.12: *Search for news and updates using Signal search filters.*

Just type keywords into the search box in the top left of the LinkedIn Signal page to bring up related results. You can filter results by network, company, location, industry, time published, geographic region, school, and more.

Signal is updated in real-time, so when new content is published related to your search, an alert is displayed at the top of the page to show you that new links and content are available. You can also save searches so you can access them quickly at any time. Want to keep tabs on what people are talking about and sharing related to your company or a competitor? Create a search and save it to review each day using Signal.

Signal allows you to more effectively use LinkedIn and LinkedIn Today to cut through activity clutter and focus on the information that matters to you most.

Polls App

In Chapters 6 and 10, you learned about a variety of LinkedIn apps that can help you enhance your LinkedIn profile and promote yourself or your business. Now it's time to introduce an app that can help you conduct market research.

The Polls app is a great tool for surveying LinkedIn audiences. You can poll your LinkedIn network or all LinkedIn members and analyze responses by industry, age, occupation, seniority, gender, and more. Want to get feedback on a new trend, product idea, or opportunity? Poll your LinkedIn network or the wider LinkedIn audience to gather some actionable metrics.

To add the Polls app to your LinkedIn account, click the **More** link in the top navigation bar when you're signed in to your LinkedIn account to reveal a drop-down list. From that list, click the **Get More Applications** link. This opens the Applications Directory where you can select the Polls app from the list of apps to open the Polls page shown in Figure 13.13. Click the **Add Application** button to add the Polls app to your LinkedIn account.

Once you add the Polls app to your LinkedIn account, it will appear as a link in the **More** drop-down menu. Just click the **Polls** link to open the page shown in Figure 13.14.

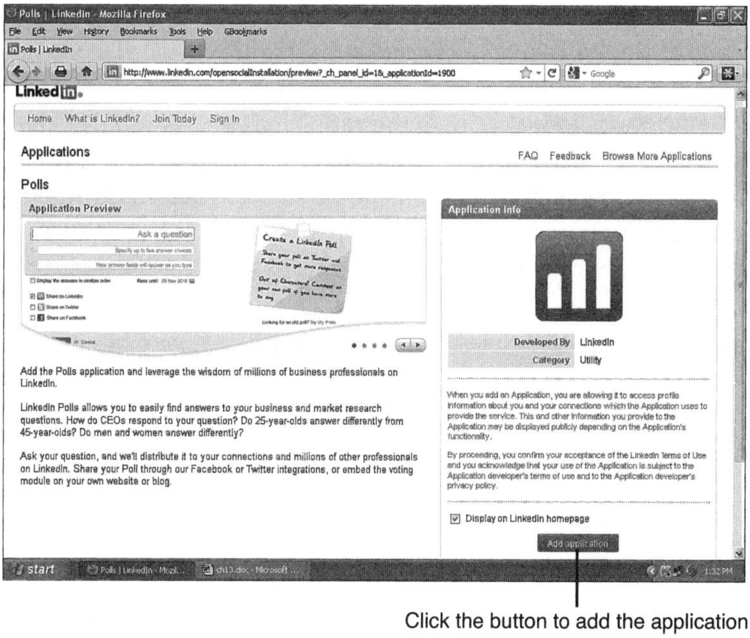

Click the button to add the application

Figure 13.13: *Click **Add Application** to add the Polls app to your LinkedIn account.*

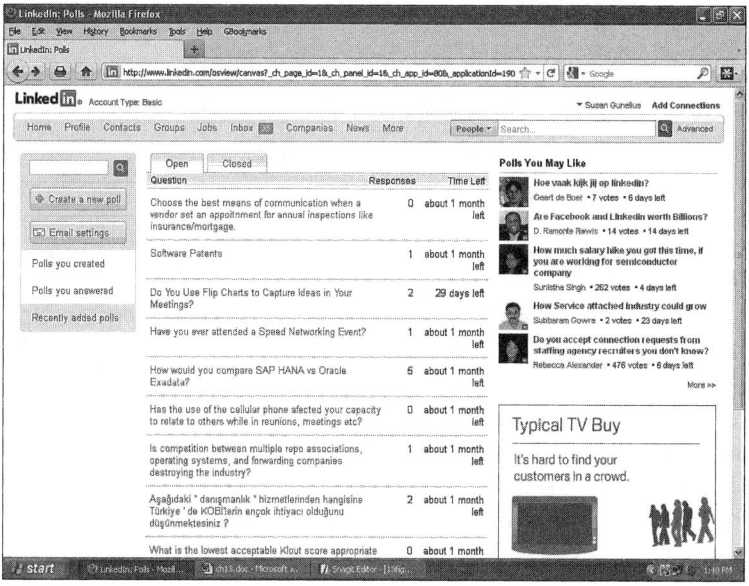

Figure 13.14: *The Polls home page.*

To start your own poll, click the **Create a New Poll** button on the left side of the Polls home page shown in Figure 13.14. The Create Poll form opens, shown in Figure 13.15. You can enter your question (75 characters or less) and up to 5 multiple choice answers (30 characters or less for each answer). To reduce bias, check the box to display answers in random order, and be sure to click the **Runs Until** date link to specify the date your poll should close. The standard duration of a poll is 30 days.

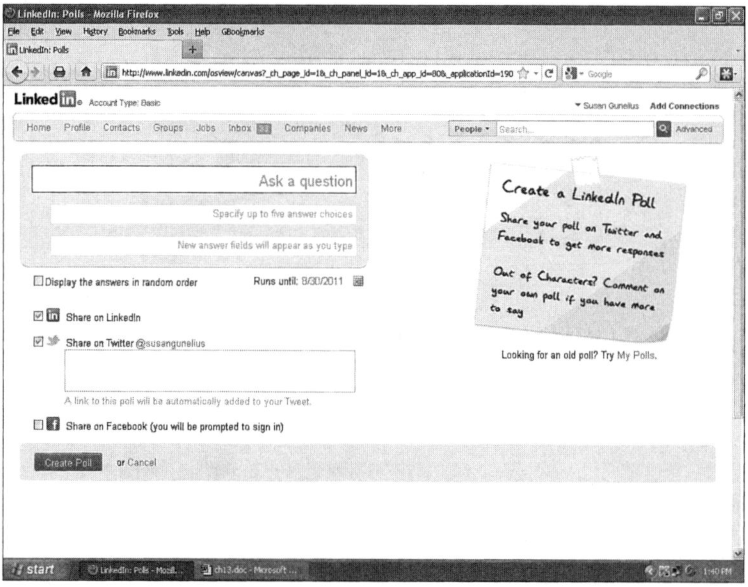

Figure 13.15: *The Create Poll form.*

WARNING

You can end a poll prior to the closing date, but note that once a poll ends, it cannot be restarted. To manually end a poll, click on the **My Polls** link from your Polls home page, select the poll, and click the **End** link.

You also have the option to share a link to your poll on your LinkedIn profile, to specific LinkedIn connections, to LinkedIn group members, on your Twitter profile, and on your Facebook profile. People won't be able to actually answer the poll on those third-party sites. Instead, they'll be directed to log in to LinkedIn to answer the poll. Click the **Create Poll** button at the bottom of the page to make your poll live and open for answers.

Once your poll is live, it will appear in the list of recent polls on the Polls home page. You also get a special link to your poll which you can use to promote the poll and boost responses on your LinkedIn profile, LinkedIn groups, Company Page, Twitter profile, Facebook profile, Facebook page, blog, email newsletter, and so on.

You can always access the poll-sharing features by visiting your Polls home page and clicking the **My Polls** button to open your Manage My Polls page. Here you can open the poll you want to promote and select one of the **Share This Poll** buttons in the upper right to get the poll link; get HTML code that you can use to embed the poll in your blog or website; or share the poll on LinkedIn, Twitter, or Facebook.

 INSIDER SECRET

You can have up to 10 polls open at the same time.

LinkedIn offers a variety of ways to view your poll responses. While you won't be able to see personal information about respondents, you will be able to view charts about how different audience segments responded to your poll question. There are a variety of categories available to you to analyze your results and make the data collected more valuable to you as a research tool for decision making. Everyone who responds to a poll will be able to see the results.

LinkedIn expects polls to be professional and transparent. That means you cannot create anonymous polls, self-promotional polls, polls that violate trademarks, polls that contain spam, or polls that refer to LinkedIn. Polls are reviewed by LinkedIn, and those that are deemed to be inappropriate or unprofessional could be removed. You're also not allowed to edit a poll once it's been published. If you make a mistake in a poll that you create, you need to close it and create a new poll.

Be sure to take a few minutes to set up your email preferences for polls by clicking on the **Email Settings** button on your Polls home page. You can choose to be notified when three events happen:

- A poll you created ends

- A poll you voted on ends

- Someone publishes a comment on a poll after you

It's easy to forget that you created a poll, voted on a poll, or commented on a poll. Stay in the conversation and make sure you see the results by configuring your poll email settings accordingly.

Legal Updates App

The Legal Updates app from JD Supra is useful to attorneys as well as to people who don't work directly in the legal field. When you add this app to your LinkedIn account, you get legal alerts from lawyers on LinkedIn.

JD Supra is a website where attorneys create profiles and upload legal articles. The site is referred to as a community-based research tool. Anyone can use the site to search for legal information submitted by legal professionals. Attorneys can boost their exposure and build their businesses by submitting useful articles that help establish their credibility and reputations.

To add the Legal Updates app to your LinkedIn account, choose the **Get More Applications** link from the **More** drop-down menu when you're logged in to your LinkedIn account. From the Legal Updates app page shown in Figure 13.16, click the **Add Application** button.

The Legal Updates app is a great tool for researching current legal trends, cases, and issues because the content is written by real attorneys. You can search for legal news and information related to your industry without leaving LinkedIn. The app enables you to customize the legal updates that appear on your LinkedIn Home page; you can follow specific subjects such as business, employment, energy, tax, insurance, and more. You can also share the content you read with your own network and reach out to the lawyers who write the content you read via LinkedIn to learn more.

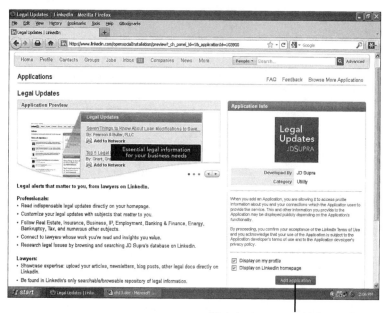

Click the button to add the application

Figure 13.16: *Click the **Add Application** button to get access to legal updates or share your own with the Legal Updates app.*

Real Estate Pro App

If you work in the real estate industry, then you need to try the Real Estate Pro app from Rofo. This app helps you keep track of local real estate markets, network with other real estate professionals, and promote your own listings and transactions.

To add the Real Estate Pro app to your LinkedIn account, click the **Get More Applications** link from the **More** drop-down menu when you're logged in to your LinkedIn account. This opens the Real Estate Pro app page shown in Figure 13.17.

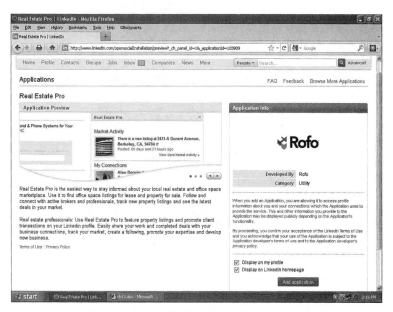

Figure 13.17: *The Real Estate Pro app page.*

Just click the **Add Application** button to add the app to your LinkedIn account and start tracking real estate news and information in the areas that matter to you. It's a great research tool.

The Least You Need to Know

- LinkedIn Company Pages provide a great deal of information about companies, employees, cultures, and activities.
- LinkedIn Today can help you cut through update clutter so you don't miss the news that matters to you most.
- Create news searches and save them for quick access at any time with LinkedIn Signal.
- Conduct your own market research by creating a free poll with the LinkedIn Polls app.

Using LinkedIn for Job Searching and Hiring

Part

4

LinkedIn has a well-deserved reputation for helping people find jobs and helping companies find talented employees. Whether you're searching for a job or an employee, LinkedIn could be a perfect fit for your search.

Part 4 covers all the details about using LinkedIn to find and apply for jobs as well as how to post a job, receive applications, and deepen your talent pool. Different LinkedIn account options offering various job search and employee search features are introduced, so you can choose the right account for you and have the best chance for success.

Finding Your Next Job on LinkedIn

In This Chapter

- Searching for jobs on LinkedIn
- Applying for jobs
- Tools and features to help you find and land a job
- Premium accounts for advanced job seekers

LinkedIn is more than just a professional networking site. It's also a tool for helping you find your next job. Companies can post job openings, which you can apply to (often without leaving LinkedIn), and you can find open jobs through informal group and company updates and discussions.

If you create a great LinkedIn profile, employers might even find you and approach you with a new job opportunity! That's why it's so important to publish content and engage in activities on LinkedIn (like the ones discussed in Parts 1–3 of this book) that tell your story, establish your credibility, develop your reputation, and build your brand. This chapter teaches you how to use LinkedIn as a job search tool, so when the right opportunity arises, you're ready to take it.

Job Search

If you're looking for a new job, then the job search feature on LinkedIn is the place to start. Just click the **Jobs** link in the top navigation bar when you're logged in to your LinkedIn account to open the Jobs Home page shown in Figure 14.1.

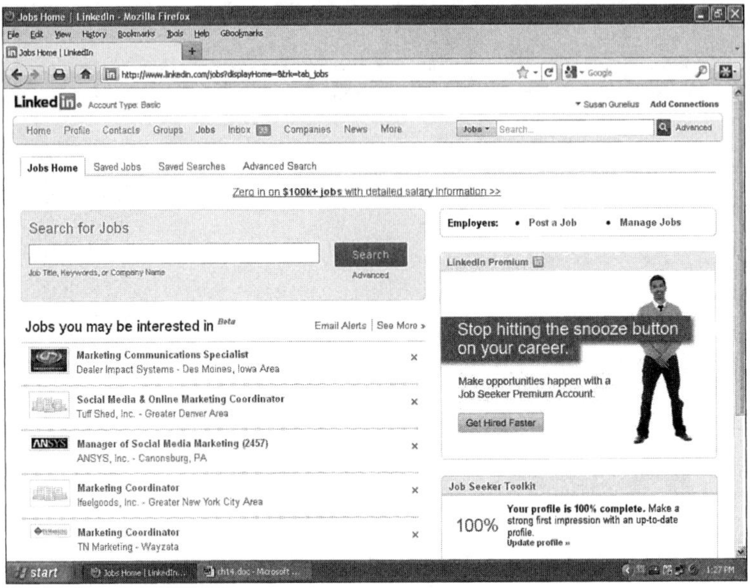

Figure 14.1: *You can search for jobs and view jobs that match your profile from the Jobs Home page.*

When you land on the Jobs Home page, you see a list of jobs you might be interested in, which LinkedIn displays to you based on the information in your LinkedIn profile. You can click through to view these jobs or click the **See More** link to see more jobs you might be interested in. The more complete and accurate your LinkedIn profile is, the more closely matched to your skills and experiences this list of jobs will be.

You can also set up email digest alerts, so a message is sent to you notifying you of job postings that you might be interested in. Just click the **Email Alerts** link at the top of the list, and select Daily, Weekly, or No Email Alerts from the pop-up box. Click the **Save** button to set up your email alerts.

It's very likely that the list of recommended jobs won't include the right job for you. Don't be disappointed. There are many jobs posted on LinkedIn from companies in a wide variety of industries. You can search through job postings by typing keywords into the search text box at the top of the Jobs Home page and clicking the **Search** button. A list of matching jobs is returned to you as shown in Figure 14.2.

Figure 14.2: *A keyword search produces a list of job search results.*

You can sort or narrow search results to get more specific results. Along the top of the list shown in Figure 14.2, you see a **Sort by Relevance** link. Click the arrow to the right of Relevance if you want to change the sort order to Relationship, Date Posted (most recent), or Date Posted (earliest). To the right at the top of the list, you see the number of matching jobs based on your search criteria as well as a Save button. Just click the **Save** link to save the search for easy access later under the Saved Searches tab.

QUICK TIP

You also have the option to receive email updates for a job search when you click the **Save** button. You can choose to receive email alerts daily, weekly, monthly, or never.

Scroll through the list of job postings delivered to you and click through to view those you're interested in. Notice that when you hover your mouse over a job on the list, two links appear to the right of the job as shown in Figure 14.3. Those links enable you to save the specific job for later viewing under the Saved Jobs tab or view Similar Jobs.

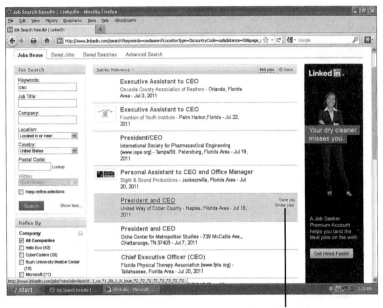

Use these links

Figure 14.3: *You can click the links to save any job or view similar jobs.*

To narrow your search results, scroll through the various filtering options on the left side of the job search results page (see Figure 14.3). You can refine your search by:

- Keywords

- Job title

- Relationship

- Company

- Location, country, and postal code

- Date posted

- Job function

- Industry

- Experience level

- Salary (available to Job Seeker Premium members only, which is discussed in the Job Seeker Premium section later in this chapter)

> **QUICK TIP**
>
> If you know you want to conduct a highly refined search, you can click on the Advanced Search tab on the Jobs Home page (visible in Figure 14.3) and immediately enter your search criteria.

Keep in mind, all of the advanced search techniques discussed in Chapter 5 apply when searching for jobs on LinkedIn, too. Go back and read that chapter for searching help and tricks to get the results you need.

Job Directory

LinkedIn offers a Jobs Directory at linkedin.com/directory/jobs/. Here you can browse for jobs by job function, industry, region, job title, or company. As you click on different categories, such as a Job Function link in the Jobs Directory, you'll be presented with additional filtering criteria such as region or experience level. When you've reached the narrowest category, a list of jobs is presented to you.

You can access the Jobs Directory even when you're not logged in to your LinkedIn account. However to view all jobs, you do need to log in. Furthermore, when the list of jobs is presented to you, you can refine your search using the same options shown on the left-hand side of Figure 14.3. It's just one more way that you can navigate through the jobs postings on LinkedIn.

JobsInsider

JobsInsider is a tool that will automatically appear as a browser pane when you search for jobs on sites other than LinkedIn. The tool requires that you use the LinkedIn browser toolbar for Mozilla Firefox or Internet Explorer (as discussed in Chapter 12). You must also be sure to search sites that work with JobsInsider, such as Monster.com, CareerBuilder.com, HotJobs.com, Craigslist.org, Dice. com, SimplyHired.com, Vault.com, and more.

For example, imagine that you're searching for jobs on Monster.com, and you find a job you want to apply for. JobsInsider tells you if there are any people in your extended LinkedIn network who work at the hiring company (referred to as "inside connections"), which can help you get referrals or request introductions to hiring managers and key employees at that company.

INSIDER SECRET

The JobsInsider tool uses information in the job posting to identify inside connections from your LinkedIn profile. Therefore, the list of connections is only as good as the job listing content. For example, if the company name isn't provided in the job listing, no inside connections will be displayed.

You can install the LinkedIn browser toolbar for Firefox or Internet Explorer at any time by clicking the **Tools** link from the LinkedIn footer, selecting the **Browser Toolbar** tab on the page that opens, and following the installation instructions provided. Details are included in Chapter 12.

Company, Employee, and Group Research

Don't feel like your job search on LinkedIn is restricted to searches through the Jobs Directory and jobs search tool. You can also find jobs through Company Pages, employee profiles, and group career discussions and jobs sections.

Companies that post job openings on LinkedIn can display those jobs on their LinkedIn Company Page. See Figure 14.4 for an example.

When companies post new jobs, those job announcements are also published as an activity update, so it's a good idea to follow the Company Page for companies that you want to target in your job search. Following Company Pages is discussed in detail in Chapter 13.

Figure 14.4: *Company Pages can include a Careers tab with job postings.*

It's also common to come across job openings through employee's personal profile updates on LinkedIn. For example, an employee might publish a job posting for her company and post it as an update in her personal profile activity stream. Employees also might discuss open jobs casually in their LinkedIn updates. If you're targeting specific companies in your job search, look for current employees that you can connect with and keep an eye on their updates. You never know what you might see!

Groups offer another great way to find job openings. Join groups related to the type of work you want to do or industries and companies you want to work with. Some group administrators set up a Jobs section where members can share jobs posted in LinkedIn jobs.

Group administrators can also add a Career Discussions section to their groups where members can post and discuss job opportunities they hear about outside of LinkedIn jobs. These discussions are always timely because they are automatically removed after 14 days.

Job Seeker Premium

If you are extremely serious about using LinkedIn to find a job, then you might want to consider paying for a Job Seeker Premium account. You can upgrade your account at any time. Just click the **Upgrade My Account** link from the LinkedIn footer when you're logged in to your account. The Subscription Plans page opens. From there you can scroll to the Looking for a Job? box in the bottom right of the page and click the **View Plans** link to see current prices and features of Job Seeker Premium paid plans.

All upgraded LinkedIn plans are discussed in detail in Chapter 16, including Job Seeker Premium plans. There are three Job Seeker plan levels with different price tags: Job Seeker Basic, Job Seeker, and Job Seeker Plus.

With your free LinkedIn account, you can only get introduced to 5 companies that you're targeting in your job search per month. You also cannot access salary information, move to the top of the applicant list as a Featured Applicant, see who has viewed your profile, or let recruiters message you for free with OpenLink (discussed in Chapter 16). An upgraded Job Seeker Premium account lets you do all of those things and more.

Applying for a Job

You can configure the job-application process in one of three ways. When you find a job that you want to apply for, the corresponding apply button will appear on the job posting based on the application process you selected.

- **Apply on company website:** Click the button to visit the company's website and apply.

- **Apply now:** Click the button to upload your résumé and cover letter to apply. You can also request referrals from people you're connected to on LinkedIn who work for the company.

- **Apply with LinkedIn:** Click the button to apply with your LinkedIn profile. You can add a note to the job poster and request referrals from your LinkedIn connections who work for the company (no résumé required).

QUICK TIP

You can create a résumé directly from your LinkedIn profile contents, save it as a PDF file, print it, and share it using the LinkedIn Resume Builder tool at http://resume.linkedinlabs.com/.

Again, the person who posts the job opening for the company determines which application—and therefore, which type of apply button—appears with the posting. Just follow the directions provided by the employer based on their application process choice to apply.

WARNING

Uploaded résumés must be less than 200 KB. Cover letters must be less than 4,000 characters.

Of course, it's important to take some time to make sure you look as good as possible on LinkedIn before you apply for job opportunities. For example, spend some time trying to get your LinkedIn profile 100 percent complete. Ask connections for recommendations (particularly those connections who can give you recommendations related to the types of jobs you want to apply to), and answer questions on LinkedIn Answers to demonstrate your knowledge. Join groups and be active across LinkedIn to establish your credibility and reputation. All of these professional activities will help you be more visible on LinkedIn and make you look more attractive to employers.

The Least You Need to Know

- Use the LinkedIn job search tools, Company Pages, groups, and employee profiles to find job opportunities.

- You can view the LinkedIn Jobs Directory when you're not logged in to your LinkedIn account, but you can't see all job listings unless you log in.

- Job Seeker Premium accounts come with additional features and fees that can help serious job seekers.

- Some job postings allow you to apply through LinkedIn without uploading a résumé. Others require résumé upload or require that you apply through the company website off of LinkedIn.

Looking for New Talent on LinkedIn

In This Chapter

* Posting a job opportunity on LinkedIn
* Searching for talent
* Using premium tools to find potential employees
* Advertising for help

LinkedIn boasts tens of millions of users who are interested in career development and professional networking. Sounds like an incredible talent pool! LinkedIn makes it easy to tap into the talent pool and find employees to join your organization through free and paid tools.

Whether you just want to post a job opening or want to create a fully functional recruiter page and profile, you can do it on LinkedIn. There are options to fit every budget and every goal. This chapter introduces you to the many ways you can find and recruit both active and passive job seekers using LinkedIn.

Post a Job

Any LinkedIn member can post a job to the site as long as they agree to the LinkedIn Jobs Terms and Conditions available at linkedin.com/static?key=pop/pop_jobs_terms_conditions. Once you read through these terms and conditions and determine that you're able to stay in compliance with them, you can post a job.

LinkedIn offers several types of accounts that provide different job posting and recruiting capabilities. This section focuses on the basic

LinkedIn account, which is free. However, you will need to pay a fee for each job you post on LinkedIn.

INSIDER SECRET

Job posting fees vary depending on the geographic area you select for targeting when you create your posting. For example, a 30-day job posting targeted to the Orlando, Florida region costs $195 (at the time of this book's writing).

Individuals can pay for LinkedIn job postings via credit card (at the time of this book's writing, American Express, MasterCard, Visa, and Discover were accepted). Alternatively, you can prepurchase job credits, which are sold by LinkedIn individually or in discounted increments of 5 or 10. Each credit allows you to post a job for 30 days, and credits expire 365 days after the date you purchase them.

Completing the Form to Post a Job

When you're ready to post a job on LinkedIn with your basic LinkedIn account, just log in to your account and click the **Jobs** link in the top navigation bar. From the drop-down menu, select the **Post a Job** link to open the Post a Job tab shown in Figure 15.1.

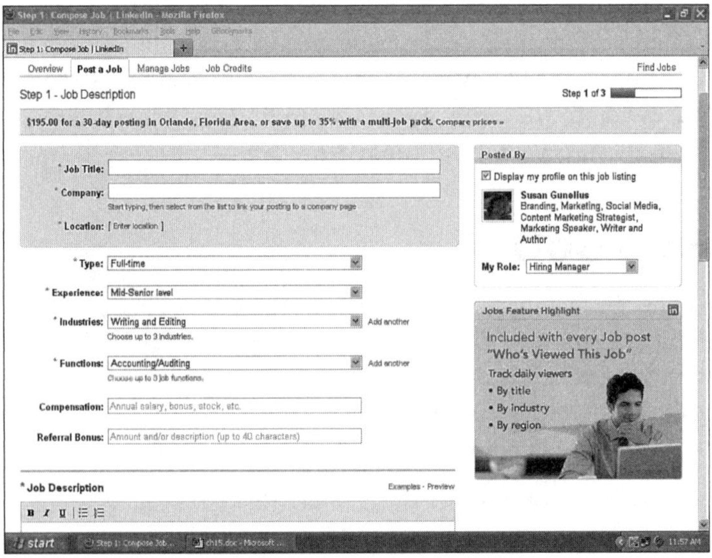

Figure 15.1: *Complete the form to post your job on LinkedIn.*

> **QUICK TIP**
>
> You can also click the Manage Jobs tab (visible in Figure 15.1) to work with job postings that you've already published. Use the Job Credits tab to purchase the credits you need to post your job.

Complete the following steps to fill out the Post a Job form:

1. Enter a **Job Title** in the text box.

2. Enter the name of your **Company** in the text box. As you type, companies with existing LinkedIn Company Pages will appear for you to select from. Create your own Company Page to add your company name to this list.

3. Click the **Enter Location** link and select the zip code you're targeting (most likely where the person will physically work) from the pop-up box shown in Figure 15.2. The price of your job posting is automatically calculated and displayed for you.

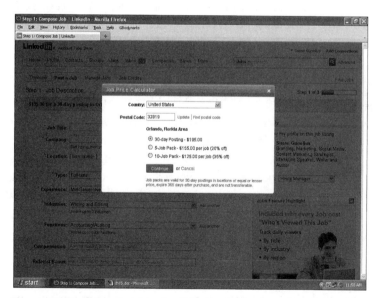

Figure 15.2: *Enter the zip code of the location you're targeting to see the price of your job posting.*

4. Choose the job **Type, Experience** level, **Industry**, and **Function** that most appropriately describes the job you're posting from each drop-down menu.

5. If you'd like to include **Compensation** or **Referral Bonus** information, you may do so in the text boxes provided. Both are optional.

6. In the **Job Description** text box, enter a great description of the position, and be sure to include keywords (discussed in the Skills section later in this chapter).

7. If you'd like to include **Desired Skills and Experience** requirements or a **Company Description** in your job posting, you can enter both in the text boxes provided. These are optional.

8. In the **Applicant Routing** section of the form, you can choose the appropriate radio button to route applicants in one of two ways: You can collect applications through LinkedIn and be notified via email (enter your **Preferred Email Address** into the box) when new applications are submitted. Your email address will not be shown to applicants. If you'd rather **Direct Applicants to an External Site** or your website to apply for the job (and your account type allows it), enter the URL in the box provided.

9. If you don't want anyone to see that you were the person who published the job posting, scroll back up to the top of the form and make sure the **Display My Profile on This Job Posting** check box is not selected in the box on the top right. If you do want to display your profile with the posting, you can modify your role using the drop-down list.

10. Scroll back down to the bottom of the form and click the **Continue** button.

Once you click the **Continue** button, you might be presented with a list of Profile Matches if you have a premium subscription LinkedIn account. These matches are provided based on members' profile information and the job description that you wrote. You can preview up to 24 Profile Matches that LinkedIn finds for you before you even publish your job posting! However, you cannot unlock the matches and use the 10 free InMails you get to contact them unless you pay a $95 fee (check current rates to ensure this amount is still accurate).

> **QUICK TIP**
>
> Profile Matches are available to premium Talent Finder and Corporate Recruiting Solutions account holders. These accounts are discussed in detail later in this chapter and in Chapter 16.

The InMails you purchase will expire after 90 days, so you have time to use them. You don't have to contact your Profile Matches immediately. If you want to continue on and post your job, then return to your Profile Matches list later, they'll be accessible in the Manage Jobs tab of your LinkedIn account. Just select the specific job posting from your list (if you have multiple postings) to see the related Profile Matches.

When you bypass the Profile Matches page (if you're presented with one), you'll arrive at the payment page where you can purchase credits and pay for your posting.

Once you pay, your job is immediately published on LinkedIn Jobs (accessible through the top navigation bar for any logged in LinkedIn member). If you chose to show your own profile with your job post, then anyone who can see your profile will see the job, too. The job posting also appears as a status update on your news stream, so your first-degree connections will see it on their home pages within their list of connections' updates. Furthermore, your job posting automatically appears in the Careers tab of your Company Page (if you have one and if you identified that company using the drop-down menu in the job post form) even if yours is a free Company Page.

As LinkedIn members view your job posting, you can view information about them through the Manage Jobs tab of your LinkedIn account. Just select the specific job posting and click the **Who's Viewed This Job** tab to see a list of anonymous characteristics about the people who have viewed your job posting.

INSIDER SECRET

By viewing characteristics of people who have viewed your job posting, you can determine if the right people are finding it and modify your job description if necessary to attract the right candidates.

Receiving Applications and Finding More Applicants

When a LinkedIn member wants to apply to your posted job, there are a couple of ways they will be directed to proceed based on the type of LinkedIn account you have and the settings you entered when you created the job posting.

For example, if you have a free LinkedIn or any upgraded account other than Talent Pro or Corporate Recruiting Solutions (upgraded accounts are discussed in detail in Chapter 16), then you can enter any email address into the job posting form to receive applicant cover letters, résumés, and LinkedIn profile information. If you have a Talent Pro account or a Corporate Recruiting Solutions account, then you can direct applicants to an external website where they can apply directly through your company's system. Again, you identify your preference when you create the job posting.

If you receive applications through LinkedIn with an email notification, then you can review that information without logging in to your LinkedIn account through your email account. However, you can always log in to your LinkedIn account and visit the Manage Jobs tab where you can click on the specific job posting and review all applications and applicant information. Here you can click the links provided to view applicants' cover letters and uploaded résumés, as well as their LinkedIn profiles. You can also click the **Find References** link to access a list of possible references you could contact to ask about specific applicants.

Sometimes your job posting doesn't deliver the applicant responses that you need. Fortunately, all hope is not lost. There are ways that you can find the type of talented people that you need to fill the open role. First, look through your employees' connections on

LinkedIn and ask them to refer connections to you who might be a good fit for the job.

Make sure your employees are listed on your Company Page. Give them the following instructions so they show up in the employees section of your Company Page, adding to your page's credibility and giving more people another way to find it through their extended LinkedIn networks:

1. Click **Profile** from the top navigation bar when they're logged in to their LinkedIn accounts.

2. Click **Edit** next to the listed position with your company.

3. Click the **Change Company** link and type the name of your company. A drop-down list of similar companies with existing Company Pages on LinkedIn is shown. Tell employees that they must select your company (based on the company name in your Company Page) from the drop-down list.

4. Click the **Update** button.

You can mention your job in groups that allow it and you can always send your job posting to your first-degree connections on LinkedIn. Of course, promoting it outside of LinkedIn is a good idea, too. Share the link to the posting on Twitter, Facebook, related forums, your blog, and so on. Sometimes people feel more comfortable applying to a job through LinkedIn than they might feel when applying through a third-party website. Bottom line: give them as many ways to learn about and apply for your open job as possible to boost applications.

However, it's also important that the applications you receive are from candidates who actually fit the job description. Don't forget, LinkedIn offers a variety of advanced search features that can help you find potential job candidates who match your job posting. Read Chapter 5 to learn about the many search tools available to you that you can use to find talented people on LinkedIn.

Closing, Expiring, and Renewing Job Postings

Job postings remain active for 30 days. After 30 days, your job posting immediately expires and is removed from LinkedIn jobs, your Company Page, and so on. You can still view your job posting and applicant information through the Manage Jobs tab of your LinkedIn account, but no one else will be able to find or apply for the job.

You can republish a job posting in the future, but once a job expires, the republished posting (even if it is identical to the original) is considered a completely new job in your LinkedIn account. That means applications received the first time the posting was published will be associated with that posting and will not appear in the new posting. All new applications received will appear with the new posting but not with the old one.

To keep all applications together in one job listing, you must renew your job posting before it expires. LinkedIn recommends that you renew your job posting at least a few days before the expiration date. When you renew a job posting, the date posted field on the published job listing changes to the date the posting was renewed, which brings it to the top of the list of job postings in LinkedIn Jobs.

> **WARNING**
>
> Renewed job postings cost the same as the original posting. You must pay the renewal fee in order for your job posting to stay active for another 30 days.

If you're fortunate enough to find the perfect candidate for your open job before your job posting expires, you can close your posting before the expiration date without penalty. Once you close your job posting, it is instantly removed from LinkedIn Jobs and all search results. You'll still be able to view the job and applicant information through the Manage Jobs tab in your LinkedIn account (assuming you received applications via email rather than through an external website). However, you will not be reimbursed for the unused time from your 30-day job listing.

Talent Finder Accounts

LinkedIn Recruiting Solutions offers several ways that individuals and large corporations can better leverage the active and passive job seekers on LinkedIn to fill open positions in their organizations. The individual and small business offering comes in the form of Talent Finder premium accounts.

LinkedIn offers three types of paid accounts for individuals or small businesses that are serious about using LinkedIn for recruiting and need more functionality than the free LinkedIn account. These three accounts are Talent Basic, Talent Finder, and Talent Pro. Each of these accounts is discussed in detail in Chapter 16. For now, it's important to understand the basic ways that a paid Talent Finder account can help you as a hiring manager.

With a paid Talent Basic, Talent Finder, or Talent Pro account you can do the following:

- Send an increased quantity of InMails.

- Use premium search filters.

- View more candidates when you conduct searches.

- Search for candidates within groups.

- Access folders to manage your recruiting efforts with your colleagues.

- Allow people outside your network to contact you with *OpenLink*, which is discussed in more detail in Chapter 16.

- See names of third-degree and group connections.

- See who has viewed your profile.

- Receive more alerts when new candidates meet your job-posting criteria.

- Use the Reference Search tool.

- Get priority customer service.

DEFINITION

The **OpenLink** network is open to premium LinkedIn account holders. If you're in the OpenLink network, anyone on LinkedIn can send you free messages (even if they are not in your extended network) and you can send free messages to all OpenLink members.

The benefits of paying for a Talent Basic, Talent Finder (recommended by LinkedIn for advanced functionality at a more affordable price), or Talent Pro account are that you have more control over your talent search and recruiting activities. The abilities to send InMail messages, use OpenLink network capabilities, view more candidates through searches, get alerts when new clients match your criteria, and use the Reference Search tool are particularly helpful in communicating with LinkedIn members who are actively looking for jobs as well as those who are passive job seekers.

Many people on LinkedIn might have the skills you need but are not actively looking for a new job right now. However, if the right job is presented to them, they might just change their minds. Premium Talent Finder accounts on LinkedIn let you fill your talent pool with the right candidates and fill positions more effectively.

Corporate Recruiting Solutions

As part of LinkedIn Hiring Solutions, large companies and corporate recruiters can pay to use Corporate Recruiting Solutions, which is accessible through the Recruiting Solutions link in the footer of the LinkedIn website. The tools offered through Recruiting Solutions aren't cheap, but they can help companies that hire a lot of professional people streamline the process and find the best talent.

WARNING

LinkedIn doesn't advertise pricing for Recruiting Solutions, and it is not communicated unless you first view a demo.

LinkedIn Recruiting Solutions offers a variety of useful tools and features (some are also offered in the individual Talent Finder premium accounts). With Recruiting Solutions, you can do the following:

- Access the entire LinkedIn network.

- Use very advanced search refinement filters.

- Target potential candidates based on company, location, industry, skills, keywords, and full user profiles.

- Contact candidates directly through InMail messages.

- Get access to InMail templates and send one-to-many InMails.

- Create project folders and reminders.

- Collaborate with team members using folders, searches, profiles, and candidate notes.

- Create automatic search alerts to find candidates that match your job criteria.

- Find candidates through your employees using the Referral Engine tool.

- Use search algorithms along with your employees' referrals to get the best referral suggestions.

- Automatically send referral suggestions to employees' email inboxes on an ongoing basis.

- Target and reach passive candidates based on the search criteria you select.

- Promote recruiting events.

- Publish recruitment ads to find talent. Just give LinkedIn your message and criteria about the person you want to hire. LinkedIn manages your campaign and sends names and information for qualified candidates directly to you.

- Publish jobs to LinkedIn Jobs, your Career Page on your Company Page, and employee profile pages.

- Advertise your jobs across the internet to the targeted audiences who match your specific criteria.

- Enhance your Career Page within your LinkedIn Company Page with videos, banners, employee spotlights, and more. You can target content and messages on your Company Page based on the visitor's LinkedIn profile. Your page automatically shows the most relevant jobs for each visitor. You can see a sample enhanced Career Page in Figure 15.3.

Figure 15.3: *Enhanced Career Pages can offer job postings, employee profiles, videos, and more.*

- Display job ads on your employees' LinkedIn profiles.
- Conduct surveys to learn from your target audience and benchmark your company against others.
- Send applicants to your application management system or external website to receive and manage the hiring process.

INSIDER SECRET

Recruiting Solutions is the biggest moneymaker for LinkedIn.

LinkedIn Recruiting Solutions is expensive, but can be effective for the right users. Most often it is useful to big companies that need to hire a lot of people frequently and to recruiters who believe the types of people they need to hire use LinkedIn. This is not an investment to undertake without a lot of research, thought, and planning.

Skills

LinkedIn Skills was in Beta at the time of this book's writing. The tool is intended to offer a way for LinkedIn members to search for the types of skills that are important to them and find other members who have identified those skills in their own LinkedIn profiles, companies tied to those skills, jobs related to those skills, and even more related skills.

When you're looking for talent to hire for a job opening, Skills is a handy tool that can help you write your job description. Click on the **More** link in the top navigation bar when you're logged in to your LinkedIn account and click the **Skills** link from the drop-down menu. The Skills & Expertise page shown in Figure 15.4 opens where you can type in keywords for the skill you're looking for. As you type, a list of related keyword skills appears which you can choose from. Search for the types of skills you think the best candidate should have for your open position.

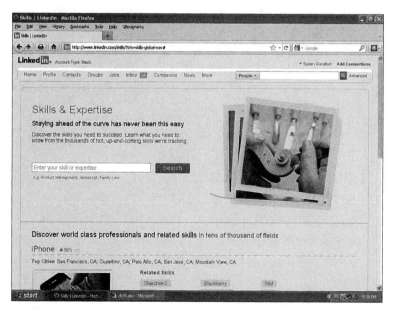

Figure 15.4: *The Skills & Expertise page. Enter keywords related to the skill you want to investigate.*

Once you've selected the skill, click the **Search** button. Poke around the results that are presented to you.

Review profiles of people with those skills, read through the list of related skills, and check out some of the matching jobs and companies. You'll find more skills, different ways to word your job description, keywords, and much more information that can help you create the best job description to attract the best talent.

Bottom line: There are many premium accounts you can pay for to execute a full-scale recruitment initiative. However, there are also many ways that you can effectively post a job, find applicants, and attract top talent without paying a huge amount of money. If the types of people who you want to hire use LinkedIn, then it's worth it to try posting a job through LinkedIn Jobs.

The Least You Need to Know

- Anyone with a LinkedIn account can post a job on the site.
- The price to post a job on LinkedIn depends on the region selected for targeting during the job post creation process.
- You can pay for job postings by purchasing job credits using an accepted credit card.
- LinkedIn offers premium accounts for individuals and small businesses as well as corporate accounts for larger companies and recruiting agencies with varying price levels and features.

Analyzing and Retooling Your LinkedIn Strategy

LinkedIn, the internet, and technology change rapidly, and what you're doing on LinkedIn today to build your brand, business, or career might not be the best thing to do tomorrow. Analysis and retooling are essential to a successful LinkedIn strategy.

Part 5 begins by introducing you to the varied types of LinkedIn accounts. Depending on your LinkedIn goals, the free Basic account is likely to be all you need to get started. However, there are several paid accounts that offer more features and can be helpful depending on your LinkedIn strategy. You also learn how to track your LinkedIn efforts so you can change what's not working and do more of what is working.

Upgrading Your Account

In This Chapter

- Choosing a free or paid account
- Understanding types of business accounts
- Paying for help to find a job
- Reviewing Talent Finder accounts
- Using a corporate recruiting account

LinkedIn separates its account types into four categories: Basic, Premium for Business, Premium for Job Seekers, and Premium for Recruiters and Employers. Within each of the four categories are various account subscriptions that you can choose from to get the features you need, at the price you're willing to pay.

This chapter identifies what the various accounts offer to you, so you can make the best decision in choosing if and how to upgrade your LinkedIn account. Note that many of the account types offer similar features overall with nuances to make them more attractive for business users as opposed to job seekers or hiring managers and recruiters.

Basic Account

The Basic LinkedIn account is the free account that has been discussed throughout this book. Unless otherwise specified, all of the features discussed in this book are available to basic account holders.

Basic LinkedIn accounts are completely free. Unless you want to post a job, purchase additional InMails, or upgrade to a premium account, you don't have to pay a cent to use LinkedIn to build your brand, career, or business.

With a Basic LinkedIn account, you can do the following for free:

- Create your member profile.

- Create a standard Company Page.

- Start and join groups.

- Send and receive private messages through your LinkedIn Inbox to and from your connections.

- Use third-party LinkedIn applications.

- Give and receive recommendations for and from your connections.

- Send connection requests to people you know or request introductions to people you don't know through your existing connections.

- Ask and answer questions using LinkedIn Answers.

- View 100 profiles when you conduct a search.

- Save up to three search alerts per week.

- Get introduced to up to five companies you're targeting per month.

- See the first names of your third-degree connections and group connections.

INSIDER SECRET

The vast majority of LinkedIn members have free Basic accounts.

I highly recommend that you start using LinkedIn with a Basic account. Like most people, the free account is likely to offer all the functionality you need to effectively use LinkedIn to build your brand, career, or business. If you find you need advanced features in the future, you can always upgrade when that time comes.

Premium Business Accounts

Premium business accounts offer advanced features to professionals who want to boost their networking efforts on LinkedIn. Three types of business accounts are available: Business, Business Plus, and Executive. The three come in a tiered pricing structure with increasing functionality to match the increasing cost.

> **WARNING**
>
> The prices and features discussed in this book were valid at the time of writing. Be sure to view current pricing on LinkedIn.com to confirm accuracy or view the pricing comparison document at help.linkedin.com/ci/fattach/get/761012/0/filename/Compare%20Account%20Types.pdf.

Business: For $24.95 per month (or $19.95 per month if you pay for a full year upfront), you can get a Business account. This account offers you all the features of the free Basic account and also enables you to do the following:

- Contact up to three people directly using InMail with a guaranteed response or your InMail count doesn't go down.

- See 300 profiles when you conduct a search.

- Use premium search filters in searches.

- See expanded profiles of everyone on LinkedIn.

- View the full list of people who have viewed your LinkedIn profile.

- Save profiles and notes in up to five folders using Profile Organizer.

- Save up to five search alerts each week.

- Get introduced to 15 (outstanding) companies in addition to the 5 per month offered through the Basic account.

- Use the Reference Search tool.

- Allow anyone to send a message to you for free using OpenLink.

- Get priority customer service.

Business Plus: For $49.95 per month (or $39.95 per month if you pay for a full year upfront), you can get all of the features in the Basic and Business accounts as well as the following or with the following modifications:

- Contact up to 10 people directly with InMail with a guaranteed response or your InMail count doesn't go down.

- See 500 profiles when you conduct a search.

- Save profiles and notes in up to 25 folders using Profile Organizer.

- Save up to seven search alerts per week.

- Get introduced to 25 (outstanding) companies in addition to the 5 per month offered through the Basic account.

QUICK TIP

LinkedIn recommends the Business Plus account.

Executive: For $99.95 per month (or $74.95 per month if you pay for a full year upfront), you get all of the features offered in a Basic account, Business account, and Business Plus account in addition to the following and with the following modifications:

- Contact up to 25 people directly with InMail with a guaranteed response or your InMail count doesn't go down.

- See 700 profiles when you conduct a search.

- Use premium search filters and talent filters when you conduct searches.

- Save profiles and notes in up to 50 folders using Profile Organizer.

- Save up to 10 search alerts per week.

- Get introduced to 35 (outstanding) companies in addition to the 5 per month offered through the Basic account.

- See the full names of your third-degree connections and group connections.

If you're not a power user, it's unlikely that you need a premium LinkedIn account, particularly an expensive option like the Executive account. Start small and work your way up, so you don't waste money.

Premium Job Seeker Accounts

All Basic LinkedIn account holders can view and apply for jobs listed on LinkedIn Jobs or company Career Pages. Basic account holders can also get introduced to up to five companies they're targeting per month.

However, if you're really serious about using LinkedIn to find a job, you might want to consider upgrading to a premium Job Seeker account. There are three types of premium Job Seeker accounts with a tiered pricing structure and features: Job Seeker Basic, Job Seeker, and Job Seeker Plus.

Job Seeker Basic: For $19.95 per month (or $15.95 per month if you pay for a full year up front), you can get a Job Seeker Basic account. In addition to the features you get with your free Basic account, you can do the following:

- Display a Job Seeker Badge on your LinkedIn profile, so recruiters notice you.

- Get detailed salary information for job postings that provide it.

- Move to the top of the list of applicants as a "Featured Applicant."

- See everyone who has viewed your profile.

- Join the "Job Seeking on LinkedIn" web-based seminar.

- Get introduced to 10 (outstanding) companies that you're targeting in addition to the 5 introductions per month you get with your Basic account.

- Allow recruiters to send you messages for free using OpenLink.

- Get priority customer service.

INSIDER SECRET

To be a featured applicant, make sure you check the **Featured Applicant** box at the bottom of the job application page. Also, be sure to turn on the **Job Seeker Premium badge** from your account Settings page or it won't display next to your name in your LinkedIn profile.

Job Seeker: For $29.95 per month (or $24.95 per month if you pay for a full year up front), you can get the features provided in the Basic and Job Seeker Basic accounts as well as the following additions or modifications:

- Contact up to five people using InMail with a guaranteed response or your InMail count doesn't go down.

- Get introduced to 15 (outstanding) companies that you're targeting in addition to the 5 introductions per month you get with your Basic account.

QUICK TIP

LinkedIn recommends the Job Seeker account for people who are searching for a job.

Job Seeker Plus: For $49.95 per month (or $39.95 per month if you pay for a full year up front), you can get all the features of a Basic, Job Seeker Basic, and Job Seeker account as well as the following additions or modifications:

- Contact up to 10 people using InMail with a guaranteed response or your InMail count doesn't go down.

- Get introduced to 25 (outstanding) companies that you're targeting in addition to the 5 introductions per month you get with your Basic account.

These accounts are not cheap, but if you're relying on LinkedIn to help you advance your career and land your next job, then they might be worth considering.

Premium Accounts for Employers and Recruiters

With a free Basic LinkedIn account, you can pay to post individual jobs by purchasing job credits with your credit card as described in Chapter 15. You can see up to 100 candidates when you conduct a talent search, see the first names of your third-degree and group connections who might meet your targeting criteria, and get up to 3 automated alerts when new candidates meet your chosen job criteria.

For individuals, businesses, and corporations that need more features, there are three premium talent account types—Talent Basic, Talent Finder, and Talent Pro—as well as a corporate recruiting account—Corporate Recruiting Solutions. The features and pricing for each are provided below.

Talent Basic: For $49.95 per month (or $39.95 per month if you pay for a full year up front), you get all of the features of a free Basic account and can do the following:

- Contact up to 10 people using InMail with a guaranteed response or your InMail count doesn't go down.

- Use premium filters when you conduct candidate searches.

- See up to 500 profiles when you conduct searches.

- Save and manage candidate information and processes in up to 25 folders.

- See expanded profiles of everyone on LinkedIn.

- Allow people outside your network to contact you for free with OpenLink, making it easy for candidates to communicate with you.

- See the first names of your third-degree and group connections.

- See everyone who has viewed your profile.

- Get up to seven alerts per week when new candidates meet your specific criteria.

- Use the Reference Search tool.

- Get priority customer service.

Talent Finder: For $99.95 per month (or $74.95 per month if you pay for a full year up front), you get all features in the free Basic account, the premium Talent Basic account, and the following additional or modified features:

- Contact up to 25 people using InMail with a guaranteed response or your InMail count doesn't go down.

- Use premium filters and talent filters to conduct candidate searches.

- See up to 700 profiles when you conduct searches.

- Search for talent within up to 50 groups that you belong to.

- Save and manage candidate information and processes in up to 50 folders.

- See the full names of your third-degree and group connections.

- Get up to 10 alerts per week when new candidates meet your specific criteria.

QUICK TIP

LinkedIn recommends the Talent Finder account for noncorporate users.

Talent Pro: For $499.95 per month (or $399.95 per month if you pay for a full year up front), you can get all of the features offered in the free Basic account, premium Talent Basic account, and premium Talent Finder account as well as the following additional or modified features:

- Contact up to 50 people using InMail with a guaranteed response or your InMail count doesn't go down.

- See up to 1,000 profiles when you conduct searches.

- Save and manage candidate information and processes in up to 75 folders.

- Get up to 15 alerts per week when new candidates meet your specific criteria.

Recruiting Solutions: For an undisclosed amount of money (unless you contact LinkedIn and watch a demo of the Recruiting Solutions product), you can upgrade to a comprehensive recruiting tool. This type of account is expensive but full featured. See Chapter 15 for a list of 20 key features Recruiting Solutions account holders get. This type of account is used by large companies with frequent hiring needs as well as recruiting agencies that need to build large talent pools and fill a large number of jobs on an ongoing basis.

Upgrading, Downgrading, and Canceling a Premium Account

You can upgrade your account at any time by clicking the **Upgrade My Account** link in the LinkedIn footer when you're logged in to your account. The Subscription Plans page, shown in Figure 16.1, opens. Here you can choose the type of premium business account you want or click the **View Plans** link in the Searching for Top Talent? box (visible in the lower left of the figure) or the Looking for a Job? box (visible in the lower right of the figure) to choose a premium Employer and Recruiter account or a premium Job Seeker account.

QUICK TIP

To access Corporate Recruiting Solutions, you must click the **Recruiting Solutions** link in the LinkedIn footer.

Your premium account is automatically renewed each month or year depending on your payment schedule. You can cancel your premium account at any time by contacting LinkedIn and requesting cancellation using the form at help.linkedin.com/app/ask/subject/ Cancel%20My%20Premium%20Account.

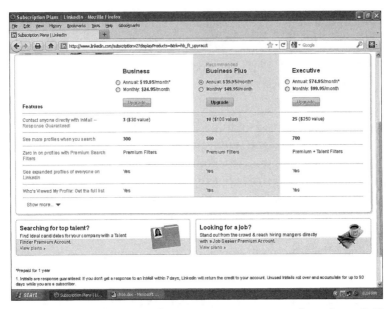

Figure 16.1: *Select the type of premium account you want from the available Subscription Plans.*

Once approved, the cancellation is effective immediately and your account is downgraded to a free Basic account. That means all premium features, such as InMails that you got as part of your premium account, will immediately disappear from your account.

If you want to downgrade your premium account to a lower-level premium account rather than reverting to the free Basic account through a premium account cancellation, then you can contact LinkedIn using the form provided at help.linkedin.com/app/ask/subject/Downgrade%20My%20Premium%20Account. Be sure to identify the type of account you want to downgrade to in the **Question** text box of the contact form.

When your request is approved, your account is immediately downgraded to the one you requested and you lose access to all higher-level features provided in your previous account.

WARNING

LinkedIn recommends that you initiate your cancellation or premium account downgrade request at least 3–5 business days prior to your account renewal date in order to avoid the automated renewal charge.

You can always upgrade your account again in the future after you cancel or downgrade your premium account. Keep in mind, when you cancel or downgrade your premium account, LinkedIn does not refund any money for unused or partially used periods. For example, if you prepaid for a full year of a Talent Finder account and decide to cancel it and revert to a free Basic account three months later, you will not be refunded for the nine months you did not use. Therefore, be sure to choose your premium account type and payment terms wisely. You don't want to be stuck paying for an account you don't need or want.

The Least You Need to Know

- LinkedIn offers a free Basic account and a variety of paid premium accounts for business people and job seekers as well as hiring managers, employers, and recruiters.

- You can pay for premium LinkedIn accounts on a monthly basis or prepay a full year to get a discount.

- You can upgrade your account or downgrade or cancel a premium account at any time.

- LinkedIn does not provide refunds for partially unused accounts. If you cancel your premium account before the renewal date, you do not get a refund.

Gathering Metrics

In This Chapter

- Learning what to track to analyze LinkedIn results
- Reviewing profile and network statistics
- Analyzing Company Page and ad performance
- Gathering metrics outside LinkedIn

If you're using LinkedIn as a tool to build your brand, business, or career, then you need to make sure that your efforts are delivering the results you need to reach your goals. How do you know if you're spending your time (and possibly your money) on the right activities if you don't gather and analyze performance data?

This chapter explains what you should track to monitor your LinkedIn performance and where you can gather the data both internally through LinkedIn features and externally through third-party tools. Whether you're trying to develop your personal brand through your LinkedIn profile or you're trying to build your business brand to increase sales through your LinkedIn Company Page and ads, you can find the data you need to ensure that your time and efforts are well invested.

What to Track

At first glance, it might seem like LinkedIn offers very few features to help you gather data about the success (or failure) of your efforts. However, with a bit of digging (and knowing where to look), you can unearth a mountain of metrics and statistics.

At the same time, you can enhance that data with information and metrics available through third-party tools and websites. Some of these tools are free and others have price tags attached to them. It's up to you to determine how serious you are about reaching your goals through LinkedIn and how much you want to track and spend to get that data. Several popular and affordable third-party metrics tools are discussed at the end of this chapter.

Of course, the metrics you track to measure your LinkedIn performance will vary depending on your LinkedIn goals. For example, if your LinkedIn goal is to land a new job, tracking ad performance would be completely irrelevant to you. It's not that common for LinkedIn members to publish ads as part of their job search plan. On the other hand, if you're a business trying to sell more products, a LinkedIn ad might be a perfect marketing tactic, and tracking the performance of that ad is critical to your overall business success.

Following are ten of the most common metrics that LinkedIn members can track using both internal LinkedIn features and external tools. You don't have to track all of these, and it's very likely that you'll track more or different metrics. That's perfectly fine. Remember, no two LinkedIn members have the exact same goals.

- Number of first-degree connections.
- Number of people in your extended network.
- Regional breakdown of where the people in your network are from.
- Breakdown of the top industries represented by people in your network.
- Number of times your profile shows up in LinkedIn searches.

- How many times people have looked at your profile (with a premium account, you can also see who looked at your profile along with the keywords they used that led them to it).

- Trends related to who has viewed your profile to track popularity (for premium account holders only).

- Who is sharing your updates and how frequently your LinkedIn updates are shared on LinkedIn and outside of LinkedIn (through external tools).

- How frequently your name or brand name is mentioned on LinkedIn and across the internet (through external tools).

- Trends related to connections, sharing content, activities, influence, and more (through external tools).

INSIDER SECRET

Some of the most valuable metrics you can analyze related to your LinkedIn efforts are trends that show your audience growing over time (particularly an audience that matches your target audience and includes influential people), your own messages spreading, your credibility building, and your influence growing over time. You can't buy that kind of sustainable authority.

Remember, LinkedIn is a powerful brand-building tool for both individuals and organizations of all kinds. Its strength comes from its ability to enable people and organizations to establish their expertise and credibility while developing relationships with people who share their content, talk about them, and build a brand buzz. This is a powerful form of word-of-mouth marketing! Those relationships and conversations typically lead to organic personal, career, or business growth.

Profile and Network Statistics

LinkedIn offers features that track a variety of metrics related to your personal profile and the network of people that develops through your connections. These features are the best place to start for tracking your LinkedIn performance. While some data is only available to premium account holders, even Basic (free) LinkedIn members can gather enough information from the Profile Stats and Network Statistics features to determine whether their LinkedIn efforts are delivering positive growth.

Profile Stats

Profile Stats is available to all Basic account holders. Visit your LinkedIn profile and notice the module called Who's Viewed Your Profile on the right side of the page, as shown in Figure 17.1. Here you can see the number of people who have viewed your LinkedIn profile in the past seven days and the number of times your profile showed up in LinkedIn searches during the past three days.

Figure 17.1: *Click the link to see who viewed your profile.*

QUICK TIP

If no one viewed your LinkedIn profile recently, the Who's Viewed Your Profile module won't appear.

Your Profile stats page displays up to five people who have viewed your profile as well as a trend graph that shows both the number of visits to your profile and the number of times your profile has appeared in search results during the previous 90 days.

WARNING

You must change your profile visibility account settings from **Anonymous** to **Your Name and Headline** in the **Select what others see when you've viewed their profile** setting to access Profile Stats.

This is a great tool to make sure your profile is attracting the right kinds of people to help you reach your goals and to confirm that your profile traffic and search performance is improving over time. If not, you might need to increase your efforts to make yourself visible on LinkedIn (e.g., connect with more people, be more active in your updates and share and comment on other people's updates, participate in groups, answer questions, and so on).

Profile Stats Pro

Premium LinkedIn account holders can access Profile Stats Pro (whether or not their visibility settings are set to anonymous), which offers more data than the standard Profile Stats feature does. For example, Profile Stats Pro provides the full list of everyone who has viewed your profile. However, if an individual has his own visibility settings configured to Anonymous, additional information about him won't be accessible.

Furthermore, Profile Stats Pro offers information about visit and search trends just as the standard tool does, but the really useful data comes from the following:

- Keywords used to find your profile

- Industries people work in who viewed your profile

- Regions where people live who viewed your profile (provided on a country level)

If you're targeting specific areas of the world or industries in your LinkedIn efforts, then Profile Stats Pro data can tell you whether people from the right countries and industries are finding your profile. You can also make sure the right keywords are leading people to your profile and discover new useful keywords that you might want to add to your profile to further leverage traffic from them.

Network Statistics

All LinkedIn members (even Basic account holders) can access the Network Statistics feature within LinkedIn by clicking the **Contacts** link in the top navigation bar (when you're logged in to your LinkedIn account) and selecting **My Connections** from the drop-down list. This opens the My Connections page. Click the **Network Statistics** tab near the top of the page to open your Network Statistics page, shown in Figures 17.2 and 17.3.

Figure 17.2: *Get data about your LinkedIn network size through Network Statistics.*

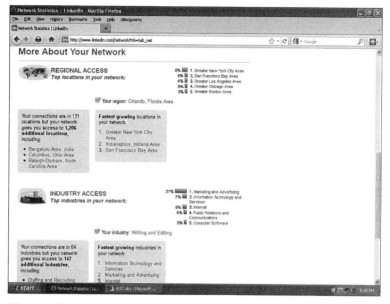

Figure 17.3: *Get data about your LinkedIn network regional and industry access through Network Statistics.*

The Network Statistics feature gives you information about the size and makeup of your extended LinkedIn network and puts into numbers exactly how broad your reach is through that network. For example, you can gather information about the following:

- Number of first-, second-, and third-degree connections

- Number of people you can contact through an introduction

- Number of new people in your network since the previous day

- Number of users you can contact via InMail

- Top regional locations in your network

- Number of locations your connections are in

- Number of additional locations your network gives you access to and a sample of some of those locations

- Fastest-growing locations in your network

- Top industries in your network

- Number of industries your connections are in
- Number of additional industries your network gives you access to and a sample of those industries
- Fastest-growing industries in your network

INSIDER SECRET

The statistics provided through Network Statistics are not intended to be a perfect measurement of your LinkedIn extended network. Therefore, use them for directional strategic planning purposes only.

The Network Statistics feature gives you a quick way to analyze your network and make sure it's growing in the right ways to meet your goals. According to your LinkedIn Network Statistics, you can probably reach thousands or millions of people through your network. Use that reach to build your brand, business, and career!

Company Page Analytics

If you have a Company Page on LinkedIn, then there is a wealth of data waiting for you to tap into! Just visit your Company Page and click the Analytics tab to access that data.

You can view 12-month trend graphs for all pages or by individual page (Overview, Career, or Products and Services) to see statistics about page views or unique visitors. You can also see how your Company Page statistics compare to similar Company Pages.

If you're interested in tracking the clicks people make on your Products and Services page, there is a 12-month trend graph for that metric, too. You can view the graph for people who clicked on the following:

- More information link
- Contact employees
- Promotional banners
- Special promotional links

INSIDER SECRET

Corporate Recruiting Solutions account holders can create Company Pages with a clickable banner, customizable modules, and additional analytics.

A 12-month trend chart is also available to track the number of LinkedIn members who are following your Company Page and a 12-month trend chart that tracks member visits by industry, function, and company.

This data can tell you what type of people are following and visiting your Company Page and whether your Products and Services page is generating enough clicks to meet your goals. Use the information to modify your Company Page promotional efforts and revise your Products and Services page to generate more interest and clicks.

LinkedIn Advertising Results

If you invest in placing ads on LinkedIn, then you certainly want to make sure that those ads are generating the results you need to earn a positive return on your investment. You can access statistics about your ad performance through your LinkedIn Ads dashboard.

Just click the **Home** link in the top navigation bar when you're logged in to your LinkedIn account and choose **Advertise on LinkedIn** from the drop-down list. Click the **Manage Your Ads** link near the top right of the page that opens to access your Ads dashboard. From here you should click the **Reporting** tab to open the page shown in Figure 17.4 where you can select the Report Type, Date Range, and View By format for your report. Both campaign performance and ad performance reports are available for download in *CSV* format.

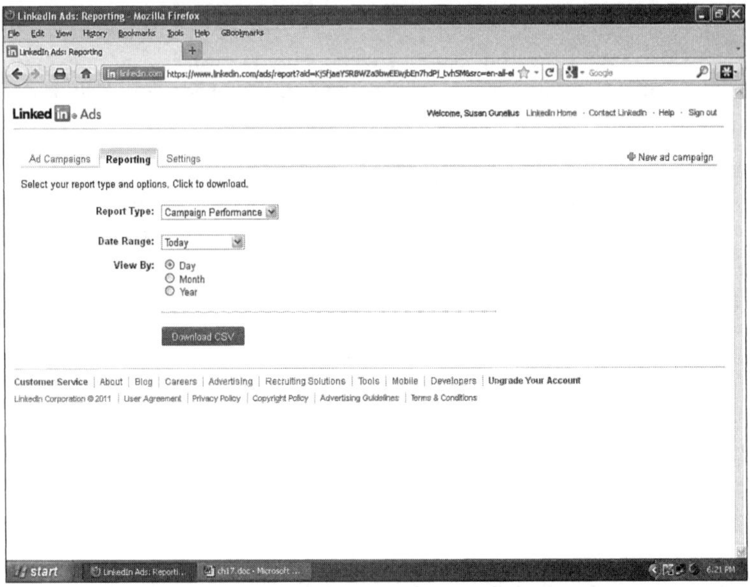

Figure 17.4: *Configure the options for the type of report you want to use to track your ad performance.*

> **DEFINITION**
>
> **CSV** is an acronym for comma-separated values or character-separated values. A CSV file is a simple text format for a database file that can easily be imported to common database and spreadsheet programs such as Microsoft Excel.

Based on the information provided through your ad reports, you can determine whether changes need to be made to your ad for better performance in the future. For example, you might determine from your analytics report that you need to revise the message in your ad, adjust your targeting criteria, or increase your maximum bid. LinkedIn only counts valid clicks on your ads in its reporting, so you can feel confident that the data provided to you in your ad reports is an accurate representation of your ad's performance.

External Performance and Reputation Management Tools

The analytics tools offered by LinkedIn are very limiting. While they can offer a great deal of information about your LinkedIn network and your reach within that network, that is only a small part of your online brand building and reputation monitoring efforts. Chances are people are talking about you and sharing your LinkedIn content, updates, and conversations beyond LinkedIn.

For many people, LinkedIn is just one piece of their online brand-building and marketing efforts. Whether you're trying to build your own reputation or your business reputation, there are many more tools, websites, and social destinations that can help you track your performance. If you have bigger goals for your brand, business, and career that extend beyond the LinkedIn network, then it's even more important that you conduct some tracking outside of LinkedIn.

There are a variety of free and fee-based tools that you can use to monitor your online reputation, your growing influence, and your success that extends beyond your LinkedIn efforts. The remainder of this section introduces you to a number of different tools that offer different types of data at different price levels. There are many more tools than those listed in this chapter, but the following tools represent some of the most popular options to get you started and many are free or offer free trials.

HootSuite: HootSuite is a social media dashboard available at hootsuite.com, which can be used by multiple contributors. It's free to use and can help you manage multiple social media profiles, including your LinkedIn profile, either from your desktop or through the HootSuite website. The free version of HootSuite gives you access to a variety of reports, so you can track click-through statistics and more. When you upgrade to a paid account, you get even more features and reporting capabilities.

Klout: Klout is a tool created to measure online influence. Anyone can register for a free account at klout.com. Just follow the steps provided after you register to connect your Klout account to your LinkedIn account, Twitter account, Facebook account, and more. You can view metrics related to your online activities and how people share your content to get a better understanding of how influential you are online. If you're trying to build your brand, business, or career both on LinkedIn and across the internet, then working to raise your Klout score is a good idea!

> **QUICK TIP**
>
> At the time of this book's writing, you have to have either a Twitter or Facebook account to register for Klout. Once registered, you can connect your LinkedIn account to your Klout account.

Sprout Social: Sprout Social is a tool that makes social media management easier. You can get a free trial at sproutsocial.com. If you like the tool, you can register for a subscription. There are currently two subscription options offered, with more features available for a higher price. However, both plans are very affordable ($9 per month and $49 per month at the time of this book's writing). Sprout Social was designed for small businesses and individuals who want to manage and monitor their brands. It also offers features to help you measure and track your success.

Trackur: Trackur is a social media monitoring tool. Visit trackur. com to learn about current packages, pricing, and features. All paid packages include tools to help you manage your various online pro-files, monitor your online reputation, and measure the influence of your audience as well as the extent of your audience reach. At the time of this book's writing, a 10-day money-back guarantee was offered with plans starting at $18 per month.

Radian6: Visit radian6.com and you'll see a lot of big brand names using the company's tools and services to monitor and track their social media activities and performance metrics. Radian6 is one of the most popular social media monitoring and tracking companies, with tools that enable you to listen, measure, and engage with customers and the online audience. As one of the leading companies in the social media tracking space, Radian6 tools and services come with higher price tags than those listed earlier in this chapter. For example, the Radian6 Dashboard product starts at $600 per month. However, if your business is extremely serious about using the social web to grow, a Radian6 investment might be worthwhile.

No matter what tool you use, remember that no tool is perfect. Look for a tool that offers the features you need at a price you can afford. You can always upgrade to a bigger, better, and more expensive tool later. At first, you'll find all the data you need within your LinkedIn account, but as your online presence and reputation grow, you'll need external analytics tools to gather an adequate amount of performance data to make strategic decisions for the future that will position you to reach your goals.

The Least You Need to Know

- LinkedIn offers data to help you track the performance of your profile, network, Company Page, and ads.
- LinkedIn analytics tools are not very detailed and not perfect.
- Look for trends related to your growing audience, reputation, and online reach to assess your success on LinkedIn and across the internet.
- For more detailed metrics, you need to use a free or fee-based external tool.

Glossary

above the fold   Content that appears in a person's internet-browser window without having to scroll is considered to be above the fold. The term originally referred to content that can be seen in the top half of a newspaper page without turning the paper over.

B2B   An acronym for business-to-business that refers to a business, company, individual, or organization that markets its products and services to other businesses. For example, an advertising agency is a B2B company.

B2C   An acronym for business-to-consumer that refers to a business, company, individual, or organization that markets its products and services to consumers. For example, your local drugstore is a B2C company.

blog   Originally called *weblogs* (from the fusion of the words *web* and *log*), blogs began as online diaries with entries listed in reverse chronological order. Today, blogs are written and published by individuals, groups, and businesses and more and allow two-way conversation between the author and visitors through comments.

blog posts   Individual entries written by a blogger and published on a blog.

blogger   A person who writes content for a blog.

blogging   The act of writing and publishing blog posts or entries.

blogging application   The program used by bloggers to create and maintain blogs. Popular blogging applications include WordPress, Blogger, TypePad, Movable Type, and LiveJournal. Also called *blogging platform* or *blogging software*.

blogosphere   The online blogging community made up of bloggers from around the world creating user-generated content as part of the social web. *See also* social web.

brand   The tangible and intangible representation of a business, service, product, or person, which includes a promise, message, and image.

browser   A program used to surf the internet. Browsers include Internet Explorer, Firefox, Opera, Chrome, Safari, and more. Also called *web browser.*

comment   An opinion or reaction by a website visitor to a specific piece of online content. On LinkedIn, members can comment on updates published by other members.

content marketing   The practice of developing awareness, recall, purchases, and loyalty through the use of content published online or offline.

cost-per-action   An online advertising model in which the advertiser pays each time an ad is clicked by a visitor and a corresponding, predefined action is performed (e.g., a sale is made or a lead form is submitted). Also called *CPA.*

cost-per-click   An online advertising payment model in which the advertiser pays each time an ad is clicked by a visitor. Also called *CPC.*

cost-per-impression   An online advertising payment model in which the advertiser pays each time an ad is displayed. Also called *CPM.*

cross-promotion   Marketing across various channels or businesses to achieve a common objective.

CSV   An acronym for Comma-Separated Values or Character-Separated Values, a .csv file is a simple text format for a database file that can easily be imported to common database and spreadsheet programs such as Microsoft Excel.

domain The part of a URL that represents a specific website. Domain names are typically preceded by *www.* and end with an extension such as *.com* or *.net.*

feed Subscribers receive the content for their various website, LinkedIn updates, and blog subscriptions in an aggregated form called a feed. *See also* subscriber.

feed reader RSS feed content is read in a single location through a feed reader. Popular online feed readers include Google Reader and NewsGator. *See also* RSS and feed.

footer The area spanning the bottom of a web page, which typically includes copyright information and may include links and other information.

forum An online message board where participants post messages within predefined categories. Other participants respond, creating an online conversation between a potentially large group of people led by one or more moderators. Forums can be public or private, or a combination of the two.

hashtag A keyword preceded by the # symbol used in a Twitter update (called a *tweet*). Hashtags help Twitter users quickly find content related to a specific subject.

impression-based advertising An ad model wherein advertisers pay based on the number of times their ads are displayed to visitors.

indirect marketing Any activity that is not intended to result in an immediate action but rather a secondary response.

influencer People who have earned trust among their audiences and can affect the way their loyal audiences think and act.

InMail Similar to an email message but accessible only through LinkedIn members' LinkedIn account inboxes, a LinkedIn InMail is a private message sent from one LinkedIn member to another.

integrated marketing The process of creating multiple marketing tactics that work seamlessly together to reach a common objective.

keyword   A word or phrase used to help index a web page, allowing it to be found by search engines.

link   A connection between two websites. When selected, a link takes the user to another web page. Also called *hyperlink*.

LinkedIn app   An application created by a third party to enhance the functionality of LinkedIn.

LinkedIn modules   The various parts of a LinkedIn profile or Company Page, which often appear as boxed, separate sections.

LinkedIn plugin   A tool created to enhance the functionality of LinkedIn.

LinkedIn profile   A LinkedIn member's personal page which includes work-related history, recommendations, links, education, and more.

LinkedIn widget   A tool used in LinkedIn to add additional features and functionality.

microblogging   The process of publishing short updates (typically 140 characters or less) through sites such as Twitter.

navigation bar   A set of links arranged across all or a portion of a web page to make it easier for visitors to find content.

new media   Any form of nontraditional media born of Web 2.0, including blogs, microblogging, social networks, and so on. *See also* Web 2.0.

online reputation management   The process of monitoring the perceived reputation of a person, brand, company, and so on, based on the content and conversations published online about that person, brand, company, and so on.

OpenLink   A network that is open to premium LinkedIn account holders only. If you're in the OpenLink network, anyone on LinkedIn can send you free messages (even if they are not in your extended network) and you can send free messages to all OpenLink members.

page view   A statistic that tracks each time a web page is viewed by anyone at any time.

RSS An acronym for Really Simple Syndication. RSS is a technology that creates web content syndication and allows web users to subscribe to websites and blogs and receive content in an aggregated form via email or a feed reader. *See also* feed and feed reader.

search engine A website used to find online content related to specific keywords or keyword phrases. Search engines use proprietary algorithms to spider the internet, index content, and return relevant results, which are typically presented in a ranked order. Google, Yahoo!, and Bing are popular search engines.

search engine optimization The process of creating content to boost its search results for specific keyword phrases on popular search engines like Google, Bing, and Yahoo!. Also called *SEO*.

segment An audience segment is a smaller subset of a larger group of people who have similar demographic or behavioral traits and are likely to respond similarly to content and messages.

SEO *See* search engine optimization.

sidebar A column on a web page to the right, left, or on both sides of the largest, main column.

social bookmarking A method of saving, storing, and sharing web pages for future reference. Popular social bookmarking sites include StumbleUpon and Reddit.

social media Any form of publishing and communications media found on the social web, including blogs, social networks, microblogging, and so on.

social media marketing Any form of direct or indirect promotion that is executed using the tools of the social web and is rooted in two-way dialogue and interaction.

social networking The process of communicating with, connecting with, and building relationships with people online by using specific tools and websites. Popular social networking sites include Facebook and LinkedIn.

social web The second generation of the World Wide Web, which focuses on interaction, user-generated content, communities, and building relationships. Also called *Web 2.0*.

spam Comments and content published online for no reason other than to drive traffic to another website. Spam can also come in other forms such as email spam.

strategy A statement that defines an individual's or business's intended direction and outlines how the individual or business will achieve its goals.

subscribe When a person signs up to receive online content via a feed to his or her feed reader, email, or other tool, he or she is *subscribing* to it.

tactic A specific effort executed in support of a strategy to help an individual or business reach its objectives.

target audience The specific segment of a larger audience that a business or person focuses on communicating with directly using specific tactics and strategies. Target audiences usually share demographic or behavioral traits.

trademark An official registration provided by the United States Patent & Trademark Office that protects a name, logo, slogan, design, or other element, so only the trademark owner can use it within its registered industry.

unique visitor A visitor to a website or blog who is counted one time regardless of how many times he or she visits. *See also* visitor.

URL An acronym that stands for Uniform Resource Locator. It represents the unique address of a web page.

visit Each time a page on a website is accessed by anyone and at any time, a visit is counted.

visitor A person who views a page (or multiple pages) on a website.

Web 2.0 *See* social web.

web analytics The data used to track the performance of a website.

web browser *See* browser.

Resources

The resources listed in this appendix will help you find additional information so you get the most from LinkedIn.

LinkedIn Help and News Sites

- **LinkedIn Help Center:** help.linkedin.com/
- **LinkedIn Learning Center:** learn.linkedin.com/
- **LinkedIn Blog:** blog.linkedin.com/
- **LinkedIn on Twitter:** twitter.com/linkedin
- **LinkedIn YouTube Channel:** youtube.com/linkedin

LinkedIn Mobile Tools

- **iPhone:** itunes.apple.com/WebObjects/MZStore.woa/wa/viewSoftware?id=288429040&mt=8
- **Android:** m.linkedin.com/android
- **BlackBerry:** linkedin.com/static?key=blackberry
- **Palm:** developer.palm.com/webChannel/index.php?packageid=com.linkedin.mobile

Social and Online Reputation-Monitoring Tools

- **HootSuite:** hootsuite.com
- **Klout:** klout.com
- **PeerIndex:** peerindex.com
- **Sprout Social:** sproutsocial.com
- **Trackur:** trackur.com
- **Radian6:** radian6.com

Social Media Icons

- **FreeIconsDownload.com:** freeiconsdownload.com/free_web_icons.asp
- **WPMods.com:** wpmods.com/ultimate-social-media-icon-list
- **WebDesignLedger.com:** webdesignledger.com/freebies/the-best-social-media-icons-all-in-one-place
- **About.com Guide to Blogging:** weblogs.about.com/od/Social-Media-Icons/Social-Media-Icons.htm

Index

T